Jennifer~

My best to you
in all your life
choices.

Mary Farrar

"Mary Farrar's stated goals in writing this book were to tackle tough issues head-on. To be real, honest and most of all, biblical—and she hits those goals and more in this outstanding book. If you're in a season of change, or simply wanting to move towards God's best instead of second best, *please read this book.*"

John and Cindy Trent
Encouraging Words

"Women who want to follow a Christian path for their lives are often confused by conflicting influences. Everything from self-esteem to submission seems to be up for urgent review. In *Choices* Mary Farrar has tackled the guesswork with a thoughtful critique of the current chaos. For her, motherhood, marriage and mentoring stand or fall in the light of the Creator. Every woman makes choices everyday which fashion the person she is now and, most important, who she will be when she meets her Maker."

Howard and Jeanne Hendricks
Center for Christian Leadership

"Finally, a woman has stepped forward to challenge the politically correct conventional wisdom and reveal the biblical bedrock for the high-calling of womanhood. Mary has exposed the depth and the width between femininity and feminism."

Tim and Darcy Kimmel
Generation Ministries

"Mary Farrar delivers a timeless perspective for the <u>choices</u> facing today's woman. By challenging assumptions and providing principles, Mary captures the heart of femininity! Part II alone, "The Great Flood...The Tide That Blinds" is worth the price of the book."

Stu and Linda Weber
Good Shepherd Church

"*Choices* is a timeless message for every Christian woman. It stirs your emotions, challenges your thinking, and passionately points you back to the holiness of God."

Dr. Gary and Barbara Rosberg
Family Legacy

"Mary Farrar addresses the issues many Christian women are afraid to face: feminism, careers, gender differences, parenting, abortion, and using our giftedness in and out of the church. Her sound logic, historical accuracy, biblical research, balanced approach, and riveting illustrations captivated my attention, challenged my preconceived ideas, and helped me form defendable answers to the tough questions."

> Carol Kent
> Speaker and author of *Tame Your Fears* and
> *Secret Longings of the Heart*

"Modern technology has eliminated many of the hardships faced by our foremothers, but has paradoxically introduced a whole new set of difficulties for women. According to Mary Farrar, the greatest hardship of the modern woman is the <u>choices</u> she must make. Farrar's analysis of woman's plight is insightful. In a personal, friendly style, she challenges women to examine the pressures in their lives and to make day to day decisions based on biblical priorities."

> Mary Kassian
> Author of *The Feminist Gospel*

"Mary Farrar provides a dose of reality to cure all the ill effects of the 'Super-Woman, have-it-all, do-it-all' myth. Her work is fresh, readable and stimulating…a must read for today's Christian woman.

> The Council on Biblical Manhood & Womanhood
> Chicago, Illinois

CHOICES

*For Women Who
Long to Discover Life's Best*

MARY FARRAR

MULTNOMAH BOOKS • SISTERS, OREGON

To my mom, Sara Jo Wilson,
best friend,
wise counselor,
astute theologian,
angel of mercy...
perfect mom.

In gratitude for forty-five years of choosing
my best over her own.

CHOICES

© 1994 By Mary Farrar

published by Multnomah Books
a part of the Questar publishing family

International Standard Book Number 0-88070-662-7

Cover design by David Uttley
Illustration by Jonathan C. Lund

Printed in the United States of America

Unless indicated otherwise, Scripture references are from the New American Standard Bible,
The Lockman Foundation © 1960, 1962, 1963, 1968, 1971, 1972, 1973, 1975, 1977. Used by pemission.

Scripture references marked NIV are from the Holy Bible: New International Version,
© 1973, 1978, 1984 by International Bible Society. Used by permission of
Zondervan Publishing House. All rights reserved. The "NIV" and "New International Version" trademarks are
registered in the United States Patent and Trademark Office by International Bible Society.
Use of either trademark requires the permission of International Bible Society.

Scripture references marked KJV are from the Holy Bible:
Authorized King James Version.

Library of Congress Cataloging-in-Publication Data
Farrar, Mary. Choices:for women who long to discover life's best/Mary Farrar.
p.cm.   ISBN 0-88070-662-7:$16.99
1. Women--Religious life.   2. Woman (Christian theology)   3. Feminism--Controversial literature.
4. Feminism--Religious aspects--Christianity.   5. United States--Moral conditions.   6. Christian life.
7. Ferrar, Mary.   I. Title
BV4527.F47   1994   94-33257
248.8'43--dc20   CIP

94 95 96 97 98 99 00 01 02 03 — 10 9 8 7 6 5 4 3 2

ACKNOWLEDGEMENTS

I have decided that writing a book is like flying an airplane. The pilot may be at the controls, but from the time you leave the ground until you land that baby, it is a total team effort. This plane would have never reached its destination had it not been for the incredible efforts of a host of key people.

Thank you, Sharon, for being a sister who has stuck "closer than a brother." Without your encouragement day and night, your belief in me, and your commitment to this book, I would have never gotten into the air, much less landed. Thanks for pulling me through the times of fuel loss, convulsive turbulence, and lost direction. You are a woman of God, and this book has your hand prints all over it.

To Steve, my husband, soul-mate, and fiercely loyal friend. You are a man after God's own heart, an exceptional dad, an astute thinker, a model of integrity, and a true champion for womankind. Because of you, I had something to write about. Thank you for making my choices so easy and the trip such a blast.

To Rachel, John, and Josh, my cockpit crew. Thanks for all the encouraging notes, late-night drinks and treats, and warm, cup-filling hugs. And thanks for never complaining about McDonald's and Domino's Pizza. You are my inspiration and the joy of my life.

To the women who took the time to read the manuscript and add their invaluable perspective: Mary Kassian, Jeanne Hendricks, Darlene Hixon, Margaret Fitzwater, Cheryl Mauldin, Peggy Tikson, Sharon Owens, Deedee Smith, Sharon Collard, Karen Boyd, Terry Biel, and Rebecca Price.

To those women who gave up their time to be in two field test groups: Sharon Owens, Terry Biel, Jenny Shell, Debbie Grisham, Jean Sehnert, Jolie Humphrey, Kelley Maxwell, Melissa Rosandich, Peggy Tikson, Karen Boyd, Marcie Thompson, Pam Tortorich, and Scarlett Burks. Thanks for your helpful feedback.

To Darlene Hixon, for a job well done in producing an excellent study guide. Women across the country will benefit from your topnotch work.

To two special men at Dallas Theological Seminary. Thanks to Dr. Howard Hendricks for your encouraging supervision of the historical research. And to Dr.

Darrell Bock; I am indebted to you for your expert and enthusiastic assistance with my research into the Greek language.

To Jennifer Treischman, for your special touch in caring for our children.

To Terry Biel, Deedee Smith, and Janis Tucker, for your expert assistance and "hole plugging" in the heat of a busy year. You were each an invaluable part of the team.

To the awesome team at Questar. I couldn't have asked for a more skillful and committed crew. Thanks for believing in this project and for making this a first-class flight.

Thanks especially to Dan Rich. You are not only the best marketer in the business, but your commitment to the author-publisher relationship goes above and beyond the call of duty.

My special thanks, also, to Rebecca Price, for giving your whole heart as well as your creative genius towards the landing of this plane.

And, finally, to my editing team, Carol Bartley and Larry Libby. Thank you, Carol, for your gracious encouragement and wise direction from day one. Without your skillful touch on every page, this book would have been 500 pages long, and better off in the trash.

Larry, I have never met a more humble word genius. Thank you for lending your magic to this book, and most of all, your heart.

CONTENTS

The Great Fire

The Great Flood

The Great Frontier

INTRODUCTION

*O*n a sweltering July afternoon in 1977, the seeds of this book were sown.

That was the day I said "I do," and then stood on tiptoes to kiss my new husband. Everyone thought Steve was crying, but it was just sweat pouring down his face. Ever since then I have lived in sweaters and socks in a 65 degree house so this man would never again be publicly accused of crying.

That was some seventeen years and another life ago. "And then I had kids," as Susan Yates' wonderful book puts it. Three of them.

In a matter of five short years, I went from being a single, career woman—free to travel and make decisions at will, free to go to bed when I felt tired and sleep through the night, free to organize and actually schedule my life, free to clean house and have it stay clean for at least twenty-four hours, free to talk on the phone without interruption—to being a wife of one and mother of three.

It was a fairly significant change.

Don't get me wrong. I loved being a wife and mother. In fact, I moved into my new life at full throttle. I felt blessed beyond measure. What more could a woman ask than to be married to her soul mate, and to give birth to three of the most precious children anyone could ever hope to have? As I saw it, my career had simply been re-routed. Independence no longer mattered. This was exactly where I was supposed to be.

But somewhere along the way, I came to a turn in the road. I entered a time of struggle that went deeper than postpartum blues or the need to get out of the house. When the struggle didn't subside, I began to feel guilty. What was my problem? Was I unappreciative of all that God had done for me? Did I have an uncaring spirit toward the ones He had put in my life? But as I looked into my heart, I could honestly say this wasn't the problem. I valued them most of all. My husband and children were top priority in my life.

As the struggle continued, I felt a sense of—dare I say it—*futility* creeping into my life. It wasn't that I minded doing the laundry or cleaning mildew out of the shower. But I was discovering something I didn't expect. Isolated from the outside world and enveloped in the daily demands of caring for a home, I was finding the gap between the home and the outside world was far greater than I had ever imagined.

It wasn't long before I discovered that other women, many of them more mature in their faith than I, were experiencing a similar quiet struggle. And as we opened up to one another, we realized we were asking many of the same questions.

In a feminized world how do we view our role as women?

How does a woman reconcile the issue of work and gifts within a culture where the role of the home has so drastically changed?

What is a woman to do with the call of God to *co*-parent her children when most men—and many women—have so little time to parent?

What about the biblical teaching of submission in light of the need of a woman to be her own person?

And what about the value of a woman's input in the church and society at large?

We found ourselves between a rock and a hard place. To our right were Donna, June, and Harriet. And to our left were Betty, Gloria, and Pat. Yet neither path seemed to be the way to go. "Traditional" roles weren't working anymore, and the answers of feminism fell short of our innermost needs. What was a Christian woman to do in such times? We needed a new path based on the timeless truths of God's eternal word. In our effort to flesh out the plan of God in changing times, we were asking the all-important question: What does it mean to be a biblical woman in the days in which we live?

And so my search began.

In the years that followed I found that God is the "God who is there." God *still* speaks to His women who seek after Him. He has not left us in the lurch. He understands us. And He has provided a way through.

Chapter One

Towering Inferno

~⁓

The strength of a nation is derived from the integrity of its homes.

CONFUCIUS (C. 551-479 B.C.)

Oh, that they had such a heart in them,
that they would fear Me, and keep all My commandments always,
that it may be well with them and with their sons forever!

YAHWEH (DEUTERONOMY 5:29)

O ne cold winter night in Epworth, England, the church bell began to ring.

Awakened from their sleep, the townspeople ran out into the night. To their dismay, the sky was illuminated by a house engulfed in flames—the house of a well-loved family in their town.

A crowd gathered to fight the fire, working desperately, feverishly. But it was too late. The house had become an unquenchable inferno.

Samuel and Susanna had escaped the flames, along with six of their children. But soon it was discovered that one child was missing. No one could find Johnny. Realizing the worst, Samuel headed toward the blaze, only to be held back from certain death by the townspeople. The loss of a child is a terrible tragedy, but the loss of both father and child? It would have been too much to bear.

And so in silent torture, they all stood by. Helpless. Watching the fire wrap searing arms around this family's most valued possession—a little child. Not a woman among us has difficulty imagining what must have been going through Susanna's mind. Forget the house. Forget everything in the house. A child's pain is a mother's agony. His death is her most profound grief.

Then someone in the crowd shouted, *"Look!"*

A little face had appeared in an upstairs window. Johnny had awakened and, unable to escape through the flames, had made his way to the window. In an instant, two men ran toward the house. One climbed upon the shoulders of the other as they stretched and distended their bodies to form a human ladder up to the child. The heat was so intense their clothes began to smoke. But within moments the child was pulled through, brought to safety on the arms of a living ladder.

The little guy who was saved that night was none other than John Wesley, the man God used to shake the world in the Great Awakening of the eighteenth century. Years later Wesley wrote, "That night I was plucked as a brand from the burning."

A CULTURE AFLAME

Why do I tell this story? I tell it because it is a vivid picture of our culture, a culture which has become a towering inferno. The difference is that in this great inferno we do not find a *house* being destroyed, but a *home*. And it is not one home, but countless homes—invisible human edifices where marriages, families, and children thrive. Homes, built on the foundations of relationships, values, and matters of the heart.

True to the nature of a fire, this inferno has shown itself to be no respecter of persons. It has hit young and old, conservative and liberal, wealthy and poor, famous and infamous. It has penetrated the doors of the church, spreading through its pews and into its pulpits. In so doing, it has discredited the integrity of the Christian faith and attacked its very foundation—the reliable, authoritative Word of God.

When we see the strongest among us fall, we begin to realize the scope of it all. There isn't a woman reading these pages whose life hasn't been touched by the destruction of the home.

Some of you are in the midst of fighting for your own home even as you read. You are fighting for your marriage, for your children. Perhaps the battle seems hopeless, the blaze beyond your ability to vanquish.

Others of you are picking up the pieces from the ashes and rubble of what was once your home. You are fighting for your future and the future of your children, trying desperately to make things work in the wake of tragedy.

Still others of you are fighting to save the homes around you. You are waging the battle in your neighborhoods, local churches, and communities. Your home may be intact now, but you know we are all vulnerable. You sense that the momentum is against us, that everything in our culture is set against committed, healthy marriages and emotionally, spiritually, and morally healthy children.

Very simply, we are *all* in the midst of the fight of our lives.

It's not that we aren't trying to protect our homes. Christians today attend more seminars, read more books, and seek more counsel than ever before. Yet with all our unprecedented efforts, we are finding less and less success. Why does the number of single mothers continue to rise within the church? Why do divorce rates within the church remain equal to those outside it? Why are our children as sexually promiscuous as those who are unchurched? And with all of our books and training, why do our parent-child relationships seem to worsen? Perhaps this is the greatest tragedy of all. Even within the church we cannot seem to save our homes.

The family is not merely changing or evolving, as some would have us believe. It is being splintered and turned into kindling. And as an institution in this nation, it is being gutted and destroyed. The alarm has been sounded and time is running out.

In a very real sense, *my* children are inside this towering inferno. *My* children are standing at the window, peering out. What's more, so are *yours*. It is our children's lives, as well as the lives of their children that hang in the balance. They are the little "brands" in desperate need of being plucked from the burning.

A woman will do wild and strange things when the lives of her children and grandchildren are at stake. She may turn and face a lion on the attack. She may throw herself in front of a moving car. She may even write a book.

A HARE AND A TURTLE

Funny, isn't it, how different people respond to a crisis. In our family, my husband is the crisis person. Steve is incredible in an emergency. Had he been in Epworth that night, he would have been one of those guys in the human ladder. No question about it.

Not long after we married, I watched him resuscitate a seventy-year-old woman who had collapsed in the foyer of the church. He broke her collarbone but saved her life. Not long after, he saved our first child from a potentially fatal fall, racing clear across the room and grabbing her before she hit the floor. He was there to catch her before I even realized she was falling. When the 1980 San

Francisco earthquake hit near our home in the bay area, Steve had our baby outside the house (still strapped in her high chair!) before I knew we were *in* an earthquake. On another occasion he snatched our four-year-old niece from the path of an oncoming car. And once when we were visiting relatives who owned a swimming pool, he became aware that our one-year-old son was missing. While the rest of us ran about the house getting ready for an outing, Steve instinctively rushed out to the pool, saw Joshua at the bottom, jumped in, and pulled him out just moments before he would have drowned.

You are probably wondering if I married a new breed of Superman. Something like Super Preacher—kindly pastor by day, hero of the cloth by night. The truth is my husband has a sixth sense for crisis, for which I have thanked God many times over. In fact, I am convinced it is this sense which has drawn him into a ministry to men. Steve believes that this country is in a crisis and that the only hope for survival is spiritual revival. And if revival is to occur, he is keenly aware that men are key. Historically, spiritual revivals have always begun through the repentance and renewal of men. So that is my Steve.

If Steve is the hare, then I am the turtle. I am the slower, more deliberate one in the family. When there is a crisis, I tend to be the calm one (once I realize we have a crisis on our hands), the one who anticipates good in the face of depressing news, the one who feels confident all will work out in the end. I am the incessant optimist.

But this time even *I* am beginning to smell smoke. Slow and steady may win the race (who are we kidding?), and a positive outlook may be an asset, but positive thinking has never put out a fire. I am not an alarmist, but I am genuinely alarmed.

In an article in January of 1994, Chuck Colson—no slouch in reading the societal weather vane of our nation—gave a rather grim prediction: "I think we have five years left (to turn the tide). What should we do? We should start by modeling the kind of families that will civilize our young people and help them form their sense of conscience."[1]

Would you say Colson is an alarmist? Let's examine the evidence.

EVIDENCE THAT DEMANDS A VERDICT

In his recent *Index of Leading Cultural Indicators*, William Bennett, former Secretary of Education and Chairman of the National Endowment for the Humanities, paints the statistical picture of our thirty-year "experiment" in devaluing the family. In the years from 1960 to 1990 our nation tripled its Gross Domestic Product and increased its governmental social spending *fivefold*. Spending on education increased 225 percent, while our allotment to welfare was upped an astounding 630 percent. What did all of this profit and spending do for us?

In the same thirty-year period, SAT scores plunged almost 80 points, while teenage suicides rose 200 percent, violent crime soared 560 percent, illegitimate births leaped 400 percent, children in single-parent households tripled, and divorce rates quadrupled.[2]

So much for the joys of affluence. While some have viewed the recent leveling out of the divorce rate as a hopeful sign, they have overlooked a crucial point. The leveling divorce rate actually indicates a loss of confidence in the value of marriage. Since 1980 the number of couples living together has increased by 80 percent, with half of those households having children. And although their breakup rate is much higher than that of married couples, those figures have not been reflected in the official divorce rate.[3]

Why the huge jump in social problems since 1960? Although numerous factors are involved, research shows that family breakdown is the one clear thread that weaves through them all. In an article citing an onslaught of new studies, *Newsweek* magazine recently noted: "There is high correlation between disrupted homes and just about every social problem imaginable." Decrying lost values and a seemingly irreversible "national unraveling," it went on to say, "The disaster that has overtaken American families has been quieter, more diffuse, but...incontrovertible."[4]

Evidence among our children is abundant and overwhelmingly clear. Long-term studies now show that children from broken homes are three times more likely to have emotional and behavioral problems, twice as likely to drop out of school, and at greater risk of becoming involved in crime, precocious sexuality, teenage marriage, pregnancy, nonmarital births, and divorce. Children of broken homes find it harder to achieve intimacy in relationships, form stable marriages, hold steady jobs, and are more likely to commit suicide.[5]

A 1990 Code Blue report published by a commission of family experts summed it up by saying, "Never before has one generation of American teenagers been less healthy, less cared for, or less prepared for life than their parents were at the same age."[6]

Women are in no less trouble.

Never have so many women suffered from marital unfaithfulness and breakdown. And despite unprecedented progress and accomplishment over the last thirty years, never have more women felt so shortchanged and disillusioned.

Mary Ann Mason, a divorce lawyer, former historian, and feminist, wrote these words in 1988: "Something has gone very wrong with the lives of women. Women are working much harder than they have worked in recent history, they are growing steadily poorer and they are suffering the brutality of divorce at an unprecedented rate.... Feminists have sadly become prisoners of their own political rhetoric, and this rhetoric is based on a model of equality which is not suited to the lives of most women."[7]

In an effort to bring about the androgynous ideal, something has indeed gone wrong. In his historical study of twentieth century women, Dr. William Chafe refers to the increasing "feminization of poverty," in which women now constitute 70 percent of the adult poor. "It is," he says, quoting from Dickens' *A Tale of Two Cities*, "the best of times and the worst of times."[8]

Many of my dearest friends are single moms. And through their eyes I have seen that poverty is only the tip of the iceberg. The truth is that women in every walk of life, whether single, married, or divorced, are finding themselves victims of the times in which we live.

Why have women become so vulnerable? The well-being of women has always been tied to the well-being of the home. As one writer put it, "When society fails to protect family, it fails to protect women."[9]

As studies continue to pour in, experts nationwide are expressing alarm. Said one well-known historian, "We have conducted a thirty-year experiment.... Everyone gets to act out. There are no consequences. It's been a disaster."[10] Karl Zinsmeister of the American Enterprise Institute was equally frank. "The data are monolithically worrisome," he said. "None of these circumstances—divorce, single-parent families, stepparent families—are healthy. There is no precedent for what has happened in any other time, in any other place."[11] Even Dr. Joyce Ladner, avid defender of alternate family lifestyles such as homosexual unions, recently stated that the current anarchic trend of family breakdown simply cannot continue. As she put it, "Everyone I know says, 'Enough is enough.'"[12]

The evidence is indisputable. The great American "experiment" has failed.

"The family," said the great Harvard sociologist Pitirim A. Sorokin, "is the heart of society."[13] The family is not just an arm or a finger. It is the very heart. And everyone knows if you have a bad heart, you are in serious trouble.

The idea of the family as the foundational unit of society is nothing new. For centuries philosophers and thinkers have noted the atomic nature of the family. But do you know where we first find the idea? God Himself declared it in the first commandment: "You shall have no other gods before Me.... For I, the LORD your God, am a jealous God, *visiting the iniquity of the fathers on the children, on the third and the fourth generations* of those who hate Me, but showing *loving kindness to thousands*, to those who love Me and keep My commandments" (Exodus 20:3, 5-6).

Do you catch what God is saying? One family—one single family—who loves God and keeps His commandments has the potential of impacting thousands with His loving kindness. What a great thought! Yet, that same family also can negatively impact the world for generations to come.

As Dr. Michael Novak once wrote: "One unforgettable law has been learned through all the disasters and injustices of the last thousand years: *If things go well with the family, life is worth living; when the family falters, life falls apart.* (italics mine)."[14]

One could go on to say that when the family falters, society also falls apart. Every great society that has devalued its families has crumbled under the breakdown of the home. Israel crumbled under the moral breakdown of its families. And so did Rome. In his *Decline and Fall of the Roman Empire*, Edward Gibbon listed the top five reasons for the fall of Rome. The primary cause? "An undermining of the dignity and sanctity of the home, which is the basis for human society."

DYSFUNCTIONAL FAMILIES—DYSFUNCTIONAL NATIONS

Dysfunctional families lead to dysfunctional nations. What is the problem in a dysfunctional family? A dysfunctional family cannot face its own illness. Its members live in a state of denial. The same is true of a dysfunctional nation.

If you are a baby boomer, you are part of a generation that has chosen the dysfunctional path. Three and a half decades ago we baby boomers made a decision not to listen to God anymore. We threw out Scripture and rebelled against its authority. We determined that there are no absolutes, no timeless right or wrong. We concluded that "right" is whatever seems or feels right at the moment. And in so doing, we refused to acknowledge what the world has known for centuries: that the absence of morality is the presence of immorality. That free sex, free choice, and free thought are never "free" when they are set free from the moral law of God.

There is another true story about a burning house. Once again, a huge crowd gathered outside to help fight back the flames. But this fire, too, was beyond quenching. Standing back, the crowd watched as the flames raged out of control. Then, unexpectedly, above the roaring crackle of the fire came the faint cries of a child. As the fire grew more intense, the cries grew more compelling.

Suddenly a man broke loose from the crowd and raced toward the house. Before a stunned audience, this hero disappeared into the flames. Seconds seemed like hours as they waited for him to reappear. And then the cries of the child stopped.

Momentarily, the man emerged through the doorway with a bundle in his arms. Then, overcome by the smoke, he fell to the ground. Out of his arms tumbled the bundle. A large safety box. The man had risked his life to rescue his life savings.

What sort of man would close his ears to the screams of a dying child for the sake of *money*? Only a morally and spiritually impoverished man.

Yet this is the story of our very own nation. "Why do you turn and scrape every stone to gather wealth," Socrates challenged his fellow Athenians, "and take so little care of your children, to whom one day you must relinquish all?"

Amazing what a crisis will reveal about the hidden character of a nation—or an individual. Values surface quickly in the middle of a crisis, don't they?

What does this mean for us as Christian women? Facing an ocean of choices in a time of genuine crisis, Christian women today often feel like tiny vessels tossed to and fro by the fickle winds of modern thinking. And rightfully so. Confusion reigns on women's issues, even within the church. The church has never been so divided on the issues that concern us—issues like biblical manhood and womanhood, career and motherhood, submission and marriage. No wonder women feel so torn.

FROZEN IN TIME

When Pompeii was being excavated, a woman's body was uncovered that had been embalmed by the ashes of Vesuvius. Her feet were turned toward the city gate and safety. But her face was looking behind her and her hands were reaching back for something that lay just beyond her grasp.

What was she reaching for?

Only inches from her frozen fingers…was a bag of pearls. Perhaps she had dropped them as she was fleeing for her life. Or perhaps they had been dropped by another. Whatever the case, though death was at her heels and life was beckoning at the city gates, she foolishly looked back to pick them up, and her fatal choice became frozen in time.

It's the same for us. Whether we realize it or not, the critical choices we make in times of crisis can become matters of life and death. Although men are key to revival, women are no less important. In fact, our role is absolutely pivotal. I believe the choices of women over the next ten years will profoundly impact the course of our nation.

Recently a great deal of fuss has been made over the accomplishments of women. But whether they call this the Year of the Woman, the Decade of the Woman, or even the Century of the Woman, what difference will it make if all that we leave behind is nothing more than the woman of Pompeii?

I submit to you there is nothing in this world more important than our homes, our marriages, and our children. Nothing. There is not one ministry or job or accomplishment or calling that is more important. And certainly not one safety box—no matter what it contains!

What profit is it if we have all the money in the world, yet raise our children in emotional bankruptcy?

What meaning is there in finding fame if our own spouse and children wish they had never heard our name?

What do we gain if we minister to thousands but lose our marriages and families?

If we build empires, yet in so doing destroy our homes, we will find ourselves alone, clutching a worthless bag of pearls.

HUMAN LADDERS

My guess is you are reading this book because you already believe this to be true. You want to make the right choices. You want your home to survive the inferno. And *more* than survive, you want to make a difference and ensure a legacy for your children and grandchildren.

If you come away with nothing else from this book, my hope is that you will remember two words: ...*but God.*

God created the atom.

God also created the family.

God holds the atom together so that the universe does not fly apart into chaos.

God can also hold a family together.

And God has a plan. A sovereign plan. "I am God, and there is no one like Me, Declaring the end from the beginning.... Saying 'My purpose will be established....' Truly I have spoken; truly I will bring it to pass. I have planned it, surely I will do it" (Isaiah 46:9-11).

In the end, God alone can save a nation. But here's the clincher. When God chooses to work in a nation, He always does it through the individual choices of people. People like you and me.

It was the sovereign plan of God that Wesley should be saved. And it was His sovereign plan to bring revival to England. But how did He do it? He used two tangible, bold, clear-thinking people to accomplish His great plan. Two people who saw the crisis, understood what had to be done, and acted with little regard for themselves.

I don't think we can expect it to be any different this time around, do you? If the little Wesleys in our homes today are to survive this inferno, it will take another human ladder. A ladder of tangible, bold, clear-thinking men and women—people who see the crisis, understand what has to be done, and are willing to step out and do what is right.

In some cases it will be a husband and wife who sacrificially choose to be committed first and foremost to their marriage and home. In some cases it will be a woman who finds herself alone—a single mother, a wife whose husband is far away from God, an unmarried woman who longs to give her best for the sake of God's kingdom—each one choosing to step out and trust God.

It all comes down to our choices.

What if you have already made mistakes in your choices? Join the club. We're all members! And take heart in this: No matter where you are in life or what mistakes you have already made, it is *never* too late. God is an awesome God. He can still use your good choices—today, tomorrow, next week—and make a difference in your world.

A DEEP, UNCHANGING CURRENT

When sailors first sailed the northern oceans, they noticed an amazing phenomenon. Oftentimes, as powerful winds were blowing the current in a given direction, icebergs would pass by them, moving in the opposite direction. How could this be, they wondered. How could an iceberg move against the current?

It was eventually discovered that these floating mountains of ice were being carried by stronger currents, deep within the sea. Since eight-ninths of their mass was below the water surface, they were caught in the stronger grip of deep underwater currents, no matter which way the wind blew.

What a beautiful image for modern women. As the powerful winds of prevailing opinion blow squarely in the face of God's wisdom, we must go down deep to the sure and steady current of God's unchanging and timeless truth. We must become anchored in God's all-wise plan for homes, marriages, and for women.

That is the goal of this book. To confront the issues directly. To be honest and, most of all, biblical. And by God's grace, as we do, we will more than discover life's best.

We will discover God's best.

Chapter Two

The Tide that Blinds

Life can only be understood backwards.

KIERKEGAARD

Save me, O God, For the waters have threatened my life....
I have come into deep waters, and a flood overflows me.

DAVID (PSALM 69:1-2)

*I*t had been a day like any other day. A quiet, warm day in the mountains
of Colorado. Dabs of color splashed across the mountainside. Aspen
leaves shimmered like feathers of gold in the brilliant sunlight. And sun-
beams shafted through the pines, giving the forest a cathedral glow.

But this was not just any day.

Marilyn Henderson-Rydberg will never forget that summer day of 1976. Nor
will Ney Bailey or Melanie Ahlquist, or any of the other thirty-five members of
Campus Crusade for Christ's women's leadership team. They had gathered at
Sylvan Dale Ranch for a long-anticipated retreat. As the sun slipped behind the
hills, they gathered inside the cabin...old friends hugging, laughing, animatedly
conversing, praying. There was a sense of God's presence among them.

Suddenly, out of the darkness came a loud voice from the road above.

"Evacuate immediately! High water is coming! Take nothing with you!"

Dropping everything, the women ran outside. On the road above them, a
policeman was shouting orders over a megaphone.

"Flash flood! Evacuate immediately! Take nothing with you! Get to higher ground!"

But where was higher ground? Where was the flood?

Piling into the nearest available cars, the women headed out of the ranch.

Newspaper accounts would later describe a freak storm that dumped four-teen inches of rain on the eastern face of the Continental Divide. Flooding the Big Thompson River, it sent a wall of water leaping down the canyon, uprooting trees, and overwhelming homes, cars, and everything in its path.

In the darkness outside the ranch, confusion set in and the cars became sepa-rated. One group followed a policeman across a bridge and up to a parking lot. By this time, it was beginning to pour. In the distance they could hear the roar of the flood as it moved down the mountain, picking up speed with each mile, and they could smell the propane gas from tanks exploding at the impact of the mighty waters.

Joining them was a crowd of people, some on foot, others in cars, all seeking escape. Above the incredible clamor of cars, horns, shouting, and explosions, the women screamed, "*Where* is higher ground?"

But there was no answer.

Ney's car finally came upon another policeman.

"Get out of here!" he yelled. "Get out of your cars and get to higher ground!"

As they jumped out of their cars, someone standing nearby said, "The bridge we just crossed—it's gone!"

Ney groped her way up the mountainside, choking on propane fume. Fighting through loose rocks, mud, and barbed wire, her group finally reached safety at the top. *Where is everyone else?* they kept wondering.

In the distance, they could see fiery bursts of light from exploding tanks, and the eerie flashing of headlights from cars being swept downstream. As they waited and prayed, they huddled together against the pelting rain and shrieking wind. It was not until the next day that they learned what had happened to the rest of the group.

Marilyn and Melanie were in another car. They came upon an officer who pointed east.

"Take this road to Loveland," he said, "and *hurry!*"

But hurry was impossible. The road was choked with traffic fleeing from the thundering water just behind. Marilyn and the driver of her car quickly switched places—her friend overwhelmed by anxiety. She could not have known she had just saved Marilyn's life. Nor did anyone know they were heading straight into the flood.

Moments later the floodwater hit. Their car was engulfed and immediately sucked into the swirling current. Miraculously Marilyn managed to roll down her window and slide through.

Instantly she was swept downstream. The force of the water propelled her like a torpedo, throwing her up against rocks, lumber, tree limbs, and nameless debris. She didn't know if she was up or down, and for what seemed like an eternity she fought desperately to find air.

Just when it seemed she couldn't last another second, she burst through the surface of the water. Just ahead of her she saw a tree. As the flood waters swept her past, she reached out for a limb. Surrounded by darkness and the violent rushing waters, Marilyn clung.

Moments later, she heard someone up above. It was an older gentleman looking for a friend. Marilyn cried out to him, and he ran for help. As rescuers pulled her from the water, she gasped, "Quick, there are others. Please try to find them!"

Melanie found herself gripped with indecisiveness as the waters engulfed the car. Should she stay inside—or—try to climb out into the black water. It was a terrifying choice. But then she, too, managed to roll down a window and slide into…chaos.

As she was sucked downstream, the water tore off her clothes, watch, and rings.

At least I know where I'm going, she thought.

And then suddenly the water grew calm. For some unknown reason the current briefly subsided. As Melanie burst up through the surface, she saw a lone tree, standing straight and tall against the sweep of the swirling waters. She fought her way towards it and grabbed hold of its trunk. Then, as quickly as the calm had come, it left. The floodwaters boiled and churned with fresh intensity.

Despite the force of the current, Melanie wrapped her arms and legs around the tree trunk, and held on, her head just barely above the water. But what would happen as the waters continued to rise?

After a few minutes, she noticed something. Rocks and debris forced up against the tree were lodging at its base, forming a mound. Melanie climbed up onto this pile of debris, finding that it made a kind of ladder up the tree. As more and more debris lodged, the mound grew higher, and the ladder moved up the tree. Time passed, as Melanie climbed and clung. This lone, sure tree had become her anchor in the storm.

Eventually Melanie's ladder grew high enough for her to reach a limb. Exhausted and shaking in the cold night air, she climbed out on the limb and waited. The night wore on as Melanie huddled there, encompassed by floodwaters. As time passed, her hope of being found grew dimmer.

Suddenly she saw a lone man walking along the road. It was Marilyn's rescuer, searching for her friends. Miraculously, even though every shred of clothing had been ripped from her body, Melanie's contact lenses had stayed in her eyes and were clear enough to see. She yelled out to him, praying he could hear her over the roar of the flood.

"I'll get help!" he yelled back.

Minutes later, a helicopter hovered overhead, and Melanie was plucked from her perch to safety.

Of all the women swept into the flood waters that day, only Marilyn and Melanie survived.

The flood was declared the worst flash flood in Colorado's history, with a hundred reported dead by day's end, and eight hundred missing.

Why were these two spared? One day, Christ Himself will take each of them by the hand and explain it all. But in the meantime, they have allowed their trauma to point everyone they meet to their living Lord.

As I listened to their account, I was struck once again by the consequences of choices—a choice of a road, a choice of a driver. And I was impressed by the awesome power of such a flood. Flash floods, you see, come in different forms. They do not always come as a wall of raging water.

THE GREAT FLASH FLOOD OF HISTORY

God willing, you and I may never have to face the power and terror of a flash flood screaming through a narrow canyon.

Yet you and I *are* in a flash flood. A monumental flash flood of change. Change unlike anything the world has ever seen. It began quietly less than two hundred years ago. But in the decades that have followed, it has picked up unparalleled power and speed.

It is a monumental flash flood of change.

Now, we all know there has been change. I can't help my kids with their math homework for that very reason. Preparing dinner in our home looks quite different from preparing meals when I was growing up. But I am not talking merely about new math, microwaves, and cellular phones.

Suppose we were to take the equator that stretches clear around the globe and use it as a time line representing all of history. If we were then to put the last

175 years on that line, they would amount to a mere ink dot. Yet the change that has occurred within this "dot" exceeds that of any tens of centuries before.

That is why I say we are in the Great Flash Flood of history. For until this time, cultural change occurred slowly, becoming absorbed into life over centuries. However, from the beginning of the Industrial Revolution until the present day, the unprecedented rate and power of change have literally turned modern culture upside down. What's more, this great flood is far from over. If anything, its peak is yet to come.

Historian William Manchester speaks of such "volcanic, tumultuous" change in this century: "One can almost say that everything that was then is not now, and that everything that was not then, now is.... It is actually possible to live today without touching anything that existed 60 years ago."[1] And as we are further told in a recent *U. S. News and World Report* article, titled "1933-1993, The Years that Remade the World and the Forces that Could Remake It Again," the next fifty to sixty years are going to move at least as fast as the last sixty.[2] In other words, we are in a raging current of change—you and I, along with our children.

Change, of course, is inevitable. And it's not always bad. I've no objection at all to running water, electricity, computers, or antibiotics. Dishwashers are just fine, and you won't find me protesting microwave ovens or electric curling irons. Truthfully, so many of the changes of the past century have bettered our lives and eased our burdens.

But just like the Colorado flood, this great flood of change has also taken victims by virtue of the sheer rate and power with which it has come. Who have been the victims?

The home has been directly in its path.

Once the center of life itself, the home has been swept off its foundations and hurled downstream. In the wake of its devastation, virtually every relationship and institution it touches has also suffered.

In short, since the home is the atom, the heart, the foundational institution of culture, *all of culture* has fallen victim to this great current of change. The inevitable result has been a gradual unraveling, an ever-increasing domino effect. The cultural revolution of the last forty years should therefore come as no surprise. The rise of feminism in the fifties, the sexual revolution of the sixties, and the "immoral revolution" of the seventies and eighties—all are natural results of the flood.

Even the church has shuddered under the impact of those crushing waters of change. Walk into any Christian bookstore today and what do you see? Shelves full of "rescue writing"—books on healing, recovery, survival. Christian writers, like the rescue team that plucked my friend Melanie from the churning floodwaters, are occupied with throwing ropes to men, women, and kids, who have been uprooted and thrashed about in our nation's deluge of change.

More than likely, the problems you face in your life today—and unquestionably the struggles you experience as a modern woman—can all be traced back in some way to the powerful flood that came roaring out of contemporary history, sweeping all before it.

THE ROCK IN THE MIDST OF THE FLOOD

In the midst of the flood there have been other great forces at work...economic, political, social, religious, philosophical. And most importantly, above and through it all, has been the sovereign hand of God.

God has not been sitting on His throne, anxiously wringing His hands as the floods of change sweep our landscape. Not at all! As a matter of fact, He is the One who has *orchestrated* the events of the last two hundred years to bring us to this place and time.

It's all part of His plan.

Knowing this great truth lends a different perspective to the events unfolding before us, doesn't it? That is why, as we look at this flood of change, our souls can take great heart. God not only knows of the flood, but His holy and merciful purposes are being accomplished through it.

Not long ago, my teenager daughter sensed a heavy spirit in me.

"What's wrong, Mom?"

Rats, I thought, *I can't hide anything from my kids.* Debating whether to be frank, I finally said, "Honey, I guess sometimes when I look at what's happening around us, I feel a deep concern for you and your children. I grieve over what you're going to have to deal with someday."

That was a nice way of saying that, at the moment, I was worried. This particular little child has always been tuned in—tuned in to me and to what is happening in the world around her.

"Mom," she said, wrapping her arms around me in a tight hug, "please don't worry. God will take care of me and my children."

What can you say to that? Case closed. We cannot hold back the forces of change. And God is perfectly capable of caring for our children in the midst of it all. He is the mighty Rock, the One who places us on higher ground.

He has also told us the end of the story! Right *will* win out over might. Good *will* be vindicated. Evil *will* be brought into the light and judged. And Jesus Christ *will* be worshiped by one and all. In the end, God's people *will* be preserved. God Almighty has a plan, and this flood of change is part of that plan.

What then, is the real task at hand? Our real task is to discern how to cope, and how to help our children cope in the midst of this great flood.

Coping always requires perspective. You and I need to get perspective in the midst of this flood. It is impossible to make heads or tails of a situation when we are swirling about in the middle of it. And so we must mentally pull ourselves up out of the flood to get the big picture.

We must ask some all-important questions: What caused this flood to begin with? Why was the home the primary victim? Why has it so affected marriage and family? Why have women's issues become so central? And, finally, how do we get to higher ground? Is there a way out?

A look at recent history can begin to give us answers.

DON'T KNOW MUCH ABOUT HISTORY

I can remember sitting in my high school history class…literally counting the minutes before it would be over. Even my thin, aging, bachelor teacher looked bored. He would sit on top of his desk, droning on and on about facts that seemed completely irrelevant to my life. The only interesting thing that happened all period was when he would occasionally take his elastic watchband and pull it towards his face to check the time. We were all waiting for the day the band would break and go flying into his face.

But when I met Steve's ninety-six-year-old grandmother, history took on new meaning. This woman had lived through all but seventy-five years of the Great Flash Flood. When Nanna was born in 1897 into her fifteen-member household, their Kansas farmhouse had two bedrooms and no electricity or running water. (Now, my brain simply cannot compute that.) Her perspective on this century's history didn't come out of a history book. It was in her diary!

Today's women need that sort of wide-angle perspective. It is the story of events that have shaped our lives into what they are today. I believe that if Christian women could get a handle on the events of recent times, the light switch would go on. Much of the present fog of confusion would clear up, and truth would begin to come into focus.

The truth is, we have been *misled* regarding our history and our contemporary plight. Christianity and biblical teaching (as well as the entire male sex) have been blamed in large part for the "oppression" of modern-day woman. Yet nothing could be further from the truth.

Understanding "our story" as women will help us to understand why women felt so trapped at midcentury, why Betty Friedan hit pay dirt with her book *Feminine Mystique,* and why the issue of work is so important to modern Christian women. It will help us to see why "roles" are such a sensitive topic in the church, and why there is so much confusion today over the place and identity of a woman. It will give us a much better understanding of modern men and equip us to respond to the crisis they too are experiencing. Finally, it will explain why Scripture has been so denigrated in recent times.

So, for the next few chapters we are going to travel back into recent times and catch the highlights as they relate to us as women.

A FEW DISCLAIMERS

Let me offer a few disclaimers. First, understand that we will be making general statements relating to a general subject. There are, of course, exceptions to every rule. There have been, and always will be, extremes on either side of the issue. But this should not keep us from drawing accurate conclusions regarding our recent past.

Secondly, this subject could fill an entire library with books. But, for our purposes, we will focus on the home and the roles and relationships that surround it. Our primary goal is to discover how homes—and the women in them—have been affected by the flood.

THE CALM BEFORE THE STORM

The storm that brought us this Great Flash Flood of history hit our land in the early 1800s. Many historians date the beginning as 1815, with the onset of the Industrial Revolution. Although this was less than two centuries ago, culturally it was more like *eons.* For this reason, we must begin with a picture of the world before the great flood hit. We must go back to the calm before the storm, to early colonial America—pre-industrial, pre-flash flood days. And if my guess is right, you are going to be surprised at what you see.

To help us get there, take the wide-angle lens of your mind's eye and focus on another time and place...

Picture a wide open prairie. A gentle breeze ripples an endless sea of grass. Not a person is in sight. Not a sound can be heard, save the rustle of the grass and the buzz of a bee nearby. Far off in the distance you can see a faint chain of smoke, spiraling upward into the sky. And now you begin to make it out. A lone log house, sitting on a small rise. It is, as a matter of fact, a...*little* house.

Chapter Three

Hub in the Middle of the Wheel

~⌒~

*In the early days of the American republic there was no emperor,
but there was moral consensus. Now there is neither an emperor or moral consensus,
and it is likely that we cannot go on indefinitely without both.*

HAROLD O. J. BROWN

hen Laura Ingalls Wilder wrote *Little House on the Prairie,* she was describing a very different world—a world of deprivation, grass fires, Indians, grasshopper plagues, and endless hard work. It was also a world of strong family life, close community ties, and deep faith in God. One thing is certain. Ingall's "little house on the prairie" was light years away from our modern-day "little house on the freeway."

For most of known history, the home has been central to woman. It has been her primary place of work and influence, and thus, the natural place to express her womanhood. Therefore, throughout history—and this is critical—*as the home has gone, so has gone woman.*

But equally as significant is that for most of known history, the home has been the center of society. From biblical times until the Industrial Revolution, this was so. Home was central to life, education, work, and religion. Whether a Roman villa or a tepee in the woods, home was the hub of the wheel of life.

The centrality of the home had significant implications for our early American foremothers. As one historian of colonial times described it, "Home was then indeed the center and heart of social life."[1] It was the place of work, the place of social comings and goings, the place of training and apprenticeship, the place of religious and academic education of children, the place of recreation and fellowship. It was the hospital, school, store, and church. And, as we will see, it was also the government.

Since the home was the hub of society, and since women's primary place of expression was in the home, women were central to society. Their work was central and their role was central. In those days, home was "the place to be."

In preindustrial times, both men and women worked very hard. But their work always revolved around the home. Men worked in businesses connected to the home, or they worked close-by in the fields, cultivating the land, caring for livestock, or hunting for food. Women assisted their husbands in these home-related businesses. They often ran them for long periods of time when their husbands were away. Or, in the case of farm life, which represented most of society, women worked out in the fields when necessary. Indeed, whenever survival was at stake, women did any and every kind of work required to keep their families alive.[2]

Midge Yearley writes: "Women taking important roles in business, politics, the army, the ministry, and the arts is not a recent phenomenon. During the colonial period, the Revolution, and the early years of our nation, women were also active in these fields. Businesses were centered in the home or in nearby offices, and women and children as well as the men worked to make a success of the family business. It was not until the 19th century when most occupations became unsuitable for women."[3]

But primarily, women worked in their homes, producing the necessities for daily living. While their husbands hunted for food and raised the crops, their lives were consumed with hours of production—grinding wheat, preserving fruit, curing meat, baking bread, making candles and soap, weaving material for clothing and bedding, hauling firewood and water, washing clothes by hand, preparing meals, and caring for the children. In conjunction with their husbands, they were the teachers of their children, and until the late 1800s, they were the nurses as well.[4]

PREFLOOD WOMEN AND WORK

Therefore, the work of preflood women in the home was absolutely paramount to survival. For this reason, they lived with a sense of challenge and value. Every ounce of energy, skill, and intelligence they could muster was required for the tasks they did daily.

In essence, prior to the Industrial Revolution, the home was a self-sufficient entity. One farmer wrote in 1787: "My farm gave me and my whole family a good living…for I never spent more than ten dollars a year, which was for salt, nails, and the like. Nothing to eat, drink or wear was bought, as my farm provided all."[5]

But this also meant that their work was very hard. Life itself was very hard, harder than you and I can begin to fathom. Just making it all happen was a tough, unending task. The struggle, therefore, in a woman's life did not revolve around a lack of value or importance. Nor did it revolve around a sense of inhibition from the man's world. Why? Because her role *was* important, and her world *was* her husband's world.

Women were not walking around with a driving desire to do a man's work, either. When it came to hard, physical labor, men unquestionably had the greater job. It was the burden of the husband to fight the elements of nature, to carry logs and build houses, to plant and raise crops, to provide when the crops failed, to hunt in the woods where wild carnivores lived, to ride for days if necessary to get supplies, to protect from Indians, to fight prairie fires and grasshopper plagues and wars.

No, the struggle for colonial women lay in the difficulty and unending nature of their own tasks in the home. It lay in the isolation they felt out "on the prairie" and in the necessity to be utterly resourceful and self-reliant. Last, but not least, it lay in the inherent dangers in becoming a mother.

Look at the difficulty they faced in motherhood. Every pregnant woman had to face the strong possibility that she or her baby would not survive the birth. Just think of that! So many women died while giving birth that in 1801 the life expectancy for a woman was thirty-five.[6]

Infant mortality was heartbreakingly common. Most mothers buried at least one child, and despite the trend of large families, it was not uncommon for parents to have no children outlive them. In the absence of life-saving drugs and vaccines, older children were vulnerable to infectious diseases. As a result, mothers spent much of their lives nursing sick children. Because of the hardships, it was a rare woman who lived to see her grandchildren.[7]

What about the difficulty she faced in sustaining the home? Once again, we cannot comprehend the enormous task of taking care of a home without electricity or running water.

Consider the task of hauling water. Although husbands and older children may have brought water in each morning, much more was needed throughout the day. So the job fell to women. One historian describes the size of this task still being done in the 1940s by women in the Texas hill country, an area that had yet to receive running water and electricity: "Since the average farm family was five persons, the family used 200 gallons, or four-fifths of a ton, of water each day—73,000 gallons, or almost 300 tons, in a year.... On the average the well was located 253 feet from the house and...to pump by hand and carry to the house 73,000 gallons of water a year would require someone to put in during that year 63 eight-hour days, and walk 1,750 miles."[8]

Now I ask you, do you have the slightest urge to go back to those days? Just one week without air conditioning in the midsummer heat of Texas is enough to make me wonder why anyone settled south of the Mason-Dixon line. But consider life without lights, water, phone, or antibiotics. No department stores. No sewing machine. Consider spending months weaving the material for a single shirt for your husband. Consider weaving all of your family's and servants' clothing, all of your sheets and curtains. Consider cooking without a stove or oven, and never being able to run to a grocery store for *anything*. [9]

Life was very hard. As I look at life in those times, I am convinced, given my health record, that I probably would not have survived, nor would one or more of our children.

THE PIONEERING CHARACTER OF PREFLOOD WOMEN

As one writer put it, the feats performed by our early American foremothers "required the strength of Hercules, the skill of Tubal Cain, and the patience of Job."[10] When a crisis occurred on the prairie, there was no 9-1-1. What's more, husbands were often out in the fields, out of earshot, or off in the woods hunting. A husband might have to be gone for days at a time on hunting trips, and the nearest neighbor was usually more than a mile away. At such times, survival depended on a woman's sheer grit and ingenuity.

Reading the true stories of these women would cause your hair to stand on end. Women fought off wolves and Indians by themselves, saved their children from floods and grass fires, doctored their husbands and children after horrible accidents and injuries, and even fought the British on their own doorstep with knives and axes. I read one woman's account of going into labor unexpectedly while her husband was out on a two-day trip. In the midst of caring for her toddler, she hauled water, boiled it, gave birth, cut the cord, washed the baby, and had dinner ready when her husband returned.

Contrary to the opinion of some, early American women were not a mindless, downtrodden sort. Nor were their daughters. Pioneering was not for the faint of heart. The early women of this country chose to leave the comforts of known civilization and take on a New World. The colonization of our country took an ingenious, spirited, and very independent woman who could hold her own—which is just exactly what she often had to do. What we find in the early records of these women is an extraordinary endurance, unyielding tenacity, deep conviction, and a strong sense of purpose. In fact, according to the men of their day, the Revolutionary War could not have been won without them.[11]

How then, did their daughters fare? In a word, superbly. The women of the nineteenth century were no less strong and resourceful, no less diligent workers, and no less influential in their culture.

PREFLOOD WOMEN AND THEIR MEN

How did the hardships and trials of these early days in our nation's history affect the institution of marriage?

It only made it stronger.

The level of commitment in marriage was extremely high. Why? In part, it was because men and women *needed each other* so much. Husband and wife were a team, working together for survival. They were each other's primary source of support and companionship. But just as binding as their need for one another was the value they placed on loving commitment. The value system of our forefathers flowed directly from Scripture, and this was the glue that held life together in such difficult times.

One of the best-known examples of the colonial attitudes toward marriage can be found in the relationship of John Adams, second president of the United States, and his wife, Abigail. This couple actually represented the fairly average family in those days; both John and Abigail came from moderate homes and backgrounds. Due to the traveling his job required, they maintained much of their relationship through letters, leaving us with an unusually rich picture of their lives and a reflection of the attitudes of the day.

In one such letter, Abigail wrote: "My dearest Friend…I hope soon to receive the dearest of friends, and the tenderst of husbands, with that unabated affection which has for years past, and will whilst the vital spark lasts, burn in the bosom of your affectionate—A. Adams."[12]

Are these the words of a prudish and stifled woman? Even in our sex-enamored society, the relationship of John and Abigail would have stood up well. Another time she wrote: "Beneath my humble roof, blessed with the society and tenderest affection of my dear partner, I have enjoyed as much felicity and as exquisite happiness, as fall to the share of mortals...."[13]

George Washington wrote to his wife: "I should enjoy more real happiness in one month with you at home than I have the most distant prospect of finding abroad, if my stay were to be seven times seven years...."[14]

And Alexander Hamilton's father-in-law wrote at the death of his wife: "But after giving and receiving for nearly half a century a series of mutual evidences of affection and friendship which increased as we advanced in life, the shock was great and sensibly felt, to be thus suddenly deprived of a beloved wife, the mother of my children, and the soothing companion of my declining years."[15]

These are not the writings of male chauvinist brutes.

The evidence is overwhelming in the early diaries, letters, poetry, and other writings of colonial men and women—preindustrial marriage was in good shape. What's more, these early colonists were quite open in their expression of love for one another.[16]

I was particularly struck by the freedom men had in involving their wives in their work. When a woman showed skill, as she often did, she was encouraged to develop and use it. Women expressed their talents through their family businesses, through art, writing, journalism, publishing, and agricultural science. In short, husbands in general placed a high value on their wives' talents and abilities.

This is not to deny unhappy marriages existed. Sin is sin is sin. There were men who harshly controlled and took advantage of their wives. Likewise, there were women who ruled obsessively and drove their husbands crazy—just like today. Such dysfunction has been present since Adam, Eve, and the boys. There were couples who undoubtedly had prudish ideas. And certain writers of the time reflected an overbearing view of a man's role in relationship to a woman. But they simply did not represent the mainstream. The bulk of the writings shows that marriage generally was characterized by the biblical mandates of mutual appreciation, commitment, and love.

Parenting was also quite different in those times. As you can well imagine, surviving children were precious to their parents. Granted, some mothers who had lost children found it hard to become emotionally attached to a child until they were certain he or she was a survivor.[17] But what we see most often is that children were highly valued and deeply loved.[18]

They were also key to the family's survival. At an early age they assumed responsibilities for helping at home and out on the farm. They were constantly with their parents, assisting and being trained. Teenagers, per se, did not exist. In fact, the word *teenager* did not enter our language until 1940. Children were pledged to family—not peer group. At adolescence, they were busy at work in the home or in jobs elsewhere, bringing home their pay for the family's use. When the time came, therefore, they simply moved from childhood into adulthood.[19]

But, most importantly, both parents assumed responsibility for the teaching and raising of their children. Mothers in preflood times did not carry the sole burden of child rearing, as they would after the Industrial Revolution. Sermons and advice books regarding the upbringing of children consistently addressed both parents. And, while the young children were usually in the care of their mother, as they came of age, fathers began to play a key role.[20]

Fathers were, in fact, the overseers of their children's education. We have a hard time relating to this in a day when many fathers don't even know the names of their children's teachers! Preflood fathers also spent considerable time with their sons, in particular, while mothers spent focused time with their daughters. Since eight-to-five workdays simply didn't exist and business was a family affair, business fathers were far more available to the home. Likewise, farmers had more time in the winter months after planting and harvesting seasons were over. Dads ate meals with their families, played with their families, read to their families, and led in the training and teaching of their families.[21]

But mothers also played a vital role in the education and training of their children. A woman's own education was therefore vital to her parenting role. Abigail Adams was sick as a child and unable to receive an education. But because it was so important in her mothering, she educated herself as an adult, becoming a prolific writer and one of the best-informed women of her day. John relied heavily on her instruction of their children when he traveled. (One of their children, John

Quincy Adams, went on to become the sixth president of the United States.) In a letter regarding her training of the children, John Sr. wrote: "Train them to Virtue, habituate them to industry, activity, and Spirit...fire them with Ambition to be useful.... It is time, my dear, for you to begin to teach them French. Every Decency, Grace, and Honesty should be inculcated upon them."[22]

Today, women who have gone to college find that their education has done almost nothing to prepare them for motherhood—and that motherhood makes little use of their education. In preflood times, however, a woman's education proved absolutely essential.

Much has been made of the fact that many colonial women did not write, leading people to assume that preflood women were uneducated. We now know this was not true. Early American women, though mostly poor, came from the educated classes of Europe. However, paper and ink were so rare and expensive in those days that penmanship was considered an art to be mastered by only a few. As a result, writing became a luxury, while reading, on the other hand, was considered a must. Men were often compelled to learn to write because of their role in society, but many women did not find it necessary to go to the expense or time. Nonetheless, those same women were often well read in the great literature of the world and could recite large portions of history, as well as translate Greek and Latin.[23] (I took Latin in high school and some Greek in seminary, and I can translate neither.)

SCRIPTURE AND THE HOME IN PREFLOOD TIMES

Scripture was utterly relevant to the preflood home. Just how relevant would surprise us in these baby boomer, baby buster days. For starters, let me give you a quick pop quiz. Who do you think could have made the following three statements?

•It is impossible to rightly govern the world without God and the Bible.

•We have staked the whole future of American civilization...to sustain ourselves according to the Ten Commandments of God.

•It cannot be emphasized too strongly or too often that this great nation was founded, not by religionists, but by Christians; not on religion, but on the gospel of Jesus Christ.

Pat Buchanan perhaps? James Dobson? How about Billy Graham? No, they were made, respectively, by George Washington, James Madison, and Patrick

Henry. The same guy who uttered the famous words "Give me liberty or give me death!" banked his liberty on the gospel of Christ.

If modern Americans truly understood the centrality of Scripture in public and private life during preflood times, they would be shocked. Today we watch the Tonight Show or Letterman before yawning and turning out the light. Yet there was a time when people, as a way of life, read Scripture before retiring at night.[24] The Bible was so prominent that leaders could quote obscure verses and the general populace would know the passages from which they spoke. Today a presidential candidate can completely misquote a familiar verse, and no one will catch it.

In the early days of home-taught children, the Bible was central to their training. Every home, poor or rich, had a Bible, and in the poorer homes it was often the only book. Children were taught to read and write their letters from Scripture. And the Bible was memorized and read together as a regular part of family life.[25]

When schools began to form, children learned the Ten Commandments, as well as other portions of Scripture. The result was an emphasis on *moral* correctness rather than *political* correctness. As historian Annegret Ogden writes, "To that generation of parents, character mattered more than a great deal of academic learning."[26]

The Bible was quoted as a way of life by generals, writers, teachers, employers, judges, and yes...even lawyers. Today, a case can literally be thrown out of court if a lawyer chooses to quote from Scripture. But in those times, legal proceedings and judgments were *based* upon the words and tenants of Scripture.

In essence, the teachings of Scripture permeated our culture, our politics, and our homes. That's why our coins were stamped "In God We Trust." That's why Ben Franklin called everyone to a time of prayer when the Continental Congress came to an impasse.[27] That's why our Constitution and every other expression of our early government acknowledged our need for God Almighty. And that is certainly why George Washington proclaimed the first national Thanksgiving Day, declaring it a day for the nation to "remember and honor the Great Ruler of the nations...(for pouring out) His mercies uniquely upon us and...(giving) us prosperity."[28]

Even corporate America once bowed its knee to the Almighty. Can you imagine thousands of businessmen gathering for prayer in the public squares of our land? Yet that is precisely what happened during the great financial panic of 1857-1859.[29]

Our forefathers understood one thing clearly. A nation is only as good as the moral convictions of the people who govern it. Indeed, they had a deep sense from Whence they had come, and a healthy fear of what might happen if they forgot it.

HOMES: THE HUB OF PREFLOOD GOVERNMENT

One final factor affected the home in preflood times. And that was government. Home was the primary government in early America. This is hard for you and me to comprehend, but there was no formal, nationally organized government as we now know it. Laws existed, as well as a lean network of government to see that they were enforced. But there was no such thing as financial security, health care, public education, or crisis insurance. Even those who fought in war received no assistance or remuneration in gratitude for the lives they gave.

This meant one thing. Men were wholly and utterly responsible for their families. Since the home embodied the primary government of early America, local families basically determined how things were run in their world. Families, not government, provided for needs. The needy were dependent on the good will and generosity of their families and neighbors.

In light of this, the laws of the day made a great deal of sense. With no one but himself to turn to in times of trouble, a man by necessity had legal authority over his home. Family property was therefore a man's responsibility. By law he was required to provide food, shelter, and clothing for his wife, children, and servants. Notably, his widow was entitled by law to one-third of his estate to ensure that she did not fall into poverty or servitude after his death.

A woman's dependence on her husband was seen as anything but weakness on her part, or suppression on his. What's more, we find nothing to indicate unhappiness with this arrangement. Women didn't feel the need to hold legal rights to family property, or income, or children. Men were ultimately held responsible, and if they dropped the ball, they were duly confronted. Every town had select men who by law were to enforce family morals and see that family government was upheld.[30] In short, communities cared for one another and held one another accountable.

It also helps to understand that our legal system was adapted from British law and underwent a period of transformation before it fully reflected democratic thinking. Our early government needed time in the birthing of democracy.

Abigail wrote to John regarding some of the antiquated British laws carried over into America that unnecessarily restricted women. And, in due time, these were brought into line with the thinking that had spawned the Constitution.[31]

Generally speaking, however, it was for the woman's benefit that a man was held responsible, as well as for the benefit of society. We must understand that as committed as the early settlers were to the idea of independence, they were equally committed to the idea of *inter*dependence within the family. And such interdependence is what made life work so well.

For this reason, the church was also important. The church was the vehicle through which families could care for one another. When special needs arose, when someone lost a child or mate, when crops or businesses failed, families turned to the church. Just as husbands and wives and children stuck together, so did the community, and so did the church.

THE FEMINIZATION OF PREFLOOD HISTORY

Have you been surprised by any of this? Quite honestly, I was. Chances are, your perspective on preflood days, like mine, has been influenced by the "feminization" of women's history. Let me explain.

The historian's job is to accumulate facts, interpret them, and then report them, much like a modern reporter—except without live eyewitnesses, video cameras, and Nielsen reports. Just as in television news the viewers are highly dependent on the perspective and integrity of the one reporting, so it is in historical analysis.

Here's the point. Until recently, political feminists have dominated the field of women's history. Carroll Smith-Rosenberg, a feminist and women's historian, says in her book *Disorderly Conduct* that "women's history is the daughter of political feminism."[32]

The word *feminist*, in its purest sense, simply means "advocate of woman." Given this definition, Jesus Christ was one of the greatest feminists of all time. And so were the apostles.

However, the feminism we are speaking of is represented by the philosophy and platforms of the National Organization for Women and other modern activist groups. These are the feminists who have been at the forefront of research into recent women's history. They have started, chaired, and run the women's studies programs in universities all over the country, and were it not for their interest and research, we would have had far less interest ourselves in the history of modern women. For this, we are indebted.

But the alliance between feminism and women's history has also given the world a skewed picture. Why? Because of their evolutionary view of women.

Historian Frances Cogen points out that the theory of evolutionary feminism—the philosophy that women began in an oppressed state and have progressed into a higher and modern consciousness—overshadows their work. Anything failing to support this evolutionary theory often is dismissed or twisted. Feminist historians have also tended to draw heavily from European writings, using the Victorian "lady of leisure" image from eighteenth and nineteenth century European culture. We know, however, that American women were a quite different breed from the frivolous, male-dominated, European stereotype. Benjamin Franklin and Thomas Jefferson, both of whom traveled widely in Europe, even wrote about the vast difference between American women and their European counterparts.[33]

The result of such feminization has been a warped and stereotyped picture of colonial and postcolonial homes as strict, prudish, repressive, and unhappy. The feminist picture has so permeated modern thinking that it persists in modern articles and books, despite more recent evidence to the contrary.

But I believe there is another reason feminist historians have tended to view history as they have. We could call it the "Scripture factor." Preflood homes found their model essentially in Scripture—the biblical model of male leadership with the wife as helpmate. Influential women often spoke of the priority of supporting and helping their husbands in leadership, while influential men spoke just as often of the value of their wives' help in their lives.

We read time and again that the woman was "held in high respect, her advice often asked, and her influence marked" by men.[34] One nineteenth century writer recorded this remarkable observation: "American men have a reputation the world over for their superior treatment of women. European men...do not understand American women's desire for education, autonomy in decisions regarding housekeeping and family, or their degree of independence...."[35] These attitudes are notably biblical.

Modern political feminists, however, consider the Bible to be an outdated and dangerous book. Unfortunately, most have misunderstood what Scripture teaches. But since it remains inconceivable to hard-core feminists that roles based on biblical teaching can lead to healthy homes, or that gifted women can find fulfillment through the biblical plan, their work reflects a certain "blindness" to the facts. They are absolutely convinced that male leadership, or "patriarchalism" as they call it, is death to women and their cause, and they are wholly committed to its overthrow. Therefore, anything that comes from the biblical model is suspect to the modern feminist.

THE DAY THE DAM BROKE

How did these roles play themselves out in preflood times? On this historians agree. Women were in essence the functioning, presiding officer in the most central component of society—the home. Men, on the other hand, were the protectors, providers, and overseers. Men held ultimate responsibility for their homes and families. And they were the primary spokesmen and defenders of their homes to the outside world.

Looking back now, we can see this era as the calm before the storm.

During the late 1700s, ribbons of steel rail line began to push through forests, cling to mountainsides and span mighty rivers. Factories rose up out of the pasturelands. Industrialization—with all of its inherent sweeping—hovered on America's horizon like a sultry storm front.

And then the storm hit. With the onset of the Industrial Revolution in the early 1800s, industry swept across our young nation, bringing with it the Great Flash Flood of change.

No one could foresee what was about to happen to the home.

Chapter Four

Whitewater Rapids

Revolution is never peaceful.

MALCOLM X

When the whirlwind passes, the wicked is no more,
But the righteous has an everlasting foundation.

PROVERBS 10:25

I grew up in a day when the idea of revolution had an exciting ring to it. Baggy-jeaned hippies roamed across our campus, wearing flowers in their hair. The rest of us wore bell-bottoms and earth shoes and lined our dorm rooms with hip posters. The music of Bob Dylan and the Rolling Stones wailed through our walls as we sat studying ancient history or modern business. You could get high on marijuana just walking down the hall.

I never knew what the next day would bring. One day a "streaker" would run past me as I sat studying under a tree. (If you don't know, ask your mother.) The next day Jane Fonda would be speaking to antiwar demonstrators as I walked by the campus quadrant. None of us had an inkling how this little revolutionary fling would impact our nation and future. Yet here we are some thirty years hence, wearing suits on the outside and freedom flowers on the inside. The hippie generation has retooled America.

Although we perceived ourselves as the new thinkers challenging the old, we were nothing of the kind. We were a tiny, somewhat inconsequential part of a much bigger revolution, the rumblings of which could be heard some 150 years before.

Perspective is a wonderful thing.

REVOLUTION!

Revolution. Economic revolution. Technological revolution. Medical revolution. Cultural revolution. Political revolution. Moral revolution. All kicked off by the Industrial Revolution.

In three brief sentences the *World Book Encyclopedia* describes its beginnings: "Industry was taken out of the home and the workshop. Handwork was replaced by machinery. Great factories managed by skilled organizers changed the way of life of a whole countryside within a few years."[1]

But why would an Industrial Revolution be the start of a Great Flash Flood? What made it so different? *World Book* says what made these times so revolutionary was "not simply change, but the speeding up in the rate of change itself."[2] Such an incredible rate of change meant only one thing—flash flood.

The flood of change started with industry. Change in industry brought change in work. Change in work brought change in the home. And change in the home brought substantial change to all of life.

"Little house" was headed into the Whitewater Rapids.

Clearly, revolution in industry was a blessing to the world. It eased our burdens and lengthened our lives. It took over the laborious tasks that had so consumed women in the home—weaving, grinding, canning. And it provided an environment of inventive competition, ushering in the age of technology.

But along with all of this blessing came a great curse. Fathers left home. It was as simple as that.

When men walked out the door to go to work in factories, the first *father-absent* society was instituted. And, even though it took a century before our country was fully industrialized, the impact of male absence was felt immediately. The result was great change in the lives of men, women, and children—a change from which the home has yet to recover.

DADS LOST IN THE RAPIDS

For the first time in history, the spheres of men and women became separated. Although men and women had been separated sporadically before for matters of politics and war, this separation was different. This time, man's business—his daily, provisionary work—was taken out of the home. If a man wished to protect and provide through industry, he had to leave his wife and children for the better part of his waking hours. (An average workday was ten to twelve hours.)

In a sense, a new world—man's working world—was created. Man's sphere became the world outside the home, while a woman's sphere remained inside the home with her children. Women didn't enter into the man's world, and men became less involved in a woman's world.

Unprecedented progress also put a spotlight on public life, causing it to become preeminent over private life and lessening the value and importance of the home—woman's world. So even though women continued to work very hard, they received less and less recognition for that work in society. With each decade of progress, man's outside world broadened, while woman's inside world shriveled.[3]

Not only did father-absence diminish the importance of the home, but it dealt a great blow to every relationship within the home. The blow was not only felt by women and children, but contrary to what some have thought, *it was also felt by men*. In short, family teamwork as a way of life—teamwork in marriage, teamwork in parenting, teamwork in the work of provision itself—became a thing of the past.

MALE ABSENCE AND WOMEN

Because women are relational by nature, they felt deeply the loss of a close working relationship with their husbands. No longer were companionship and communication natural parts of life. They and their husbands had to work much harder at keeping unity in marriage. They had to go the extra mile to stay in tune with one another. As a result, it was inevitable that marriage would suffer...and divorce would increase.

The loss of fathers also meant that mothers were left holding the bag at home. By necessity, the responsibilities of educating and rearing the children now fell solely to mothers. They became the primary caregivers, primary disciplinarians, primary teachers, primary role models, primary *everything* to their children.[4]

Beyond this, something else happened that was a great disadvantage to women. Women had generally had servant help with washing, cleaning, cooking, caring for children. Sometimes that help came through neighborhood young people, earning keep for their families. Sometimes from hired hands. Women had been managers, in a sense, of a small corporation. But with the rise of industry, mothers gradually began to lose that vital help. Since pay was better in the factories, people who had once been an integral part of the woman's work force were now lured to work in industry.[5] This left mothers even further isolated and alone.

Oddly enough, in the midst of all this unprecedented expansion and growth, women became increasingly cut off and lonely in their diminishing world. "City life," said Henry David Thoreau, "is millions of people being lonesome together." But for a woman whose work was at home, and whose participation in city life was minimal, the isolation was even more pronounced. Common sense tells us that removal of such a relational creature from the world at large, from her husband, and eventually from her own children, could never work over the long haul.

As society took over production and simultaneously attributed less value to their work, women began looking elsewhere for their sense of influence, purpose, and self-esteem. It should not surprise us that the first Women's Rights Congress was held in 1848. But these early feminists could not gain the ear of the mainstream woman—for three good reasons.

The first was that in the early industrial years, a woman's work was still essential to life and society. Until the late 1800s, there were no public schools, no department stores, no restaurants, theaters, or malls, no antibiotics or hospitals. Women still sewed their family's clothing, fed them, nursed them when they were sick, and raised and educated the children. Though the home was losing its position as the hub of the wheel, women sensed the overarching value of their work in society. In fact, the great wheel of society could not have turned without them.[6]

Secondly, women enjoyed their work in the home as never before. Freed from many of the laborious tasks of production, they could give more attention to their home and children. With every new invention came new opportunities for creativity in their cooking, sewing, and decorating. Work in the home, at least for now, was still challenging.[7]

Finally, for the better part of the 1800s, men continued to underscore the value of women. We know this from many of the writings of the men in that day—Ralph Waldo Emerson, Nathaniel Hawthorne, Henry Wadsworth Longfellow, William Andrus Alcott. Unlike today, women were praised, even put on a pedestal, for their invaluable role as mother and caregiver of the home. Therefore, until the late 1800s, women continued to flourish, and marriage held strong.[8]

By the turn of the century, however, polarization was taking its toll, and a woman's work had fallen sharply in its "market value."

MALE ABSENCE AND CHILDREN

Children also suffered from the loss of relationship with their dads. Granted, children thrived under the increased time and energy their moms were now able to give them. And, likewise, by the turn of the century, a child's life span and quality of life had greatly improved.[9] But, despite these blessings, the loss of their dads proved more devastating than anyone might have imagined.

In short, children no longer received the on-site supervision, training, and discipline of their fathers. They no longer *saw* their fathers model character, virtue, and the ethics of hard work. And, worst of all, they no longer knew their fathers, nor did their fathers know them.

They say absence makes the heart grow fonder. Well, perhaps for a day or two. But absence throughout a childhood creates strangers. We simply cannot parent a child whose heart we do not know. And so it was that children were no longer "fathered" in the true sense of the term.

Unfortunately for boys, father-absence also meant male absence. In preflood days, families generally lived in close association with extended family. But as the flood of change began to rumble through society, families lived in smaller, nuclear units that moved about as industry required. Uncles and grandfathers became a less vital part of families. As a result, a young boy did not have another older man in his life to offset the absence of his dad and to serve as a male role model.[10]

For a boy, this absence was devastating. No longer did he accompany his dad into the family business or out into the fields. No longer did he have a template upon which to place himself as he became a man. The one he needed most in his growing-up years was simply not around. Whom could he talk to about the issues of his male life? Whom could he observe in forming his own patterns of fathering and husbanding? How would he learn to relate to other men on a deeper level?

The results of father-absence became increasingly pronounced as the generations passed. Each generation of boys grew up with a deeper void than the one before, until eventually it was a rare man who had a clear picture of what it meant to be a man, and a rarer man still who had not grieved over the dad he never had. Such grief was quiet, often unspoken, but nonetheless real. It was also cumulative. Lost fathers have been by far the greatest tragedy for boys growing up in the Great Flash Flood.

Young girls also suffered from this lost relationship with their fathers. It took longer for the effects to be seen, since girls were blessed with the presence of their mothers as they grew up. But eventually father-attention-deficit and father-love-deficit began to show up. Young girls began to search elsewhere for the love and affirmation they lacked from their own dads. The isolation and resulting void felt by their mothers was also passed on to them. As young boys grew up to withdraw into their own success-driven worlds, girls grew up more and more envious of men. It appeared that only in a man's world could they find affirmation and release from isolation. In the end, father-deficit and polarization from men in general would contribute to an inevitable revolt among women.

THE PRICE MEN PAID

Often overlooked, however, is the price that men paid for the great progress of the world. An industry worker's life was a year-round job, usually with poor conditions and pay. Men, therefore, had less time with their wives and children and, consequently, less influence in the home. They also lost control over their working world and were increasingly at the mercy of employers and big business. Since most business in those days was "new business," failures were common and without benefits or guarantees to those left jobless.[11]

In short, with the mentoring role taken out of a man's work, the focus shifted to promotion and success. Work now served the primary purpose of self-actualization and affirmation.[12] American men latched on to this idea with such gusto that European writers noted the unhealthy work frenzy and addiction among the early industrial men of our land.[13]

But let's not kid ourselves. Men missed their families, too. Often desperately. The nature of the world of business allowed only one part of a man to be expressed—his warrior side. Business drew heavily on his aggressive, competitive, protective instincts, all the while holding his tender side at bay.

As a result, relationships of depth and meaning in a man's working world were rare to nonexistent. He certainly could not express his feelings of anxiety or fear at work. Nor could he freely express emotions of love and affection. Conversation at work centered around the job at hand—success, competition, winning the race—not around relationships or personal feelings and needs. A man learned to ignore his deeper emotional and relational needs in order to function in the dog-eat-dog world. And so, in due time, the relational and emotional side of man literally began to starve. Tenderness gave way to a hard exterior. Affection gave way to aloofness. Enjoyment of family gave way to drive for success. And, finally, teamwork and companionship gave way to authoritarianism.

It is almost impossible for modern Americans to comprehend the loss of a man's role as father. Consider a day in the lives of these two men: one on a farm in Kansas a century ago, and the other, a thoroughly modernized man.

Sunrise in Kansas, 1890

A father rises early with his family and oversees the morning prayers and chores. Together with his older children, he cuts firewood and hauls water. When breakfast is finished, he heads out to work alone in the fields. On the horizon he sees a storm brewing. His back and arms ache, but time is of the essence. He must stay with it. Remembering the floods of the previous summer, he prays that God will spare him this season. Their survival depends on it.

At noon, he breaks for lunch and returns home. The children rush up to hug him and sit in his lap. His wife prepares lunch, and, as they eat, he converses with these, his "significant others." The baby cries and he takes a moment to rock him. Then a moment more to fix a broken toy or discipline a wayward child. If time permits, he will read to the children, discuss a history lesson, or work a problem of math. Then grabbing his oldest son, off they go to work shoulder to shoulder until dusk. The storm holds off until a full day's work has been done.

As dark settles in, the rain begins to fall. Inside, family conversation gives way to music and the telling of stories. Dad pulls out his violin and plays a little tune. Finally the children go to bed, dozing off to the patter of the rain. He stokes the fire, pulls up his rocker, and looks into the eyes of his wife, his companion.

Sunrise in Kansas, 1990

A father rises before his children awaken. He puts out the cat, showers, and dresses, then grabs his coffee and paper. Communing with the radio and rush hour traffic, he finally arrives at work twenty minutes late. How could he have guessed traffic would be backed up this morning? Starting his day on the run, he flies to his first meeting. The rest of the morning is filled with phone calls, dictation, a minor crisis over an employee's incompetence, and yet another meeting. Got to keep moving if you plan to get ahead.

Just before lunch, a memo crosses his desk. The rumor is confirmed. Yes, the company is downsizing, and, yes, jobs will be cut. A sense of panic tightens his chest and increases his heart rate. But over lunch with a client, it disappears into his subconscious. It is absolutely critical that he exude calm and confidence. Everything depends on the sale. Shaking hands for the tenth time that day, he returns to his desk and calls home. Everything is fine, but it will be another late night at work. No one else is leaving the office—especially now, when the company is taking stock. Why should he leave and risk his job?

As darkness blankets the city, he hangs up his car phone and pulls into the driveway. Momentarily out from under the pressure, all he can think of is getting off his suit and sinking into a comfortable chair. The children race up in their jammies and jump into his lap. But he is tired. He really needs a break. A few words about school and baseball, a kiss and a hug, and the kids are off to bed.

After a warmed-over meal, Dad sinks into his chair and flips from channel to channel. He has talked all day and has nothing left to say. Staring blankly into the tube, he gazes into the eyes of…a plethora of beautiful and sexy women.

It's tough for today's father to be a father. It is tough because he has to fight every day to maintain balance, to stay in touch, to be involved, to save energy for the relationships that are most important to him. He must fight the impulse to push toward success, and resist the urge to succumb to passivity at the end of the day. Not to mention temptation.

Dr. Frank Pittman, author and psychologist, summarized this struggle that has been rooted in the Great Flash Flood:

> For a couple of hundred years now, each generation of fathers has passed on less and less to his sons—not just less power but less wisdom. And less love. We finally reached a point where many fathers were largely irrelevant in the lives of their sons.…
>
> In addition, over the same 200 years, each generation of fathers has had less authority than the last. The concept of fatherhood changed dras-

tically after the Industrial Revolution.... As a result, masculinity ceased to be defined in terms of domestic involvement—that is, skills at fathering and husbanding—and began to be defined in terms of making money. Men stopped doing all the things they used to do. Instead, they became primarily Father, the Provider, bringing things home to the family rather than living and working at home *within* the family.... Once a father had moved out of family life and become part of a work crew, family values ceased to be his primary definers of himself.... His work ceased to be something he did for the sake of his family and became work for the sake of work.... In his mind, he had moved out. He had gone to conquer the world....

Life for most boys and for many grown men, then, is a frustrating search for the lost father who has not yet offered protection, provision, nurturing, modeling, or especially, anointment.[14]

Fathering, says Pittman, is the most masculine thing a man can do. Yet of this, men have been deprived. Suffice it to say that men have paid a steep price for the revolution of work in our country.

Despite all of this, we can say that the home remained in tact through the Whitewater Rapids. Scripture still held its grip in everyday life, a factor that was soon to change. Women still felt a sense of value, another factor that would change. And family was keeping its head above water. Somehow home had managed to keep from drowning.

But in 1870, the scene changed. For it was then that a second wave of change hit the nation. A wave so fast, furious, and powerful we could easily compare it to a great waterfall.

Something like the mighty Niagara.

Chapter Five

Niagara Falls

～⌒

*It is ridiculous to call this an industry. This is rat eat rat. Dog eat dog.
I'll kill 'em, and I'm going to kill 'em before they kill me.
You're talking about the American way of survival of the fittest.*

RAY KROC, BUILDER OF MCDONALD'S EMPIRE

Storms make trees take deeper roots.

CLAUDE MCDONALD

*F*ifty years ago, when couples got married, they honeymooned at Niagara Falls.

Today, forget the Falls. They'd rather go to Bermuda or Hawaii. You can see the falls any old day, right? As a result, chances are that most of you have never seen Niagara Falls. Neither have I.

They say that Niagara Falls is one of the great wonders of the world. Its waters flow out of the Niagara River at the northeastern border of Canada and America. In the summer these magnificent falls plunge 500,000 tons of water every minute into a steep-walled gorge 165 feet below. In the winter, the falls are transformed into a white fairyland of ice, forming great icicles that hang down from the brink. It's a sight to behold. (I've seen the pictures!)

But there is yet another point of wonder surrounding these falls. Every year, like clockwork, an average of six or seven people die while sightseeing at the park. Not from heart attacks or suicides.

These people die from curiosity.

Despite continual warnings from the park, there are always a few people who decide to flirt with danger. Stepping over the ropes, they slide up to the edge to get that one perfect picture...and then, in the blink of an eye, they are gone, never to be seen again.

Could this be why honeymooning couples go to Maui these days? Something like that would certainly put a damper on a marriage (no pun intended)! In all seriousness, a fall into the Niagara is deadly on two counts. Not only must you survive the fall, but you must survive the swirling current below. For at the base of Niagara Falls are the world famous Whirlpool Rapids, a swirling funnel as violent as any current in the world. Even if a person could withstand the 165-foot fall, the swirling currents at the bottom would get him.

The eighty years from 1870 until 1950 were just like the mighty Niagara. Just as fast. Just as turbulent. Just as powerful. And just as treacherous.

These years made the rapids of the 1800s look like bathwater bubbles by comparison.

THIRTY-FIVE YEARS: A GENERATION TO REMEMBER

If you are a forty-something woman, your great-grandmother grew up during this amazing time. Talk about a generation gap—look at this:

- 1870s—invention of electric generator
- 1876—invention of the telephone
- 1878—invention of electric lighting, leading to use of electric power
- 1887—invention of first car
- 1903—first plane flown
- 1905—atomic energy discovered

In thirty-five years we went from the discovery of electricity to the release of the atom. We went from lugging water up the hill to flipping light switches, driving cars, making phone calls, and flying planes. I would imagine that if a person had a difficult time with change, these years were like a wild coaster ride. Your great-grandmother had to be as flexible as Play-Doh and as tough as cement to endure such turbulence.

Along with this technology came unprecedented breakthroughs in medicine. With the introduction of antibiotics we entered an age of life-saving discoveries. And by the turn of the century, infant mortality had dropped, while the life expectancy of a woman climbed to forty-nine years.[1]

Our increasing ability to preserve life was outpaced only by our new ability to destroy it. Tanks and fighter planes replaced horses and wagons. The atomic bomb replaced rifles and cannons—just in time for a world at war.

Knowledge was mushrooming at such a rate that in each *year* following World War I, we acquired more knowledge than in any previous *century* of history.

With phones we could communicate at a moment's notice, and with cars we could move about at will. Two decades before, such activities had taken days and months. Granted, it took time for these discoveries to become part of daily life, but we became enamored—you could even say bewitched—by our accomplishments. Suddenly we were on our way to the top. The sky was the limit...and after 1903 and Orville Wright, even that no longer limited us. Scientists became almost godlike to us. Mankind was now capable of the impossible.

In this flurry of progress, we had an unprecedented boom. Boom in education. Boom in research. Boom in business. Boom in large cities and corporations.

But life was also very unstable in these times. Potential for great achievement was surpassed only by the potential for great loss. While there were vast amounts of money to be made, there was just as much to lose. Economic instability led our country through a series of five nationwide depressions (1873-1886, 1894-1896, 1907, 1914, and 1920-1925) before the Great Depression finally hit in 1929.[2]

Indeed, the byword of the times could easily have been *instability*. How do you gain your equilibrium as you pitch headfirst over Niagara Falls? There was instability in nations, instability in business, instability in communities, instability in relationships, instability in the home. But when we look at all the change of that time, one person appears to have remained fairly stable.

And that person was woman.

As "little house" was falling headlong over the falls, women held on tight. Women were the constant, the anchors in the home, throughout this whirlwind age of science and technology. In the midst of such change and upheaval, through two world wars and a terrible depression, our foremothers just plain hung in there. They continued to value their husbands, their children, and their homes. My guess is they sensed the great need for stability in such times. And they refused to do less than what was needed for their families.

The education of women began to equal that of men, and more and more women entered the work force. Yet what is often overlooked is that the majority of women who entered the work force during this period were single. If they married, women usually chose to care for their families at home. Historians record that even Rosie the Riveter, the media-crowned heroine of the war, was primarily single or came from among the thirteen million women who had no children under sixteen. Just as quietly heroic were the host of mothers who continued to hold down the fort at home.[3]

In short, even as career opportunities grew in the outside world, the majority of women still chose to care first and foremost for the needs of their families. Even those women who did step into careers tended to do so in the areas that naturally flowed out of their original roles in the home: education, literature, medicine, design and clothing, social work, or a business that flowed out of generational family businesses.[4]

So what happened to the "little house" in the midst of such progress?

WHEN HOME FELL FROM GRACE

In the years that ensued, the home fell from grace. And as it careened over Niagara Falls, it took with it the women and children who remained inside.

By the early part of this century, farm life declined and factory/business life became the mainstream lifestyle of our culture. Multimillion-dollar corporations rose up and commanded great power. Businesses moved families, set hours, required extra time, pushed for success from early morning until late at night, and, most importantly, provided the ticket for the home to survive. The *hub* of the wheel of life became *business.*[5]

One by one, the primary functions of the home became absorbed by society at large.

Religious life was centralized in the church. Children's *education* was handled by schools. Sick people were cared for by *health care* professionals. *Production* was moved out of the home. And, finally, *social life* moved into the public arena. In fact, by midcentury, families were being pulled in so many directions that they rarely spent time together.

Cities eventually became so congested that people began moving out in droves, forming a new segment of society known as the "suburbs." Enter Donna, June, and Harriet. By 1950, home had been relegated to a minor status in society. Sure, it was still necessary. We still needed a place to eat and sleep. But the centrality of home was already a fading memory in the national psyche. Like a piece of neglected real estate in a forgotten part of town, home had lost its value in society.

WOMAN'S FALL FROM GRACE

Remember the equation? As the home goes, so goes the woman. But how did woman fall from grace?

First of all, the *essential roles* that a woman had played were taken away. Except for the raising of young children and the maintaining of home life, a woman was becoming...disposable.

Secondly, the *serving roles* of society began to lose their value. The roles of teacher, nurse, child-caregiver, and home manager simply lost out to the skills and roles that drove a technological society—skills like mechanics, marketing, and research, and roles like corporate manager, electrical engineer, and research scientist.[6] To put it simply, professions of *character* building lost out to professions of *capital* building.

That was two blows against her. The third came in the very language we used. By the early 1900s, *work* was no longer a term for what a woman did in the home. *Work* was now synonymous with "paid work."[7]

The impact that language has on our values struck me just recently. I was having a conversation with a young woman who had just moved here from a third world country. As I asked her about her home and family, she told me there were fifteen children in her family. I was stunned.

"What kind of work does your father do?" I asked.

"Oh," she quickly responded, "he doesn't work."

"Is he ill?"

"No, he's well."

I decided the only other alternative was that he must be a lazy bum, so I dropped the subject.

Later in the conversation she mentioned an immense garden her father tilled for the family. Then it dawned on me. Since her father doesn't work for money, she didn't think it counted as real *work*—American style—even though the man labors from dawn to dusk to provide for his family. This woman had clearly picked up on the meaning of *work* in our culture.

So it went for the woman in the early part of this century. She no longer "worked." In truth, she worked as hard as ever. There were still young children to care for. There were still meals to cook and wash to do. There was a community with needs. And there were standards to maintain. The suburban housewife was continually measuring up to standards, now set by television and the world of advertising.

Which leads us to blow number four—perhaps the most powerful of all. The woman had gone from *producer* to *consumer*. As the primary consumer with the potential of making or breaking a business, her value to society shifted. What society valued most was her purchasing power. And her home became a sign of that purchasing power—or the lack thereof.[8]

Despite the fact that women are driven by relationships, we do draw a great deal of significance from our work—just like men. Our work is an avenue for expressing who we are, for using our gifts, and for contributing to life and society. Ultimately, it is our way of contributing to the needs of people. But the clear message from society by 1950 was that a woman's work in the home had become peripheral, a sideline to the "real work" to be done.

The second clear message was that society could now do for itself what a woman had always done and, in fact, could do it much better. The *professionalizing* of the work a woman had always done through the home was inherent in her fall from grace.[9]

But the fifth and final blow came with the *de-skilling* of the work left to her at home. The jobs of cleaning, cooking, and sewing were enhanced by her touch no doubt, but they required an inkling of the skill needed by the preflood or even early industrial women. There is a huge difference between sewing a shirt and actually weaving the material. But by mid-century, most women could now go to a shop and simply pull one off the rack. The narrowing and de-skilling of work in the home caused the challenge to disappear.[10]

The upshot of it all was that woman was eventually shut out of the mainstream of life and cut off from the influence she had always enjoyed in the world at large. The "village well" had moved out into corporate America, while woman was left sitting at home by a "well gone dry."

But what about the children? Didn't she still see to the needs of her children? Yes, this was the one great magnet still drawing her to the home. But, given the growing sense of despair in women, it didn't take a whole lot to finally convince her that she was not really needed even by her children—that even *this* job could be done by someone else, someone "professional."

MARRIAGE FALLS FROM GRACE

A half-century before, women had offset their isolation by coming together in organizations of their own. This led to a new age of activism for women, much of it very good for society. Little did anyone suspect that such polarized organizations would eventually push male-female relationships over the brink.

Some of these organizations were very positive in their influence—such as the Congress of Mothers (which became the national PTA) and the YWCA.

Others started on a positive note and then turned sour. One of the best illustrations of this was the WCTU.[11]

The Woman's Christian Temperance Union began as a male-female organization in the early 1800s. But as men became more consumed in business and separation between the sexes grew more pronounced, this group dissolved to form a new, all-female activist organization with one primary goal:

The changing of men.

The WCTU was a powerful, influential group. These women were concerned with the rising evils of society, attributing it in large part to the increase in drinking among men. Part of their strategy, therefore, was to become the moral policewomen of society.

Although their intentions were sincere, the means they used only added to the problem. In 1873, armed with Bibles, WCTU women marched into saloons in over twenty-three states and in a matter of a few weeks closed a thousand liquor-selling establishments. This stunned the male world. The WCTU's fight continued until a law prohibiting alcoholic drink was passed by Congress in 1919, only to be repealed a few years later.[12]

The tension that had been created, however, went unresolved, exacerbated by a increasing resentment among men of moral "preaching" and "scolding." Their response, in general, was to pull back further from women and see them as morally overbearing. Evidence of the strain showed up everywhere in the literature of the times. A new genre of books even appeared, called the "bad boy genre," represented by such books as *Tom Sawyer* by Mark Twain.[13] Meanwhile, women resented the unwillingness of men to listen to reason.

Early radical feminism got its second wind in this period, with one of its few successes—that of gaining the vote for women. And though this resurgence in feminism was still weak, it did reflect the growing schism between men and women.

Perhaps the final blow to the relationships of men and women came in three events that occurred between 1914 and 1945: World Wars I and II and the Great Depression. These dark days, wedged within an era of tremendous affluence and success, pushed us back into a survival mode. Men were called upon to fulfill their preflood role of protecting their homes and families. And they did it well. Women were called upon to insure the survival of the home, just as in preflood times. And they also did it well.

The difference was that these tough times occurred in the context of the

Niagara Falls. Men had already gone through a century of loss. And the tough times of the twenties, thirties, and forties only served to intensify the vacuum. The horrors of those world wars were beyond anything previously experienced in the history of man. And in order to survive, the emotional and relational side of man was further deadened.

Sandwiched between those two apocalyptic wars came the Great Depression. The depression hit men where it hurt most deeply—in their ability to provide for their families. Many men lost everything but the shirts on their backs. Yet, because manhood had come to be identified with rock-solid strength and the withholding of emotions, it was socially unacceptable to express intense stress and grief. It's no wonder so many men turned to alcohol or suicide in these years. Such an experience not only diminishes self-esteem, but it sickens the soul.

In lieu of such self-destruction, however, the only socially acceptable emotion for a man was anger. Displaced anger upon those he loved became a common means of coping in such difficult times. As would be expected, children growing up in those angry homes propagated that anger in their future homes.

You can see why men at midcentury had lost much of their biblical manhood. They had grown up with fathers who were coping with war and depression, not to mention accumulated loss from post-industrial father-absence. As a result, while our nation returned to normalcy, the young husbands and fathers who returned with it were anything but "normal." They were strong and capable, but generally speaking, less free to express emotion, ill-equipped in relationship building, and therefore at a severe disadvantage in relating to those they loved and needed most. Not only so, but many of them carried inside a hidden anger and grief.

Think though the ramifications of this in marriage. When a man experiences a disappointing relationship with his father growing up, he will tend to compensate through denial or an air of superiority. And when he is unable to expose his heart and soul, he will tend to compensate by aloofness. Such compensations enable him to avoid facing his hurt or admitting his inabilities. But while this may appear to satisfy for the moment, nothing could be worse for a marriage.

Good marriages are built on vulnerability and trust, on mutual appreciation and value. We women do not need our husband's success or his "togetherness" as much as we need his vulnerability and soul companionship. And so a woman misses out on the thing she longs for most in a marriage—a soul mate.

The daughters of depression fathers were also at a disadvantage. Since the perceived importance of the home seemed to be in free-fall, their own sense of importance and challenge plunged to an all-time low.

Not a pretty picture for healthy men and women.

Not a pretty picture for healthy relationships.

Marriages at midcentury may have been "traditional" marriages, but they were an empty shell of God's original plan.

Were all men and women in dire straits? No. But many were. I have been astounded at the consistency of this trend in the 1950s. Unemotional and unrelational men. Distraught and unfulfilled women. Men and women who were worlds apart, unable to appreciate or understand one another.

THE BIBLE'S FALL FROM GRACE

When Scripture fell from its position of honor in our country, it took with it the few remaining values that held the home together. It is impossible to overestimate the impact of that fall.

G. K. Chesterton once said: "It is often supposed that when people stop believing in God, they believe in nothing. Alas, it is worse than that. When they stop believing in God, they believe in *anything*."

Indeed, this is exactly what happened.

What caused the fall of Scripture in this century? First of all, the climate was ripe. Progress had elevated and expanded man's view of himself. God was no longer needed to survive in this world. And secondly, Scripture had come under the scrutiny of skeptics who had fled the restrictive environment of Europe during the 1800s to teach in our seminaries and universities. Slowly but surely their influence was now being felt.[14]

And then came Darwin.

Darwin entered the world at a time of great vulnerability in the church. While Judeo-Christian beliefs were under attack, science, on the other hand, was in its heyday. Science had done it all. Science had fueled progress, prolonged life, exploded the field of knowledge, and given the competitive edge in a technological society. Science was what man felt he needed most. In the most pragmatic of terms, science was fast becoming the new religion of modern man, and the scientist, his new god.

When Darwin published his *Origin of the Species* in 1859, his theories met with such worldwide approval that by the turn of the century Darwinism dominated every discipline of study. Before long his ideas had filtered from academia into society as a whole, creating a new world-view of "cultural Darwinism."

In a nutshell, the Darwinian-evolutionary world-view envisioned a world without God. Although Darwin himself began with evolution of living things, his disciples carried the evolutionary theory farther back, asserting that life rose up from lifeless matter, slowly evolving upward over eons of time. This leap of faith was necessary if we were to eliminate God. In Darwin's world-view there was no need or place for the spiritual. All that existed was matter. Consequently, there was no meaning or purpose in life, no significance for human life. All was molecular substance, in a fatalistic world of chance. The only real meaning, then, came in the "struggle to survive." And in this struggle to survive was the heart of Darwin's theory.

Whether we realize it or not, this view of life has totally permeated our culture.

Women, this is critical for you to see. Under Darwin, women were not only dehumanized, but they were assigned a certain value in the system of "survival." The ramifications were absolutely profound to our gender.

You see, according to Darwin, *men* had the edge. Man was by far the superior creature. He detailed his reasoning in *The Descent of Man*:

• Aggression, a fighting spirit, energy and strength, courage, and inventive genius are the superior traits that have given the edge in natural selection.

• These are primarily male traits. Therefore, men are superior to women.

• Feminine traits of nurture and responsiveness have given woman the weaker, less dominant position. Childbearing and the reproductive process have drained a woman's intellect, and diminished her power to reason and judge objectively.

• The male struggle to mate, the energy that struggle produced, and the skill it required have enabled him to come out ahead. Men are therefore both biologically and intellectually superior, the primary force in human evolution.[15]

Now, after learning of the fall of the home, the fall of woman, and the fall of marriage, I felt a little depressed, this could really get a woman down! Can you begin to understand the anger of the modern feminist?

On the heels of these ideas, a new field of science, known as "craniology," added to the perception of males as superior. Craniology was the study of the size, shape, and characteristics of human skulls. Craniologists suggested that since a woman's brain was smaller than a man's, she was intellectually inferior. This theory was widely acknowledged for some time—until scientists recognized something else: in terms of sheer brain mass to body size, a woman was actually ahead.[16]

Now, I ask you—is the Bible primarily responsible for the devaluing and suppression of women? Yet, the Bible has been blamed. Let me underscore something here and now. Darwin's world-view could not have been further from the biblical view of woman. Or more devastating. Darwin not only belittled the traits of femininity, but he belittled the value of the feminine role.

Few had the gumption to question him, but one who did was Antoinett Brown Blackwell. In her book *The Sexes throughout Nature* she defended the role of "nurture" in woman, saying it was as vital to life as the role of "struggle" in man. Then Blackwell went on to challenge Darwin's assertion that men were superior, by asking an astute question. Was Darwin suggesting that women, in their continual loss in the evolutionary struggle, were actually moving downward while men were moving upward? And would that not eventually lead to the extinction of the human race? Blackwell went on to suggest that women were superior morally, because they would never let go of something so valuable as the home.[17] Had there been "talk" radio, Blackwell might well have been the female Rush Limbaugh of her day!

Here is the point. While modern feminists have blamed biblical teaching for the problems of women at mid-twentieth century, *early feminists actually found their spark in Darwin.* Charlotte Perkins Gilman, a well known early radical feminist, expressed it well: "Women have been left behind, outside, below.... We are the only animal species in which the female depends on the male for food.... (We are) primitive woman, in the primitive home, still toiling at her primitive tasks." To Gilman, the home was the lowest, most outdated institution in the evolutionary process. It was so useless that she recommended the de-institutionalizing of the home—turning its functions over to society at large. She suggested having eating places where cooking could be done professionally and people would come to eat. (We have done better—we have drive-through.) She recommended putting children in large centers where professionals could raise and train them. (Our centers send children home to sleep at night.) While most people laughed off her ideas, the academic community praised her.[18]

Do you know when Gilman said these things? Almost 100 years ago. Here we are a century later, watching these very ideas become reality.

There is a tragedy behind Gilman's passionate hatred of the home, as is often the case among militant feminists. Gilman grew up in an unhappy home. Her father was irresponsible, and her mother was so miserable that she took her daughter, Charlotte, and left him, only to end up in poverty herself. Throughout her life, Gilman fought severe bouts of depression. Eventually, she abandoned her own husband and daughter to become a writer and national lecturer.

If I haven't missed my guess, you are already putting the pieces of the puzzle into place, just as did the feminists. The prescription for rebellion according to the gospel of Darwin went something like this:

- A woman needs to compete with a man.

- A woman needs to prove her intellectual prowess and superiority over a man.

- A woman needs to become just like a man—since his traits are more desirable—and de-emphasize her feminine traits.

- A woman needs to take on a man's role.

And there you have it. Modern feminism in a nutshell.

THE PROBLEM THAT HAS A NAME

At the end of this second great wave of change, "little house" had plunged over the edge of Niagara Falls into the swirling current of the Whirlpool Rapids below.

In the world at large, life was looking up. The second world war was over. Business was thriving, and the baby boom was out of the chutes. But in the world of the home, things were not good. A still-quiet sense of hopelessness tinged the lives of many women who found themselves alone, undervalued, unchallenged, and depressed. Many women who had nourished the home for so long found themselves now on the point of starvation. And amidst the Whirlpool Rapids, a certain panic set in. Their own survival was at stake.

When Betty Friedan wrote her book *The Feminine Mystique* she spoke about "the problem that has no name." Friedan started her book by saying: "It is no longer possible to ignore that voice, to dismiss the desperation of so many American women."[19] About this, Friedan was right. There was a problem. At midcentury we had a group of women in crisis. To dismiss this crisis would have been to cut our own throats.

But Friedan's answer was the straw that broke the camel's back.

Her answer? Women are trapped. Their minds and talents are rusting at home. They must get up, shake the dust off their feet, and get out and work. Women, she proclaimed, needed to be "liberated" from home.

Home was going under. If women did not want to drown, advised Friedan, they must turn loose of the home, give it one final kick, and simply let it drown. Of course, no one really thought that it actually could drown, least of all Friedan. Some forty years later, Friedan would suffer rejection by her own disciples for calling them to a reconsideration of womanhood and the value of the home.

But at midcentury, when the "world" and "fulfillment" and "happiness" were all "out there," women who until then had clung so tightly to the home found themselves listening. In the decades that followed, millions of women rose up and said, "I am important. I count for something. I am intelligent, strong, and capable. Give me a job and I will do it. I will do it better than any man has ever done it."

The Second Industrial Revolution was born, and the *first mother-absent society* was instituted. Undergirded by the academic elite and armed with ambition, their leaders penetrated society, pushing the limits and defying convention. Within a quarter of a century, feminism had infiltrated and virtually dominated every part of our society.

In their rush for fulfillment, however, the unexpected happened.

The home went down, pulled under by the current, taking all of society with it.

Now, we must recognize a pragmatic truth. In the wake of the Great Flash Flood of history, such a revolution was inevitable. Inevitable, that is, in a culture no longer clinging to God's word.

But we must also recognize another truth. Ask any man or woman what is most important to them, ask them what they value most in life, and do you know what they will say? Ninety-nine times out of one hundred, they will say what you are thinking. They will say, "My family is most important. My husband, my wife, my children.

Yet there is only one institution in the whole of society that undergirds, nourishes, promotes, and secures those very relationships we value most. That institution is the home.

In the rush to make our mark in the world, we forgot something. We forgot that society's price tag does not determine true value. I may see your diamond ring and say, "That diamond is worthless. It's just an overestimated piece of crunched-up coal from the ground." But that has not in the least bit affected the true value of the diamond stone on your finger!

Societies and nations come and go. But God set the stars in their courses. God conceived the patterns of healthy relationships. And God determines value. In the economy of God, the home is no less valuable today than the day when it was created. Just as God's eternal truth never changes, His eternal values never change. There are no half-price sales, no auctions, no changing of price tags in the economy of God's kingdom.

That means only one thing. When the home went down, something of great value went down. And with it, those relationships we value most.

Think about the marriage relationship. What was the feminist answer to modern-day women? "You can have it all. Go out and compete in the biological struggle. Prove yourself. Be successful. Go for the gold." Corporately women were encouraged to do the very thing men had done for a hundred years or more. Men had left the home. Men had poured their lives and energies into the world outside their homes. Did such a choice prove beneficial to men? Did it promote unity in marriage? Likewise, has the feminist solution promoted an environment for men and women coming together?

Corporately women were told to prove their self-sufficiency and independence. "A woman needs a man like a fish needs a bicycle," said Gloria Steinem. Men were told they were not needed, that their role in marriage and family was not vital. It was the feminists who pushed for no-fault divorce, allowing a man or woman to walk away at will. Men were shut out of decisions regarding the birth of their children. In time, their presence was not even required at the conception of a child. While women had felt dismissed at midcentury, men were now dismissed, let off the hook. The result has been disastrous to the family and the institution of marriage.

In due time, those views infiltrated the church. The question, "Who needs a man?" mutated into another question within the church—"Who needs male leadership?" Another prescription for disaster.

But when the home went down, there was more than marriage at stake. There was more than church leadership at stake. Something else was forgotten— something absolutely critical.

You see, "little house" was not empty when it went down.

Someone was inside that house.

Someone vulnerable, unable to swim alone.

When "little house" went down, the *children* were still inside. Everyone had forgotten the children!

Read feminist writings. *Where are the children?* Read the best-selling books of the sixties and seventies. Where are the children? They're not there. Or if they are, they are insignificant, creatures to be cared for by society. Children simply do not enter the feminist picture. No wonder abortion-on-demand and national child-care have been such passionate demands of the feminist movement. Modern feminism cannot survive without them.

Remember the equation? As the home goes, so goes the woman. And as the woman goes, so go the children. *Children* have been the true victims of this last great wave of change. And with them, our future.

This must not be! For the sake of our precious children, we must not let go of the home. For the sake of our marriages and families, we must not let go of the home. For the sake of God's kingdom and His great eternal purposes, we must not let go of the home. We must not allow society to dictate its value, nor squeeze *us* into its own mold.

When the flash flood hit Colorado that day in 1976, all of those caught in its path were issued one instruction: "Get to higher ground." Higher ground was the place of safety.

Our Lord spoke to us about the firm rock of His word. "Build your house on the rock," He said. Hundreds of years earlier, King David also spoke of higher ground.

Save me, O God, For the waters have threatened my life.

I have sunk in deep mire, and there is no foothold;

I have come into deep waters, and a flood overflows me.

But as for me, my prayer is to Thee, O LORD, at an acceptable time.

O God, in the greatness of Thy lovingkindness,

Answer me with Thy saving truth.

Deliver me from the mire, and do not let me sink;
May I be delivered from my foes, and from the deep waters,
May the flood of waters not overflow me,
And may the deep not swallow me up....
May Thy salvation, O God, set me securely on high (Psalm 69:1-2, 13-15, 29).

David understood that salvation from the flood could be found in God's saving truth, that the truth of God would set him on higher ground. Like Marilyn and Melanie, many of us are feeling the waters rise, feeling the strong tug of the current. Our homes are already being undercut by the swirling waters of change. Yet we can take heart in David's words.

When Melanie was swept into the flood that day in Colorado, her life was saved by one lone tree. But that tree was not just any tree. Other trees had been uprooted and dashed to pieces. What made this tree different? This tree had strong and sure roots, roots that went down deep into the earth, so deep that even a mighty flash flood could not wrench them loose from their grip. David spoke of such a tree in the first Psalm:

How blessed is the man who does not walk in the counsel of the wicked,
Nor stand in the path of sinners,
Nor sit in the seat of scoffers!
But his delight is in the law of the LORD,
And in His law he meditates day and night.
And he will be *like a tree firmly planted* by streams of water,
Which yields its fruit in its season,
And its leaf does not wither;
And in whatever he does, he prospers (Psalm 1:1-3).

You and I need such a grip. We need to become trees. Trees firmly planted with roots that go deep. Roots drinking from the Word of the Lord and holding fast to its truth. If you and I become such trees, we will not perish in the flood. We will prosper.

We have His Word on it.

Chapter Six

Truth or Consequences

Lies, though many, will be caught by the truth as soon as she rises up.

OLD AFRICAN SAYING

In the end, truth will out.

WILLIAM SHAKESPEARE

S he had been waiting for over an hour when we finally sat down. Our last session of the day had been on the topic of women and work, and as soon as I finished, a crowd of conferees lined up with questions. So many, in fact, that an hour later we began making appointments for the next day. But this particular young woman had insisted on waiting.

Steve and I were three days into a post-Christmas conference with a thousand college students in Denver, Colorado. It was our first college conference in fifteen years. And I'll be truthful, we were a little tired. Actually, we were exhausted. Okay, we were dead.

We were also the only ones who had slept at night. These students just never seemed to stop. Their boundless energy totally amazed us. Somewhere in a past life I vaguely remembered being like that.

But there was something else that amazed us more. In our hours of counseling the last three days, we had been struck by the depth and complexity of pain in their lives. It was far greater than anything we remembered seeing in our early days of college ministry. As one long-time staff worker explained, things indeed have changed. Today a typical college freshman has already gone through a lifetime's worth of sorrow.

As I looked into the young woman's troubled face, I wondered what had kept her here. What weighed so heavily on her mind?

"I'm sorry to have kept you so long," I apologized, sinking into a chair beside her.

"That's okay, " she said. The shadow lifted for a moment from her features, her deep blue eyes reflecting a tired smile. Then, just as quickly, the troubled look returned.

"I hope you don't mind...I—I just had to talk to you. In your last session you said something no one else has ever said to me, and it just blew me away. In fact...," she paused, "I guess I'm still in a state of shock. I don't know what to do."

What could I possibly have said that would have been so shocking?

"You said, 'No one can have it all.' You said the idea that 'you can have it all' is a lie. Mary, I was so stunned I felt paralyzed in my seat. I just sat there holding my pen. I couldn't write another word in my notebook for the rest of the session. Honestly, it was as if I'd just run into a brick wall. I felt like...my world had come to an end.

"You see, I've been told all my life that I *can* have it all. I've lived my whole life on that philosophy. Everything I've done, every decision I've made has been to that end. And I've worked so hard—just to make it happen! This last year I was finally accepted into law school, and that's where I was planning to go next year...."

Her voice broke. Tears streamed down her face.

"The thing is," she went on, "I know you're right. I *know* it. As soon as the words were out of your mouth, I knew in my heart you were right. But...what do I do now?"

I wanted to reach over and give her a hug. The dreams of this young woman had suddenly been shattered. Her life was over. Yet in reality, it was only beginning. How blessed she was to have happened upon the truth so early in life! How fortunate to look forward to a life based on truth and crowned with the promise of God's blessing. Life is too short, too precious to be spent on a path of futile lies.

"YOU CAN HAVE IT ALL": A LIE FOR THE TIMES

Unfortunately this young woman is not the exception. We are raising an entire generation that has been nursed and fed on the lie.

I am constantly amazed at the number of teenage girls I meet who come from Christian homes, attend conservative churches, are heavily involved in their youth groups, and even have mothers who live by the truth—yet are totally seduced by the lie. In fact, it is rare to meet a young woman who has even begun to think through these issues from a biblical perspective. That is a scary thing. These precious ones are slipping right through our fingers.

If you have a daughter, this should greatly concern you. Your daughter lives in an invasive culture, more powerfully present in her everyday life than any culture in history. She is surrounded by unprecedented peer pressure and subtle indoctrination, the likes of which you and I never knew. Unless we teach our daughters to ask good questions and take the time to give them a biblical grid, there will be nothing to prevent them from blindly walking into the trap. And a terrible trap it is.

Nor can we forget the sons. If you have a quiver of boys, I pray for you. First, that you will survive! And, second, that as their mother you will give them what they need. Boys desperately need to see a woman who finds her strength and wisdom in the Lord. They need to learn respect for women from you. They need to catch the picture of biblical womanhood from your life.

My husband had two brothers, and they practically killed each other growing up. There were days his mother was certain she was raising juvenile delinquents. (I have since learned that every mother with boys has had the same thought at some point.) But she was also a saint. She gave her three daughters-in-law and all five of her granddaughters the greatest of gifts—she lived and taught biblical womanhood to her boys.

By the time Steve was grown, he had the truth so cemented in his mind that he could see straight through the lie. And he has been my greatest champion, my strongest supporter in the journey towards biblical womanhood. A woman can use that kind of support these days.

But where do you begin in exposing a lie? You begin by asking two questions. First, *what does real life say?* You see, somewhere along the line, a lie breaks down in real life. Life was meant to be lived by God's standards and rules. And when the rules are broken, life becomes broken. Inevitably, life always tells the truth. Second, *what does Scripture say?* Scripture is the ultimate test for truth. It is the light shining in the darkness, exposing lies and proclaiming the truth.

Let us look, then, at the first question. What does real life tell us? How has life itself exposed the lie? We begin by going back to its earliest conception.

THE WOMB OF THE LIE

Where did the lie come from? It was conceived and brought forth from the womb of modern feminism. Feminism…rooted in a Darwinian world-view, grounded in atheistic humanism, and fueled by bitterness. Feminist philosophy has not only mothered this lie, but a host of other lies that have deluded Western culture.

But there is something else we must make immediately clear. Modern feminist philosophy actually spoke a great deal of truth. Feminists were right regarding the problem. "Traditional" roles as we knew them at midcentury *had* failed in a postflood world. Women *were* in need. The gap between the world and the home *was* a seemingly insurmountable gap.

Feminists were also right concerning the value of modern women. Women *are* equal in the sight of the Almighty. They *are* gifted and intelligent, and they *do* need to express their gifts and exert influence in the world. In short, feminists understood the need of postflood women to find their place of significance in the world once again.

There is no question but that modern feminism has sought to address the need, raise the value of women, open the doors to social equality, and in so doing, find a way out of the flood.

But at the heart of their solution was an utterly destructive lie.

You see, a lie never works alone. A good lie wraps itself around just enough truth to draw its listeners in. And, just as certainly, life has a way of peeling back that cover, like an onion, one layer at a time.

How did so many women become so deceived? One thing is for certain. It didn't happen overnight. Although modern feminism has enjoyed widespread acceptance in the last few decades, its roots go back into the nineteenth century. Satan often takes a long time to lay a trap. And in this case, he took 150 years. But when the time was ripe and our guard was down, the trap was sprung—and we were dead meat.

Let's pause a moment for a feminist-identification break. Because there are so many terms describing feminist philosophy, it can become confusing. And so it would be helpful to distinguish the differences.

SHADES OF FEMINISM

A "militant feminist" takes an uncompromisingly hostile position against certain patterns and institutions of culture—things like marriage, men, motherhood, family, male leadership, and traditional religion. *Feminism's roots are in these ideas.* Because this is so, feminism eventually leads its converts back toward these roots.

A "radical feminist" is philosophically just to the right, believing that Judeo-Christian culture is the source of women's oppression. She is very concerned with rights, supports abortion and day care, and accepts the androgyny of men and women (the belief that men and women are not innately different).

A "political feminist" is primarily concerned with social reform, rather than ideology.

And the "biblical feminist" seeks to wed feminist philosophy with Scripture, rather than throwing out Scripture altogether as the hard-core feminist has done.

Finally, there is what I call a "cultural" or "mainstream feminist." This woman doesn't really wish to be identified as a feminist, yet embraces her own version of feminist philosophy. A recent survey has shown that the majority of modern women fit into this category. They do not identify themselves as feminists, yet they reflect strong feministic influence in their daily life.

As time has gone by, the distinctions between feminists have become fewer. Many radical feminists today are also militant in philosophy but have disguised their militant views for a better sell to the mainstream woman. And most feminists have become political in persuasion.

When I speak of feminism, I will usually be referring to the modern radical/political feminist, strongly influenced by her militant roots. She is the woman who is actively forging the trails and pushing an agenda for change in the culture.

OUT OF SYNC

From the beginning, feminists have struggled to gain widespread acceptance. Why? Because historically they have been "out of sync" with the everyday wife and mother. The values they have embraced have been consistently at odds with the values of mainstream women.

From its inception, hard-core militant feminism despised the home, men, the feminine role, and male leadership in society. Reproduction and children were considered obstacles in a woman's ascent to power, deterrents to her achievement of success and fulfillment. And families were viewed as dysfunctional gatherings of sick people. Ann Sexton, a well-known midcentury feminist and writer, summed up some of these feelings:

HOUSEWIFE;
Some women marry houses.
It's another kind of skin; it has a heart,
a mouth, a liver and bowel movements.
The walls are permanent and pink.
See how she sits on her knees all day
faithfully washing herself down.
Men enter by force, drawn back like Jonah
into their fleshy mothers.
A woman *is* her mother.
That's the main thing.[1]

Such cynicism simply was not shared by the majority of women. In fact, I believe that earlier lack of interest in the feminist movement indicates the healthy nature of the majority of homes and marriages in those days.

One thing is certain, however. Those homes that were unhealthy were a breeding ground for early radical feminism. According to feminist writer Mary Austin, early nineteenth century feminists referred to family unhappiness when sharing their testimonials at suffrage conferences, with comments like, "Well, it was seeing what my mother had to go through that started me," or "My father was one of the old-fashioned kind." The problem most often referred to was the dominant father who ruled by "mere whim" and the mother who was "impotent and powerless."[2] To this very day, hard-core feminists continue to share the common experience of unhappy homes in which biblical roles were distorted or abused.

The poet Ann Sexton is an extreme case of one such woman. Sexton was a rebellious teenager who grew up in a repressive home, eloped at nineteen, and was finally hospitalized for suicidal depression at twenty-eight. Like Charlotte Gilman, she eventually abandoned the care of her home and children, becoming a writer and poet. She went on to receive the Pulitzer Prize in 1969 but ended her life in suicide in 1974. Sexton's story, like that of so many other feminists, is a story of tragedy.[3]

Because of the disparity between feminism and mainstream women, feminists had to learn to speak another language. Persuading our tough-minded American grandmothers, who were equally tough in their commitment to home and family, was...well, tough! In the early 1900s, it was all feminists could do to get these women even interested in the right to vote—not because they had no ideas to express, but because most women still saw their husbands as adequate spokesmen and viewed their homes as their bully pulpit of influence. Feminists were so befuddled by these women that it took them some time before they finally came up with the right language.

When suffrage rights leaders Lucy Stone and Elizabeth Smith Miller coined the slogan, "Reformer *and* housewife!" they finally hit their target. Appealing to a woman's influence through her home, they campaigned on the argument that the woman's vote would save and protect the home. It was this new "home-speak" that finally brought women on board to win the vote for suffrage.[4] Even so, it was years before most women actually exercised their right to vote—a fact which caused feminists to simply throw up their hands.

But as we've seen, the mood had changed by the 1950s. Housewives were looking for answers, and feminism was eager to provide them. Yet, while Friedan and a few others were able to touch the everyday woman, the feminist movement as a whole was still out of touch. Modern women could not identify with the anti-male, anti-family, masculinized version of woman found at the forefront of the feminist movement in the fifties and sixties.

BENEFITING FROM RADICALISM

Oddly enough, however, feminists have actually enjoyed being different. In fact, radicalism has helped the cause of feminism in two arenas: the arena of public discussion (the media) and the arena of academia.

Look at public discussion for a moment. For the last fifty years, the media has become the forum for public discussion. If you can win the eye and allegiance of the media, you can win a platform for change. Yet, it is media's nature to be drawn to the irregular, the flamboyant, the shocking. And feminists have certainly fit that bill—living on the edge, challenging conventional wisdom, demanding anti-social reform. And so they have caught the eye of the media. And in time, they have won its allegiance.

As a result, feminists have had the privilege of shaping our public discussion. They have used the media well, first by stating the extreme, creating a reaction, and forcing their agenda into discussion. And then it has only been a matter of time before society has followed in the age-old domino effect—moving from discomfort, to discussion, to apathy, and finally to resignation.

Heather Booth, director of the Coalition for Democratic Values, explains NOW's philosophy: "First they're ridiculed, then attacked, then dismissed. Then what they're pushing for occurs and becomes the accepted norm. By then, they are on to the next level of debate."[5]

This is clearly why in 1992 Pat Ireland, lauded as NOW's first "traditional, mainstream" president, could be forced to admit her involvement in a long-time gay-lesbian relationship while still married to her husband of twenty-five years, and only months later be lauded by the same organization for her clarifying leadership in the "expanding of lesbian rights." (A gay-lesbian magazine threatened to "out" her if she did not come clean.)[6]

It is also the reason that NOW (which boasts a 30-40 percent lesbian membership) can push for an overtly militant gay rights agenda—calling for marriage and adoption/parenting rights for homosexuals, punishment of groups like Boy Scouts who exclude homosexuals from leadership, removal of age-consent laws which presently inhibit homosexual recruitment among children, and the implementation of mandated sex education programs promoting the gay lifestyle as normal and acceptable. Although these views have been strongly resisted by society, they believe it is only a matter of time before we will relent.

In response to a reporter's question regarding her lesbian lifestyle and its appearance to the American public, Ireland responded, "What was yesterday's radical idea is today's given."[7] She had just stated feminism's strategy in a nutshell.

How many years will it take before her words are proven true? Not many, it appears. Feminists have seen the dominos fall in favor of their agenda for unrestricted abortion. They have enjoyed huge success in pushing for appointments to high positions in government. And they have gained unprecedented victories on such specialized issues as the outlawing of pro-life demonstrations at abortion clinics. Given where our country was even a decade ago, their string of recent successes has been nothing short of remarkable.

What about the arena of the academic community? Radicalism has had a history of success among the academic elite, and feminism is no exception. From early on, feminism has enjoyed the applause and acceptance of higher education. Therefore, when atheistic humanism permeated our institutions of learning earlier this century, feminism became a shoo-in.

By the time baby boomers entered college, the university campus had become a veritable tent-grounds for the feminist crusade, and the university classroom its pulpit. And its converts? Disillusioned baby boomer daughters who walked in as traditional girls and left as feminist women.

Perhaps you remember those days. The sixties were the glory days of Gloria and the bawdy days of bra burnings. I remember loud angry speeches, flyers and petitions, student newspaper articles, and heated classroom debates. Many of the girls I knew joined the movement and took up the cause. It was the start of a revolution that pushed feminism into the forefront of our culture.

GOING MAINSTREAM

This surge of feminism as a political movement was exciting. But the problem remained. Feminism had not yet won the mainstream woman. Feminists began to realize that if their goal was to liberate the entire gender, not just an "elite" or "out of sync" group within society, they must again find a way to speak the language of the conservative woman who valued hearth and home.

Thus entered CR groups—or Consciousness Raising groups—as part of a widely successful consciousness-raising campaign. These groups were started in cities and towns all over the country. At the outset they were much like a weekly Bible Study—without the Bible Study. The thrust of these groups was to encourage a woman to "speak bitterness" and find hope for change in her life through feminism. The idea caught on so rapidly that by 1970 it was hard to find a feminist group anywhere in North America that did not engage in this practice.[8]

The CR idea actually originated with Mao Tse-tung of China as a political technique used by his revolutionary army in its invasion of North China in the late 1940s. The townswomen were gathered in town squares to "speak bitterness and pain" by reciting the crimes their men had committed against them. Their initial reluctance gave way to collective anger as woman after woman recounted stories of rape by landlords, physical abuse by husbands, and on it went, leading to support groups for the reduction of oppression against women. This strategy to purge out Japanese and Kuomintang influence brought full control to Mao Tse-tung.[9]

The tragedy behind this bit of history is that these unsuspecting women soon became victims of even worse atrocities under Mao Tse-tung's oppressive dictatorship—atrocities only now coming to light. You see, CR groups *persuaded*, but they did not *enlighten*. Even as you and I were watching democracy spread and flourish in the 1980s, horrors were occurring behind the Great Wall. Tianamen Square was only the tip of the iceberg. Mao Tse-tung was mandating sterilization of women, condemning countless thousands to death on trumped up charges, and controlling every aspect of the lives of the people of China, whom he blamed for the deep problems his own regime had brought upon them. The only free thought in China was Mao Tse-tung's.

One gripping account can be found in a recently released book, *A Mother's Ordeal*, which tells the story of a young Chinese nurse. Chi An was won to the cause of the Cultural Revolution and recruited as a population-control worker under Mao Tse-tung's one-child policy in the '80s. She used coercive peer counseling, hunted down runaway "illegally pregnant" women, and administered forced sterilizations, late-term abortions, and in cases where women carried their illegal babies to term she gave lethal injections at birth. Her hardened heart eventually softened to the horror of their experiences when she unexpectedly became pregnant herself with their second child. Chi An defected to this country and soon after found forgiveness in Christ. She has spent her time since in the promotion of the value of life.[10]

Drawing from the Chinese model, therefore, feminists formed CR groups of everyday housewives who came together all over America to "speak bitterness." Under the direction of a quietly confirmed and well-trained feminist leader, these unsuspecting women were led from commiseration to conversion. CR groups proved to be the most potent tool in building membership into the movement.[11]

HOW FEMINISM BECAME A HOUSEHOLD WORD

But the most effective campaign of the feminist movement took place through the '70s and '80s. It was then that feminism finally hit upon the language of twentieth century, mainstream women.

And it came in the form of a lie.

Women weren't necessarily joining the club, or even calling themselves feminists, but that didn't matter. They had bought into the lie, and that was what counted.

What was this lie? In a phrase it declared, "You can have it all." All of what? You can have a successful career, great sex, a wonderful marriage of equal partnership, and happy, well-adjusted children. You can have prestige and power out in the world, along with fulfillment and happiness at home. You may have to stretch, and you may have to re-train your husband, but…you can have it all.

We all watched this lie beautifully unfold. Propaganda literally flooded the market. Commercials ragged on men and flaunted powerful women. Does anyone remember the "W-O-M-A-N" who could bring home the bacon and cook it, too? She was sexy, smart, and lived on two hours of sleep at night. And could she ever sing.

Magazines and television interviews featured women from every walk of life who had achieved it all. Experts raved about the health and wealth of this philosophy. They prescribed it as a cure for everything from sex problems to depression, citing all sorts of studies to back them up. Books like *Being All Things*, by Jeanne Deschamps Stanton, and *Having it All* , by Helen Gurley Brown, filled the bookshelves and sold us what we wanted to hear.

The idea was brilliant. Who wouldn't want to believe in the immeasurable ability of woman to conquer and achieve? It appealed to the creative, intelligent, achieving side of our natures. Women have always responded to a challenge, and this was a challenge.

The peer pressure created in this great campaign was enormous. Women were told on every hand that they deserved it, needed it, and should have it. Why shouldn't they have everything, just as men had had for so long? The top M.B.A. programs became flooded with women. Working women began to stay on at work after the birth of their first child. In time, a mother who stayed home to raise her children felt like the exception to the rule. Metropolitan neighborhoods became empty during the day, while the demand for day care rose to a crisis point. American women were fueling a new lifestyle of affluence, a lifestyle many American men were beginning to like. New catch words like *yuppie* and *dinks* entered our vocabulary. But the peer pressure didn't end there.

It reached all the way down to the kindergarten class. Joining forces with like-minded groups such as the National Education Association and Planned Parenthood, feminists made a concerted effort to infiltrate the classroom. Funded by parents' tax dollars, they implemented a plan of indoctrination, bypassing parents and winning the minds of the next generation.

By the mid '80s, textbooks from K-12 had been completely purged of images of a woman as wife or mother. In a 1985 survey of over one hundred textbooks, Dr. Paul Vitz, professor of Psychology at New York University, could not find a single story or theme celebrating motherhood, while sex role reversals were common. One major textbook publisher's code of guidelines warned authors, editors, and illustrators to avoid material that "reinforces any sense that girls and boys may have of being categorized as a sex group." It also forbade images of women as peace loving, compassionate, or nurturing. Another publisher's editorial guidelines offered examples to writers, such as "The boys are in the sewing class," and "Her aunt scored a touchdown."[12]

And so, while young girls were encouraged to rule the male world, a vital part of woman's life and work was expunged from official record.

The problem was, however, that this hugely successful campaign was based on a LIE. Feminism was building a case for Superwoman, a woman who does not exist, never has existed, and never will exist. She was a figment of our media-enhanced imagination, fed by our own intense need for achievement and success. But beneath her glossy and glamorous veneer, was a very hard truth. The realities of life did not mesh with the image. Feminism had simply denied the realities of a life of career, marriage, and mothering, just as modern industrial man had done. And so, downplaying the needs of children and ignoring the requirements for a healthy home and marriage, feminists were selling a bold-faced lie. And very effectively, I might add.

THE LIE REVEALED

By the end of the '80s, however, the truth was emerging. Child care studies were pouring in, indicating negative, long-term effects of substitute care. Women were not finding the fulfillment they had hoped for in career.

They felt deprived in their womanhood.

They felt a deep sense of loss in their family relationships.

They felt torn between family and career demands, and worn down by the stress of managing both.

The true price of building a successful career was beginning to come clear. And a period of disillusionment rolled in like fog off San Francisco Bay.

I remember well when *Fortune* magazine ran a cover article in 1986 entitled "Why Women Managers are Bailing Out," with the caption "One out of four of the best women MBA's class of '76 have quit the managerial work force." The article began by reporting "a cloud hanging over the horizon.... Many women, including some of the best educated and most highly motivated, are dropping out.... A disquieting number of the dropouts are the pioneering women.... Yet the fact that many of those who led the way ten years ago have begun to bail out presents worrisome auguries not only for the female MBAs, but also for women of all kinds in the work force. If the MBAs cannot find gratification there, can any women?"

Woman after woman interviewed in the article expressed her disillusionment with the dream of having it all. Eleanor May, Virginia Business School professor, surmised: "My perception is that women have given up the goal of being super-women because it is impossible. Only a few people can cope, and if you talk to them you discover that they aren't coping satisfactorily, and the stress is greater than they should be handling."[13]

Prior to *Fortune*'s news, journalist Liz Roman Gallese had spent a year inter-viewing the country's first elite class of female graduates from Harvard Business School—the class of 1975. Her resulting book, *Women Like Us*, revealed that one decade later, every woman—without exception—had made trade-offs. Trade-offs in marriage. Trade-offs with children. Trade-offs in their careers.

No one had it all.

Other books were beginning to appear, like *Success and Betrayal: The Crisis of Women in Corporate America*, by Hardesty and Jacobs, and *A Lesser Life: The Myth of Women's Liberation in America*, by economist Sylvia Ann Hewlett.

Things were rapidly falling apart, and feminists brooded that there might be a mass abandonment of ship. At the height of the strain between reality and the feminist dream, *Harvard Business Review* ran an article stepping up the debate. It was written by a warmly embraced feminist, Felice N. Schwartz, president and cofounder of Catalyst—a profeminist research and advisory organization for women in careers. In this article Schwartz very honestly brought forward the realities of career life and suggested the need for a career track (later dubbed the "mommy track") for women who valued both family and career.[14] Though this suggestion had arisen before, it was the first time a prestigious magazine like the *HBR* had forced the issue into the corporate arena for debate.

Rarely has the *Harvard Business Review* received such a response as they did to this article. Feminists all over the country were up in arms, and a reaction rip-pled through magazines and media coverage across the land. In response Nan Stone, senior editor of *HBR*, wrote a follow-up article. Acknowledging the feminist fear that Schwartz's ideas would only harm women's careers nationwide, she persisted by saying that we still must confront the "uncomfortable question: What happens at home—to family, to children—when both father and mother work full time?" She urged her readers to look at the reality of fast-lane living for two-career couples and its ramifications for marriage. She went on to cite the research of Arlie Hochschild in her book *The Second Shift*. Hochschild had discovered that upper middle class professional couples were victims of "workaholism a deux," that uniformly their marriages and children came second to work and that in the end the children usually paid the highest price.[15]

These writers were honest enough to ask the questions that women—and men—were now asking all across America. But when college girls bent towards career finally began to ask those same questions, it became clear the jig was up. Despite the fact that collegians were still being indoctrinated with the lie, doubt was now invading the world of academia, the feminist's strongest safe haven. The first public revelation of this doubt happened before the entire nation in the spring of 1990.

Do you remember the Barbara Bush-Wellesley College flap? Most of us read about the student petition that was passed around the Wellesley campus to protest the invitation of Barbara Bush as their commencement speaker. Peggy Reid, coauthor of the petition, told reporters that Mrs. Bush did not represent the student body. She had achieved her position of prestige and power due to her husband. They wanted to hear from someone who had earned her position, who represented them, their feminist ideals, their dream.

But the most meaningful insight came from a reporter for *U.S. News and World Report* who dug a little deeper into the mind of Peggy Reid. Peggy told him frankly: "I think we have our eyes open. And what we see kind of scares us. We have been told we can do everything, and maybe we can't. We're told we can have the Bloomingdale's wardrobe, a job in the executive suite and also be a mother and wife. I just don't know how I'm going to do that balancing act."[16]

Young Peggy had smelled a lie.

EVOLUTION OF A LIE

Lest we think this was the end, we are sadly mistaken. Such a lie does not die so readily. Scrambling to accommodate the awakening reality among postcollege America, the lie mutated and evolved. It became a new, more palatable lie for the twenty-first century woman.

What does the newest form of the old lie sound like now?

"You can have SOME of it all."

The rationale goes something like this: "Well, true. You can't have it all. But you can have some of it all. Some of career, some of marriage, and some of mothering. Your employer, your husband, your children may suffer, but that's okay. That's life. If you really want to be personally happy in a career, if you want to provide the best for your children (education, vacations, a nice home), and if you and your husband want to be financially secure, you along with your family must make compromises in life. Besides, you deserve to have some of everything. It's your right."

This lie is even more deceptive, harder to nail down. The woman who bought into this lie was recognizing a certain reality. She couldn't do it all. But in order for her to have "some" of "everything," "everything" would have to suffer. Under the original lie, a woman tried to address the needs of her children and husband. This lie downplayed those responsibilities. In real life, said this lie, those responsibilities just cannot be fulfilled. Women, along with their families, must simply lower their expectations.

Along with this rationalization came the "I'm OK—my kids are OK, and my marriage is OK" philosophy. According to this philosophy, a woman's personal happiness is the most important element for happy children and husbands. The problem with this line of thinking, however, is that hosts of "happy" women have unhealthy children and miserable marriages.

I am deluded if I think that what my child and husband need most is for me to be "happy." What a can of worms this opens up! What about a man who decides to leave his wife and children for the sake of personal happiness? Men have tried to argue the same point—that everyone will be much better off in the long run. Not so, life tells us. My personal happiness simply cannot be the plumb line for family decisions. Personal responsibility *always* precedes personal happiness if a family is to survive and thrive.

This lie deceives us about the means and the price of happiness. What is the means to happiness? Happiness can never be found through shortcuts. It can only be found through following God's plan. What about the price for happiness? We live in a fallen, sinful world. This means that personal sacrifice will always be part of personal happiness. The greatest rewards in life always come through some degree of pain, do they not?

How vividly I remember when my daughter was grasping this truth. She loved to play beautiful music fluidly and freely on the piano. But because she hated the process and the price of learning to read music, she relied on my help and her good ear to get through. Her piano teacher and I knew that if she didn't go through the painful process of learning to read for herself, she would never be free to fully use her gift of music. And so every day for a part of her practicing time, I insisted that she work alone. I could hear her moaning and groaning and banging her hands on the piano. So much so that there were times I was tempted just to forget the whole thing and help her out.

One day as Rachel was doing her "alone" practicing, I came in to find a note over the kitchen sink: "Mom, please don't make me play the chords all by myself. PLEASE...it's torture!!! If you feel sorry, help me! Your child in agony, Rachel Farrar."

Who was being tortured here? Because I loved her, I could never have let her agonize if I didn't know of the joy it would eventually bring.

Yes, children do flourish under a happy mother, and, yes, husbands are drawn to a happy wife. But feminism and God's word are worlds apart when it comes to the means to such happiness. The truth is, happiness can never be found apart from embracing God's plan. When we throw out His plan, as John Piper says, we settle for mud pies instead of infinite delight.

And so this lie is every bit as deadly as its foremother. It is a dishonest compromise, a pragmatic answer still rooted deeply in rank deceit. At its roots is the same deceptive goal of *moi*, as Miss Piggy would say. It is earthly, temporal, self-oriented, and short-sighted.

Both of these lies have simply missed the point. They have danced all around the truth, never quite hitting it. As a result, they are incapable of meeting the innermost needs of a woman.

In the final analysis, these lies have flunked the first question of our test—the test of reality. But since a lie changes and adjusts at will, continuing to make reality elusive, we now come to the second test.

Scripture reveals the evolving lie.

Scripture shines light where there is no light.

What then, about the test of Scripture?

Chapter Seven

Roots

⚬⚬⚬

Tell me what the world is saying now,
and I'll tell you what the Church will be saying seven years from now.

FRANCIS SCHAEFFER

After all, what is a lie? 'Tis but the truth in masquerade.

GEORGE BYRON

*I*f you want to find the roots of a little flower, you can dig into the soil with your fingers or a trowel.

If you want to find the roots of a shrub, you'll need to bring a shovel.

If you want to trace the roots of a great cottonwood tree, you'd better move in some heavy earthmoving equipment.

If you want to find the roots of an idea—be it truth or a lie—you'd better be prepared to dig even deeper still.

Fortunately, the Bible already reveals both the roots of our culture, and the roots of God's truth. Let's trace a couple tendrils of those long, long roots for a moment. Let's follow them back, back into a distant time and place...

⚬⚬⚬

The year is A.D. 32.

The dusty streets of Jerusalem swarm with Passover crowds. Finding ourselves in the heart of the city, we travel along its narrow corridors, past its teeming marketplaces and houses until we reach a steep hill.

There, on the crown of the hill, stands a marvel of the ancient world. The great Temple. It's walls of gold and white marble flash and sparkle in the morning sunlight.

The air is redolent with incense as we pass through the temple gates. From the inner courtyards, we hear the voices of penitent worshipers. Jews, young and old, scuttle past us, cradling a dove or dragging a bleating goat or lamb. Just ahead, in the Court of Women, is the great Treasury. It is lined with thirteen, great, horn-shaped chests, overflowing with the gifts of the people.

As we enter, we notice a crowd straining to hear and see a young man. He is plainly dressed, but his shoulders are broad, his expression arresting, and his voice full of power. As he speaks, he holds forth a scroll of the Holy Scriptures.

Off to the side of the crowd, a group of scowling, finely-robed, well-manicured men huddle, clutching large, weighty scrolls beneath their arms. The holy men. Why are they so angry? Why the scarcely concealed hatred and rage darkening their faces?

Drawing nearer, we begin to catch a few of the young man's words as he raises his voice. "You shall know the truth," he is saying, "and the truth shall make you free!"

You and I have walked right into the middle of John 8, one of the greatest chapters in all of the Bible. In this chapter Jesus tackles head-on the subject of truth and falsehood. In forty of the fifty-nine verses of this chapter Jesus makes a series of claims, asserting His emanation from God, His total and utter truthfulness, and His deity.

Yet within this same chapter Jesus also makes his strongest indictment ever. Stronger than any words ever spoken to adulterers, thieves, or murderers are His words to these holy men who balk at Jesus' suggestion that he might know some truth they didn't.

Listen to what He says: "You are of your father the devil, and you want to do the desire of your father. He was a murderer from the beginning, and does not stand in the truth, because there is no truth in him. Whenever he speaks a lie, he speaks from his own nature; for he is a liar, and the father of lies. But because I speak the truth, you do not believe me" (John 8:44-45).

Strong words from a strong man.

We're drawing near to a root of the truth...and the root of a lie.

THE ROOT OF A LIE

Do you want to find truth? Do you want to discern a lie? This passage is filled with insight about deception and truth. Jesus tells us where it all comes from. Just as all truth originates with God, every lie originates with Satan. Satan is the father of lies. He is the wellspring of lies, the creator of falsehoods, the master lie teller. It was ultimately because of Satan that death entered the world. From the beginning of human history, the devil had murder in his heart. He actually plunged the human race into the ocean of death—physical, spiritual, and eternal. The fall of man, with all of its ramifications, points back to the devil as author.

Not only so, but Satan hates the truth. Why? Because the truth reveals his damnable character. Anyone who speaks the truth is a threat to Satan. Because Jesus was the light of the world and spoke the truth, Satan hated Him. And so did his children of darkness (John 3:19-21). It didn't matter that Christ loved them and was ready to die for them. Their love for the darkness blinded them to His great mercy. All they could see was the exposure of their sin. So it is with us when we speak the truth in love today. We can expect to be hated, just as was our Lord.

In the end Satan leads his followers down a path of death. The death he has in mind takes every shape and form—broken relationships, broken health, broken dreams. In short, a woman who follows after the lies of Satan finds herself on a path of death. And if she propagates his lies, she becomes a *dealer* of death, and the blind leading the blind. She doesn't know her father is a murderer and that he plots *her* end as well.

Satan is not to be taken lightly. It behooves us to know his ways, to recognize his deceit. Our Lord has given us three tests for uncovering a lie, and each of them uses the unfailing litmus of Scripture:

- Know the truth intimately (the test of the real thing—God's Word).
- Observe the deeds of those who speak (the test of deeds).
- Look for the hook (the test of partial truth).

1: Know the Truth Intimately

When the Secret Service trains its agents to identify counterfeit bills, they never study a counterfeit bill. Instead, these agents undergo a thorough study of the real thing. They become so familiar with a real dollar bill—its feel, smell, texture, markings, print—that when a fake bill crosses their path, they can recognize it immediately.

The correlation is obvious. In fact, this is precisely the point of Christ's words in John 8:31-32. Look closely again at those famous words of Jesus—this time in context: *"If you abide in My word, then you are truly disciples of Mine; and you shall know the truth, and the truth shall make you free."* The context tells us there is a stipulation to knowing truth. What is the stipulation? We must *abide* in His word, thereby becoming true disciples.

I love Jacuzzis. I love just to sit there and soak, absorbing the heat into every muscle and joint until my body temperature soars to 105 and I can't stand it anymore. That's what it means to "abide." It means to soak in His word, filling your heart and mind with His truth until you become so saturated you cannot help but reflect and emulate His word in your life.

Do you spend time "abiding" in His word? When you abide in the word, says Jesus, you will become intimately acquainted with the truth.

As a result, you'll smell a lie a mile away.

When a lie crosses your path, you'll know it for what it is. Almost *instinctively*. The word of God that fills your heart and mind will detect the lie and send out radar signals to your soul!

What happens when we apply this "test of the real thing" to feminism? What happens when we lay the teachings of feminism alongside the timeless truths of Scripture?

On every major point, feminism and God's word are in direct conflict:

- Feminism pursues personal rights, promising fulfillment.

Scripture calls for personal responsibility, promising abundant blessing.

- Feminism views work as a means of fulfillment.

Scripture views work as a means of glorifying God.

- Feminism denies the importance of the home.

Scripture embraces the home as central.

- Feminism degrades feminine virtues, pursuing male traits instead.

Scripture uplifts feminine uniqueness and calls for honoring women.

- Feminism says that, except for their sexual organs, men and women are essentially the same.

Scripture says that men and women are equal in emotions, intellect, and spirit, yet designed differently for the purpose of completion in marriage and God's unique callings in life.

- Feminist philosophy calls for independence in marriage.

Scripture calls for interdependence in marriage.

- Feminist philosophy leads to competition in marriage.

Scriptural teaching leads to oneness in marriage.

- Feminism teaches the overthrow of male leadership.

Scripture teaches the servant leadership of man in the home and church.

- Feminism sees biblical submission as victimizing and demeaning.

Scripture teaches balanced and healthy submission of the wife in marriage.

•Feminism minimizes God's call to parents and denies the needs of children.
Scripture calls parents to the sacrificial work of teaching, training, disciplining, and nurturing their children.

•Feminism denies the special nurturing role of the mother.
Scripture calls mothers to the bearing and nurturing of children.

•Feminism embraces a lifestyle of sexual sin and perversion.
Scripture teaches a lifestyle of sexual purity and marital commitment.

The disparity between feminism and Scripture is an unbridgeable chasm. Why? Read on.

2: Observe the Deeds of Those Who Speak

Jesus said to look carefully at the deeds of those proclaiming to have truth. What about the Pharisees' deeds? The Pharisees lived a mere shell of righteousness; Christ's scrutiny burned through their little facade like a laser. Beneath their thin glaze of piety and religiosity was a world of deceit and selfishness. They were more than ready to murder the One who dared to even point it out.

What does it mean to "see through" a lie? Is it being "judgmental"? No, it is being *discerning*. "I send you out as sheep in the midst of wolves," said the Lord, "therefore be shrewd [smart, perceptive, wise] as serpents, and innocent as doves" (Matthew 10:16). Again, the apostle John tells us to "test [or discern] the spirits" (1 John 4:1).

How do we test them?

"You will know them by their fruits," Christ said in the Sermon on the Mount. Then He continues: "Not everyone who says to Me, 'Lord, Lord,' will enter the kingdom of heaven; but he who does the will of My Father who is in heaven. Many will say to me on that day, 'Lord, Lord, did we not prophesy in Your name, and in Your name cast out demons, and in Your name perform many miracles?' And then I will declare to them, 'I never knew you; Depart from Me, you who practice lawlessness" (Matthew 7:20-23).

Jesus is saying to us, be discerning, be astute, look beyond the veneer, the slick exterior. Satan and his followers will gladly claim a great love for Christ if they can impress us by doing so. Look beyond the impressive gifts, the persuasive prophecies, and the amazing miracles. Satan is not God, but he can do some dazzling things. The day will come, says Jesus Christ, when these deceivers will be revealed for who they are.

AN "OTHER" THOUGHT

Would you humor me a moment with just a minor tangent? When I was in seminary, I could always tell which students were studying Theology Proper. Their eyes were glazed over, their minds were miles away, and they walked slowly and deliberately, as if in another world. I wondered why they acted so strangely, until I took the course myself. The only other time in my life that I have acted that strangely was the day after Steve asked me to marry him. Why would a class in Theology Proper cause such weirdness?

Theology Proper is the study of God. Our professor, Dr. Robert Cook, was (and still is) one of the most astute theological minds of our time, a man who knows God so intimately he hardly needs a note. He would stand before us and lead us into the vast and profound study of God, just as he had done with countless students before us. In a matter of moments we were transported to another dimension, outside of space and time—the dimension of God.

It is impossible to describe what it was like to plunge "into the Godhead's deepest sea," as C. H. Spurgeon describes it, for a full sixty minutes. We became drowned in His infinity, lost in His immensity, overwhelmed by His power, and struck dumb by His wisdom. We could not help but walk out different people. In the wise words of Spurgeon, "There is nothing so improving...so expanding...so eminently consolatory to the mind, than the study of God."

Of all the things I learned in that class, one particular truth has molded my thinking over the years and preserved my personal sense of awe of God. What would you say is the most central, most fundamental attribute of God? His love? His wisdom? His power?

No, we learn from Scripture that God's most foundational attribute is holiness. God is holy—perfect, pure, completely "other" and unlike any created thing. All of His essence flows from His holiness.

In Isaiah 6 we have a remarkable account. The prophet Isaiah is lifted up into the presence of God, and in his vision he describes seeing the Lord, sitting on His throne, high and exalted, with the train of His robe filling the temple. And seraphim are all about Him. Each of them has six wings—two covering their face, two covering their feet, and with two they fly. And what do they cry out? They do not cry, "Love! Love! Love!" or "Mighty! Mighty! Mighty!" No. They cry out continually, "Holy! Holy! Holy!" (Isaiah 6:3). Isaiah is so struck by God's awesome holiness that, seeing his own wretchedness, he falls down in mortal fear, certain he will die. That vision drove Isaiah eventually to write some of the greatest passages in all of Scripture describing our great and holy God.

Jesus taught us to pray, "Our Father, Hallowed (or Holy) be Thy Name." Throughout Scripture, we read scores of references to the holy name of God. And to the Hebrew a person's name was significant, reflecting his very essence. There is no mistaking the fundamental essence of our holy God.

Why is this so important? Because all of God's attributes flow forth from and are filled with His holiness.

When we embrace love without holiness, we are left with a washed out, spineless, cotton candy kind of love. *But there can be no love without holiness.* Holiness preserves love. Holiness protects those who are loved. Holiness keeps us from the very things that destroy love. *God's love is holy.* When we teach love without holiness, we get into serious trouble.

This is why a pastor of a growing evangelical church in our area was recently shocked to find that a large percentage of his singles' group were sleeping together during the week, then attending church on Sunday. There was so much "love" floating around, and so little holiness, that it made them feel good to come to church. This is why adultery and divorce are so rampant in the church. This is how the homosexual movement has made such inroads into the church.

Love they are crying. But there is no holiness. Such "love" is a stench in the nostrils of God.

Holiness is the key. There is no mercy, no justice, no wisdom, no act of power which emanates from God that is not filled with His perfect holiness and used for His holy purposes.

YOU SHALL KNOW THEM BY THEIR FRUITS

If holiness is the primary attribute of God and every other attribute flows from His holiness, then those who truly belong to God will pursue a life of holiness. Their deeds and words will reflect the holiness of God. On the other hand, those who lie, who hide behind the skirts of religious cover-up, will be far from the holiness of God in their personal deeds and walk. And those closest to them will know it.

The greatest tip that you have a liar in your midst is his attitude toward the holy law of God. Does he pursue the will of the Father? Does he live a life of integrity? Or does he advocate a lifestyle that violates the holy word of God?

Does he promote a philosophy that is at odds with His expressed will?

Let us then ask, at its roots what does hard-core feminist philosophy think of the word of God? Very little. Because at the very heart of feminism is an outright denial and overt defiance of God's holy character and word. For this reason, even the mildest embracing of feminism pulls us away from a lifestyle of holiness. It also pulls us away from confidence in Scripture.

Because the roots of modern feminism are at direct odds with Scripture, any attempt to wed the two inevitably leads to a compromise of Scripture and the lifestyle it teaches. The "biblical feminist" would say that a person can embrace feminism and Christianity, too. But mixing Scripture with feminism is like mixing oil with water. The very idea of "biblical feminism" as it exists today is a misnomer, an oxymoron.

This is important because hosts of Christian women have fallen into this trap. In fact, for those of us who love Christ, the lie of the biblical feminist is the most dangerous of lies. It would lead us to believe we can continue on a path of Christian faith, all the while embracing an antithetical philosophy.

THE MOST DANGEROUS LIE

The woman most vulnerable to this lie is the gifted woman in the church, the woman who takes action, who is a leader, who wants to make a difference in this world.

How could someone like that become seduced? Let me suggest three subtle steps:

1. She would begin her journey by *struggling*.

Every woman struggles. *Every* woman. This very book you hold in your hands was born out of deep struggle. But when we struggle, we must realize that we are also vulnerable. It is natural to desire to escape the struggle and to let that desire control our thoughts.

How might a woman struggle? She might begin to rightfully struggle with the idea of biblical leadership and submission in marriage. Perhaps her husband is a jerk. Maybe he doesn't value her. Maybe he's distant, self-serving, or authoritarian. Perhaps he is not fulfilling his calling of God through servant leadership. Or perhaps she has a strong bent towards leadership, and her skills clearly supersede her husband's.

Or she might find herself struggling with motherhood and a natural sense of inadequacy. Perhaps she has become depleted, exhausted, depressed. Perhaps her own mother was miserable. Perhaps she feels undervalued, unfulfilled. Surely God does not wish her to spend her life shut up at home. Surely He wants women to use their gifts. Surely He understands how much better it would be for the children to be with someone more patient and caring.

Or a woman might begin to struggle with the concept of male leadership in the church. She might begin to feel that men have too much authority. Or she might wonder why a woman's gifts should not be used as a man's gifts are. Women can think and teach as well as men, can't they? A woman can see things a man cannot see, can't she? A man could learn from sitting under the teaching and leadership of a woman. Why then *shouldn't* a woman be allowed the premier positions of church leadership?

2. From struggle, she would move to *questioning* the validity of certain biblical teachings.

To question is also natural. When life and Scripture as we understand it just don't seem to mesh, we must be honest. We must search out the truth. But the search here takes a wrong turn.

She might find other women with these same questions. Strengthened by numbers, she may feel free to question more openly and defiantly. Whether in a group, or on her own, she may begin to question Scripture in the light of her negative experiences. Certain teachings simply "don't work" in marriage, she concludes, and they are clearly "not fair." Surely God would not expect us to follow such principles.

3. In light of her experience, she would begin to *rewrite* the Scriptures she now finds herself questioning.

She would begin to look for a way around them, a way to reinterpret them and explain them away. She would be tempted to ignore good hermeneutics—sound principles of interpretation such as context, setting, original language—and become convinced that these passages of Scripture say something more to her liking or, are simply irrelevant in modern times. Perhaps she may conclude they are not inspired at all but are the ideas of men. Chauvinist men. In the end she may surmise that Christians have grown beyond the need for such teachings, that clearly our Lord actually intended the egalitarian model for the home and church all along.

These are precisely the steps taken by many genuine women in the church.

THE SLIPPERY SLOPE

When a Christian woman has reached this point, she has come to a very slippery slope. As Mary Kassian says in her excellent book *The Feminist Gospel*, "[Biblical] feminism is a slippery slope that leads towards a total alteration or rejection of the Bible."[1]

How is it slippery? Kassian describes the slide. First comes the reinterpreting and dismissal of certain Scriptures. The door is then opened for the reinterpreting and dismissal of other Scriptures that do not flow with the person's own philosophy. This leads to a denial of the divine inspiration of Scripture, which enables the person to slide into a lifestyle which is in defiance of its teachings.

A brilliant scholar in her own right, Kassian carefully follows the teachings and writings of early influential, biblical feminists. She shows how their writings reflect this pattern of departure, inevitably leading them away from Scripture and into defiance of God's word. Many of these women who started out as struggling believers ended up in a far different place—practicing witchcraft and goddess worship. Are you shocked? The lie has simply led its followers back to its roots.

Mainline denominations across the country have become the sanctuaries of such "femininological" debate. Denominations that once would not permit divorced ministers now find themselves debating whether to accept avowed lesbian ones. Feminist versions of hymnals and the Bible are replacing the old ones in church pews. Feminist theologians are taking their followers on a search for new ways of conceiving God as Mother (or Sophia, or Goddess), as well as ways of blending New Age beliefs with feminist ecological, neopagan, and Christian elements.[2]

One such group, supported by the World Council of Churches, came together recently for a "Re-Imagining Conference." Among them were Presbyterians, United Methodists, Lutherans, Catholics, and members of the United Church of Christ. In one of their sessions, a leader of CLOUT (Christian Lesbians Out Together) was joined by an estimated hundred lesbians who flocked to the stage to lead the group in a celebration of the "miracle of being lesbian, Christian, and out together."[3]

Re-imagining *what?* Re-imagining evil. Let's call a spade and spade, just as our Lord did.

And yes, there are those who have followed this long, winding root back to its very origin...the father of lies himself.

One news report covered such a group in St. Louis, Missouri:

> Hundreds of women across the St. Louis area are gathering in small groups in the bright light of the day or when the full moon is high and offering devotions to a sacred female—their Supreme Being. They call her Goddess, and they are her daughters. Dancing, drumming, singing, and casting spells, at these women's gatherings are lawyers, secretaries, teenagers, teachers, Jewish mothers, ex-Christians, current Christians, therapists, housewives, divorcees and grandmothers....No one has any firm figures on how many Goddess-worshipers are in the United States. But Starhawk, a witch and author of several popular how-to books on contemporary Goddess-worship and witchcraft, said the number ranges from 'a hundred thousand to a million.'[4]

Here is the thing. The church or believer that compromises at any point along the slippery slope pays a heavy price. Weaken God's plan for male leadership in the church, and you weaken every member in that church. Weaken God's plan for male leadership in the home, and you weaken a nation. Weaken a woman's resolve to fulfill her call in motherhood, and you weaken the next generation. Inevitably, biblical feminism weakens those who embrace it.

The truth is evident. Modern feminism finds its roots in Satan himself. A strong statement? Not in light of John 8 and Matthew 7.

#3: Look for the Hook

Inside of every lie is a hook.

This has been the fundamental strategy of Satan since the beginning of time. How does he do it? Second Corinthians tells us: "Even Satan disguises himself as an angel of light. Therefore it is not surprising if his servants also disguise themselves as servants of righteousness; whose end shall be according to their deeds" (11:14-15).

Satan's strategy is that of clever disguise. Satan can hide a lie better than anybody can (and some of us are pretty good at it!). He can disguise it so well that even mature Christians are deceived.

You see, Satan knows the word of God, too. He knows it better than you. He knows it better than I. He knows it intimately. And hate it as he does, he loves to use it—twisting it, reshaping it, changing it ever so slightly into untruth. Perhaps his greatest skill is that of making his argument look good, sound good, and, above all, feel good. You've often heard the phrase, "It just feels right to me." And that, of course, is his goal.

Go back to the very first sin, and watch how Satan laid his trap.

First, he told Eve that she could "have it all." She could eat of every tree, and, what's more, she could be like God. Now that is what I call "having it all."

Second, he appealed to her senses. He took her right over to the tree and pointed out how good the fruit looked, how desirable it was. How often Satan does this today. He pulls us alongside his followers who seem happy; he entices us with the potential of delight, and he incites our desires. Our lives begin to look drab in comparison, and discontentment sets in.

Third, he questioned God's loving character. "You cannot trust the word of God," he said. "God does not have your best interests in mind." That big, stern, chauvinist party pooper in the sky is the invention of Satan!

And finally, ever so carefully, Satan tucked his lie inside of a partial truth, as one would place a hook inside of bait. Satan used two partial truths with Eve.

Bait #1: "You will not die!" he said. Eve took a bite of the fruit, and lo and behold she didn't die! So she took the fruit to Adam. Adam could see she hadn't died. They decided there must be some truth to this guy's claims. And so he too ate.

But the moment they sinned Adam and Eve began the process of dying. Death had entered the world. And, more importantly, at the moment of sin they died spiritually. From that point forward they and their descendants were separated from holy God.

Bait #2: "You will become like God!" he said. And lo and behold Eve did gain a conscience which told her good and evil. But what a trade-off for innocence! Her knowledge caused her to want to hide, to cover herself. And mankind has been hiding from God ever since. The complete truth was that Eve was less like God than she had been before.

We, too, must look for the well-disguised lie slipped right inside of a partial truth.

What is the partial truth of feminism? Women *are* equally valuable. Women *are* capable. And women are in a tight spot when it comes to choices.

"Traditional" roles as expressed in modern times *have* failed. Women do need to be understood. Honored. Encouraged to influence the world. Free to express their gifts and abilities. Strong in their femininity. Feminists have pegged the need.

But what about the hook?

The hook is the idea that God's word is inadequate. That God's word does not meet our needs. That God's word is not relevant today. The hook suggests that we must abandon God's word because our needs can only be met outside of God's plan.

How, then, can we avoid the hook? We must hold fast to the truth. We must cling to it as we would cling to our very lives. We must allow His word to interpret our experience. When we struggle, we must be honest, but we must also use a sound mind. We must take a good argument and hold it up to the light. We must look for the lie behind the articulate rational. We must pursue the wisdom of God.

ALL, SOME...OR THE BEST

Let me suggest God's answer to feminism. God says to us, "You cannot have it all, but...you can have the best."

Now that's something you can sink your teeth into. That's a truth worth hanging on to for the long haul. In a fallen, sinful world, God says to us, "No one can have it all. Every woman must make choices in this life, choices that require a price. Choices that will lead to the road of life or the road of death.

"But I love you. I made you. Make your first choice to trust Me and follow Me. And, in My perfect way, in My wise and sovereign timing, I will give you the very best."

Do you remember Matthew 6:33? Look at the words which just precede "Seek ye first": "Do not be anxious, then, saying, 'What shall we eat?' or 'What shall we drink?' or 'With what shall we clothe ourselves?' For *all these things the Gentiles eagerly seek;* for your heavenly Father knows that you need all these things. *But seek first His kingdom and His righteousness; and all these things shall be added to you*" (Matthew 6:31-33).

This is God's answer. Don't seek it all. Don't seek some of it all. That's the world's way. Don't even seek to have the Christian life on your terms. But "seek first Me and My kingdom...and the very things that the world is scurrying about so frantically to get—I will give to you, outright."

TREES

During my own time of struggle Steve recognized my need for outlets. Early on he encouraged me to take charge of various ministries and to continue developing my interests. He spent every Monday, his day off, caring for the children while I went in to the office as part of a particular church ministry. When I directed a music ministry, he got the children ready for church while I went in early. When I became involved in teaching women, he freed me up to study. But I think most importantly of all, he valued my input on projects, planning, or the writing he was doing. We were a team, and I was blessed to have a husband who so valued me.

But ultimately I was the mother. The care of the children and home environment was primarily mine. This was our commitment, and I felt that great weight. I was amazed at how much each child needed and required. How much one-on-one listening time. How much of my availability and help. How much basic care. It was a time of great stretching and often of frustration, a time of setting goals and sometimes getting absolutely nothing done because all chaos would break loose. Often I felt overwhelmed and wanted to cry out with Patrick Henry: "Give me liberty or—at least give me a good, long break!" At times the temptation to buy into the lie, to set my own agenda, was very strong.

It took me a while to come to grips with the big picture. To see that God is not as impressed with us as we are. Yes, He is well aware of our desires and gifts (He put them there in the first place), but He is far more concerned with growing us up, stretching us, humbling us, accomplishing a deeper work within us.

He can do it through illness, through failure, through disappointment. He can do it through unexpected hardship. And without question He does it through the process of sacrificial motherhood. God uses such times in our lives to accomplish His greater purposes, to prepare us for a work we simply cannot see from our ant-like perspective.

I remember flipping on the TV at one o'clock one morning. Before me an entourage of beautiful women flashed across the screen. I looked around me. In the kitchen was a sea of dirty dishes. On the unvacuumed floor before me was an ocean of laundry—seven loads worth. My only goal in life was to fold it all and get a few hours of sleep before the baby woke up. That was the best I had to offer as a long-term personal plan for my life. I was sitting on a beat-up couch that had been virtually destroyed by two young gymnasts preparing for the Olympics.

And I knew the finances were going to be very tight that month. My hair was a mess, and what little makeup I had put on that day was completely gone.

Staring for a moment at the TV screen, I suddenly found myself saying right out loud, *"These women don't exist! Nobody like that really exists!"*

There was nowhere else to turn but to the Lord. And in the midst of the struggle, God met me. As I searched and studied the Scriptures, He began to answer my questions and meet my needs. He began to show me a path between the rock and the hard place. Not only so, but He has made good on His word. He has blessed the socks off of me.

Don't think that I don't continue to struggle. Struggle sticks closer than a brother. But that's life in a fallen world, isn't it? In fact, I have since learned that struggle is actually a vital part of the process of growing.

Consider a tree. Its roots are empty hands stretched out to the earth. It is dependent on the sun, the air, the clouds, and the soil. But a tree doesn't sit there passively. No, in order for a tree to be healthy and grow, it must struggle. It must put forth an enormous amount of energy every day to raise the water and minerals from the soil to its leaves. It has been estimated that the work of a large tree on a given day equals the amount of energy expended by a person carrying three hundred buckets of water, two at a time, up a ten-foot flight of stairs.[5]

That's what I call effort. That is major struggle. You see, struggle is okay. Struggle is part of growing up. The key in the midst of our struggle is that we have our roots tapped into the right source—the pure, unpoisoned, vitamin-rich water of God's truth.

What did I say to my young college friend that day in December a few years ago? I asked her a simple question.

"Do you desire to follow Christ and His word, first and foremost in your life?"

"Yes. I do, Mary," she said from her heart.

"Then, He will let you know when you get off track. Go to law school, develop your gifts, hone your abilities. And stay very close to Him. Let Him decide how and when He will use it all in your life. Don't let the lie deceive you. Every choice extracts a price. Don't let the initial price of a choice keep you from choosing His best."

In a world where deception surrounds us, let's cling first and foremost to this great truth. The best we can ever have will come from the hand of God—as we follow hard after Him.

Chapter Eight

Blazing a New Trail

*The reason mountain climbers are tied together
is to keep the sane ones from going home.*

GERHARD FROST

*Thy Word is a lamp to my feet,
And a light to my path.*

PSALM 119:105 (NASB).

S ome people are survivalists by choice.
They actually plan the whole thing.
These folks strap on their backpacks, leave civilization, and head out into the wilderness for the sheer sport of it. Their "just-do-it" mentality makes them prime candidates for a Nike commercial.

Other people are survivalists purely by accident.

Their boat sank, and they got stranded on an island. Their plane crashed in the Himalayas. Their car ran out of gas on a back road in the Rockies. Then there are those who took a wrong turn in Cincinnati on their way to visit Aunt Matilda.

Whatever the case, this is no sport. Their primary goal is to "just-get-out-of-here-alive!" These folks aren't really Nike material. Sign 'em up for a Hush Puppy commercial.

Can you guess which group I identify with? I like the Nike spirit, but I live the Hush Puppy life.

If you were to come upon these two survivalists out in the wilderness, you would immediately notice three differences:

1. Hush Puppy survivalists are totally ill-equipped and unprepared...*Nike survivalists are equipped to the hilt. But if by chance they*

lose their equipment, they can live off the land.

2. Hush Puppy survivalists have no idea where they are...*Nike survivalists have a compass and map. Even so, they're trained to find their way without them.*

3. Hush Puppy survivalists are trying to keep from going nuts...*Nike survivalists are already nuts!*

At least that's what I thought until I met Patty Daily. Patty is the last person you would expect to be a Nike survivalist. She is a five-foot-five, blue-eyed, natural beauty. A pastor's wife. A mother of three. She is also one of the gentlest, most caring people you will ever meet. Perhaps that is why women clamor just to hang around her and be her friend.

However, as is often the case, this ordinary woman has an extraordinary side. Patty is actually a survivalist on two counts. Each day for her is a battle with a debilitating and life-threatening disease. Yet she endures it with a strength of spirit that keeps it from becoming the focus of her life.

But some twenty years ago, "in another life" as she would say, Patty was also a bonafide, premeditated, Nike survivalist. While in college she trained for wilderness survival. She became a whitewater canoeing guide, and she trained in the art of rock rappelling. She learned sailing , spin casting, and fly-fishing. By the end of her training, she could cross raging rivers, live off the land, read a topographical map, and create shelter for survival. Yet as thorough as her training was, Patty would tell you there was nothing quite like going out there and doing it. Every trip out she learned valuable life-saving lessons. Some of her tales would permanently curl your hair.

Now I have had some wild experiences. I was once stranded at midnight in an airport in Kenya with the wrong kind of visa. The plane had left, the airport was closing, and they wouldn't let me into the country. Somehow I managed to talk my way through security, find a cab driver, and get to a hotel. My guess is that I paid the guy five hundred dollars for the ride from the airport (I knew nothing about Kenyan money). But it was better than spending the night on the runway. Or sleeping in a tent in subzero weather as my friend Patty did once.

Her first wilderness trip out, Patty trekked across a frozen lake with a team of three others. They had gone to prepare camp for a group they would be bringing back the next day. During the night she woke up to discover that her legs and arms would not move. Somehow she was able to make enough noise through her frozen vocal chords to gain the attention of a team member sleeping in the next tent. Her body had gone into hypothermia, and if someone hadn't heard her, she would have died that night.

The amazing thing is that after they thawed her out, she returned the next morning to finish out the week. This time, however, she brought the right kind of sleeping bag. "It was sort of like getting back up on a horse," she explained.

With each trip out Patty improved her survival skills. And each time she's learned something new. Her most vivid experience occurred on the final trip of her class. All twenty-five members packed up and headed out to live on an island for a week. They took less food than they would need—on purpose. The boats were then sent back, and the group made a pact that, come what may, they would stick together. They would *all* stay or *all* leave the island together.

The first night on the island was so beautiful they decided to sleep out under the stars. But the ice on this northern Wisconsin lake had thawed earlier than usual. As a result, while they lay there enjoying the beautiful starry night, the black fly larvae were quietly hatching all around them. Next morning at sunup suddenly there they were. Swarms of them. The sky was black with them.

Now these black flies were not just pesky little bugs. They were *biting* flies. The team had not come prepared to ward off the black fly. And so, on their first day out, these little black flies became the focal point of survival. At one point Patty looked down to see her arm—from wrist to shoulder—covered solid with flies. And because they could bite through clothing, by the end of the first day her skin was like raw meat.

At night the flies settled and gave them relief. But by daybreak they were back, hungry and persistent as ever. A few days into this trip, things got a little tense. The group split up into two factions. One group accused the other of eating more than their share of a can of peaches. The whole thing soon got out of hand. Facing off against each other, these soon-to-graduate college students began screaming at one another. The two groups polarized, huddling together and conniving. Before the week was out, one of the groups threatened to leave the island without the other. And they did. Patty, of course, was in the group that stayed.

"How did you endure those biting flies?" I asked Patty.

"Oh, I just put them out of my mind," she replied.

Of course. Why didn't I think of that?

"And then I would occasionally bathe in the freezing water," she went on. " I couldn't do it too often, though, because it would practically knock me out."

Certainly. That would make sense.

"But one girl accepted Christ on that island. It actually turned out to be a wonderful experience," she said.

This woman is clearly a better woman than I.

Let me put it to you this way. I am not a Nike survivalist. But if I had to survive out in the wilderness, you better believe I would want a seasoned Nike survivalist on my team. Someone like Patty.

TRAILBLAZERS

Christian women today are a like a group of Hush Puppy survivalists, caught in a situation we never anticipated. Our culture has come through a great flood of change. The place of the home has been all but lost in society, and we are all the worse for it. In the wake of the flood, many Christian women have lost their sense of clear direction. They feel torn, uncertain of their choices. They long to find a biblical path. The feminist answer to the dilemma has proven to be a wrong trail, one that only leads us further into the wilderness. The only way we are going to survive is to strike out into new territory.

It's time to blaze a new trail.

Do you know what we have become? You and I have become the *new pioneers*. We are the new trailblazers entering the twenty-first century.

How will we be able to blaze this new trail? The only way is to become seasoned survivalists ourselves. We need to gather our wits about us and think soundly. We must become equipped, trained, and prepared for the task. And we had better pull together as a team, as isolated and as different as we may be in our own little worlds. College women, single women, women changing diapers, women seeking to survive divorce, women who have kicked all the birds out of the nest—each one has a unique perspective that the rest of us need. Each one has strengths needed by the whole group. Come what may, we must pull together for the long haul.

So how does a woman become a seasoned survivalist? Let's begin with the advice of a few seasoned gurus of wilderness survival.

THE BARE ESSENTIALS

Do you know what distinguishes a seasoned survivalist from the novice? A seasoned survivalist has learned to exist on the bare minimum. Experience has taught him what the essentials are. It has also taught him a hard lesson: *the heavier the load, the harder the trip.* And so the rule of thumb for equipment is this: lighter is better.

Thoreau once said: "It is some advantage to lead a primitive life if only to learn what are the necessities. Most of the luxuries and many of the so-called comforts are not only dispensable but positive hindrances."[1]

My husband wishes I could learn this bit of wisdom. My tendency is to pack everything I could possibly need for a trip…and more. You know, just in case. As a result Steve ends up lugging a trunk when a lightweight duffel bag would have done just fine.

According to the pros, there are a few necessities that a smart survivalist would never leave home without. And an American Express card doesn't happen to be one of them. For example, the "bare essentials" list of Bradford Angier, an outdoorsman and survivalist of forty years, has thirty basic items. It begins with most important and moves down to least important.[2]

1. matches
2. compass
3. adhesive bandage
4. glasses (extra pair)
5. watch
6. map
7. mirror (for signaling, etc.)
8. magnifying glass
9. knives
10. ax
11. saw
12. Carborundum (small stone which sharpens edged tools)
13. gun and ammo
14. sleeping provision (made of eiderdown)
15. tent or tarp
16. flashlight (extra bulbs and batteries)
17. whistle
18. binoculars and telescope
19. insect repellent
20. fishing gear
21. writing materials (for mapping)
22. water purifier (comes in 2-ounce bottle)
23. survival rations (in waterproof bags)
24. rope or chord
25. cooking kit
26. medicine kit
27. toilet kit (no, he means things like toothbrush, etc.)
28. repair kit
29. extra clothing
30. survival manual

But there is actually an even lighter way to travel.

The Hudson Bay Company, which has been in the survival business for three hundred years, has come up with an eleven-pound survival kit, measuring twelve inches by three and a half inches and capable of floating. This kit is designed to sustain an individual for one week in the wild. They say if he is conservative, it will sustain him for four weeks.[3] It will also make him very thin. Weight-Watchers might want to look into this program for their most eager members.

Whatever the case, all of the experts seem to agree on one point. There are five basic needs every survivalist should prepare for: *shelter, clothing, food, water,* and most certainly, *direction.* Those five needs are the very bottom line.

What are the fundamental needs for us as we blaze the trail of life? They are really not much different. We need shelter from the storms of life that hit us and threaten to tear us apart. We need the outer covering of the "new man in Christ." We need sustenance that nourishes our souls and gives us spiritual health and strength. And we need direction to keep us on track and tell us which way to go at each fork in the road.

Now, I am holding in my hand a most amazing kit. It weighs less than a pound and is absolutely wear-proof, waterproof, and fireproof. It has equipped its users to survive every possible hardship and has proven reliable over literally centuries of time. With this tool in my backpack, I am equipped to the hilt.

"All Scripture is inspired by God and profitable for teaching, for reproof, for correction, for training in righteousness; that the man of God may be adequate, *equipped* for *every* good work" (2 Timothy 3:16).

We need look no further. The Bible is the Hudson Bay Company Survival Kit of the new pioneer woman. It has everything we need for the trip ahead. Everything. Let me illustrate.

The Word of God is a shelter in the storm, living water and bread, a sharp, two-edged sword, a lamp and a light, a rock, a hiding place, a strong foothold, a path to life, a song in the night. It is pure milk, sweeter than honey, more valuable than gold. It provides protective clothing and shoes. It cleanses. It restores the worst injuries back to health. It wards off enemies, even the devil himself. It gives wisdom and direction. It renews our minds. No other book can do all these things.

Christian bookstores are great. Christian counseling is a blessing. Teaching from the pulpit, Bible Study leaders, retreats, tapes, and radio speakers are all stimulating. I don't wish to minimize these things or to suggest that you throw them out as useless. But when it comes to the bare essentials of survival, God's word is *more* than the manual. It contains all that we need for the trip.

In a Christian culture so rich with resources, it's easy to lose sight of this fact. We tend to forget our primary resource, our most valuable asset for survival on the trail. We tend to rely last, feed last, flee for shelter last, look for direction last—from Scripture itself. And when our only contact with Scripture is through the words of someone else, we cannot help but become anemic, stunted, too dependent upon people, and vulnerable to wrong teaching.

If you and I are not feeding directly on the Scriptures ourselves, we are vulnerable and ill-equipped. And so, as we prepare ourselves for the trip, we have but one bare essential. The living Word of God. Now that's what I call traveling "light."

MOST IMPORTANT TOOL IN THE KIT

Tom Brown is the founder of the world-famous Tracking, Nature, and Wilderness Survival School. At the age of eight Tom was taught tracking and hunting by the Apache elder Stalking Wolf. Over the years he gained fame for his various travels and writings. One year, after being featured by *People* magazine, he completely disappeared. It was later learned that he had gone into the wilderness with only a knife—to hone the skills he now teaches.

We could probably learn a few things about survival from this guy. I was fascinated to learn the single most important tool recommended by Brown for survival. Can you guess what it is? No, it isn't the knife. Nor the compass, or water, or matches. Brown insists that there is one tool more important than any of these.

That tool is attitude.

Attitude?

Yes, says Brown. Attitude makes the difference between those who survive and those who don't, no matter what skills or physical strength they may possess. "I am not talking as much about physical strength as a quality of spirit and character that is often hidden in modern society. Sometimes the physically strongest person is the first to give up, while the weakest may show a determination that can give new heart to an entire group. What is it that makes a person decide to live rather than to give up and die? There is no simple answer. Sometimes it is a burning desire to see loved ones again or to push on toward an unrealized goal. But just as often it is the ability to accept the present situation and to deal with each moment as it comes."[4]

Brown tells the story of a friend who survived a storm off the shores of Alaska in a small canoe. As his friend looked at the endless walls of water coming at him, he realized he didn't have a chance. But he also knew he could not allow that thought to consume him. The only way he would survive was simply to take each oncoming wave, one wave at a time. Brown goes on to say:

In the wilderness it is the same thing: one survival problem at a time. Don't compound your problems into an ocean of troubles and you will come through just fine.

If you are in a particularly bad situation and can do nothing about it, your only alternative is to endure it. John Muir, the naturalist, and a friend were once forced by a blizzard to spend a perilous night on the summit of Mount Shasta. They were so cold they had to call to each other every few moments to make sure they didn't drift off and die. Yet in spite of his agony, Muir was still able to appreciate the beauty of individual snow crystals and the 'marvelous brightness' of the stars.

In all, Muir and his friend lay thirteen hours in the open, covered with ice and snow. Every hour seemed like a year. But they survived those hours a minute at a time. So can you. Sometimes you may be so uncomfortable that you will have to back off every few minutes and ask, "Am I all right?" If you are all right in the moment, that is all you need. The next moment will take care of itself.

One wave at a time. One minute at a time. One problem at a time. One day at a time. The next moment will take care of itself. Brown's advice has a familiar ring.

"But seek first His kingdom and His righteousness; and all these things shall be added to you. *Therefore, do not be anxious for tomorrow; for tomorrow will care for itself. Each day has enough trouble of its own*" (Matthew 6:33-34). Amazing that we would find ourselves coming back to Matthew 6. As a seasoned survivalist Himself, Jesus advised us to blaze the trail, *one day at a time.*

"Present Tense"

It was spring...but it was summer that I wanted.
The warm days and the great outdoors.
It was summer...but it was fall I wanted.
The colorful leaves and the cool, dry air.
It was fall...but it was winter I wanted.
The beautiful snow and the joy of holiday season.
It was winter...but it was spring I wanted.
The warmth and the blossoming of nature.
I was a child...but it was adulthood I wanted.
The freedom and respect.
I was twenty...but it was thirty I wanted.
To be mature and sophisticated.
I was middle-aged...but it was twenty I wanted.
The youth and the free spirit.
I was retired...but it was middle-age I wanted.
The presence of mind without limitations.
My life was over. But I never got what I wanted![5]

This poem, written by a fourteen-year-old boy, has captured the value of living in the present—one day at a time. A woman who learns to live this way increases her chances of survival tenfold.

Perhaps you are saying, "I find it hard not to worry about tomorrow. I struggle to enjoy the moment in the midst of its difficulties." Mothers of young children know what this is like. When the kids are little, there are times when one moment seems like a year. Mothers who like to accomplish things, who are leaders and visionaries, movers and shakers, have a hard time taking the slow, tedious, daily periods of their lives one day at a time.

Others of us find this attitude hard because we have found life to be exceedingly hard. Like a quarterback who has been blindsided, we have been hit so hard by life that it is difficult to move forward without looking for the next hit. The hardships of life can destroy our ability to trust.

Which leads me to the second most important tool suggested by our guru of survival. That is the tool of perspective.

When someone is unexpectedly trapped in the wild, the very first thing he must do is to gain perspective. How does he do this? He climbs to a high point. He then notes land features, trees, rocks—whatever would help him in determining his location. He makes a mental map of his surroundings. By so doing, he will be less likely to go in circles and he can begin to make clear forward progress.

Perspective affects our attitude. If I have a perspective on the big picture, then it's much easier to take life one day at a time. It's much easier to have hope. But if I have lost perspective, I begin to lose hope. And if I lose hope, chances are I will more readily panic and yield to the crisis of the moment.

Earlier we gained a certain perspective from looking back at history. But what about the future? Can we gain a future perspective that will help us to live life one day at a time?

Of course, no one can know the future. Or can they? There are at least four certainties we can expect in this life:

- Life will be *hard*.
- Life will be *unpredictable*.
- Life will be *unfair*.
- Life will be *short*.

What kind of perspective is this, you may be asking. How in the world can this help? Don't we try to avoid such hard truths in this life? Don't we try to make life comfortable so it won't be hard? Don't we seek to control life, to offset its unpredictability? Don't we insist on fairness, even in the face of life's inequities? Don't we try to extend life and youthfulness?

In themselves, these truths about life can lead us into a cynicism and despair. But when we see that these truths are only *half*-truths, the picture changes drastically. There is another side of the coin of life, a side the world doesn't see. If you and I are going to survive and thrive, we cannot afford to miss either one.

This "other side of the coin" I speak of is engraved with two words.

It's also the title of my next chapter.

Chapter Nine

...But God

> *"If life is a bowl of cherries, what am I doing in the pits?"*
> ERMA BOMBECK

> *Thou art my hope in the day of evil.*
> JEREMIAH 17:17, KJV

Life is not a jelly doughnut.

As we set out to blaze a new trail, God has been good enough and honest enough to tell us the truth. Ahead of us will be hardships, unexpected turns, and setbacks. That is the nature of life. Life is hard, it is unpredictable, it is unfair, and it is short.

But what about the nature of God?

Because there is a God, and because He is the unparalleled God of Scripture, we have great hope.

You see,

• Life is hard...*but God is Good.*

• Life is unpredictable...*but God is Sovereign.*

• Life is unfair...*but God is Just.*

• Life is short...*but God is Eternal.*

For the sake of perspective we would be wise, then, to find a high point, pull out our manuals, and get a handle on these four truths.

LIFE IS HARD...

Life is difficult. And life's hardships come in all shapes and sizes, don't they? The most common hardship comes in the form of the everyday "hassle." Jesus could just as easily have said, "Every day has enough hassles of its own."

Hassles eat away at us in little bits and pieces. Isn't it often the little hassles of life that cause us to lose perspective? It's the little things that pull us away from a close walk with Christ—subtly, unsuspectingly. Many a woman has been first pulled off course, even derailed, by a preoccupation with these daily hardships. Most of my struggles have certainly begun there.

Hassles remind me of mosquitoes. Sometimes they bug you one at a time. And sometimes they come in swarms.

- Flu bugs
- An abscessed tooth
- Overflowing toilets
- Computer breakdowns.
- Car breakdowns
- Did I mention air conditioner breakdowns in 110 degree weather?

- Lost luggage
- Traffic jams
- Fussy babies
- Babies who won't take naps
- Bickering siblings
- Did I mention bickering siblings in the backseat of the car?

Mosquitoes are a nuisance, but mosquitoes can be managed. Yes, they wear you down, and sometimes they can get in your underwear and make you lose perspective. But in most cases, perspective can eventually be regained.

It's when the level of hardship deepens that our pain can begin to turn to despair. This is when we find our greatest need for the perspective of Scripture.

A few years back psychologist Dr. Scott Peck wrote a book that struck a chord with American readers and, surprisingly, hit the bestseller list. It is particularly surprising when you read the opening statement of *A Road Less Traveled:* "Life is difficult. This is a great truth, one of the greatest truths. It is a great truth because once we truly see this truth, we transcend it. Once we truly know that life is diffi-cult...then life is no longer difficult."[1]

Peck is not a believer. Far from it. But he has observed a portion of truth. The expectancy that life should not be difficult or that we can eliminate difficulty actually creates all sorts of unnecessary difficulty and pain. Many people have been plunged into depression because they simply did not *expect* life to be so hard. Knowing and accepting that difficulty is part of life is the first step in the right direction.

But I differ with Peck on one point. Accepting pain doesn't remove the pain. Accepting difficulty doesn't take away the difficulty. Pain and difficulty will keep right on coming, whether we have accepted them or not. To say otherwise is wishful thinking—the very thing Peck is admonishing us not to do.

Sometimes life hurts badly. And nothing—absolutely nothing—can take away the pain. To deny that there is pain or berate ourselves for feeling the pain is foolishness. And it is living a lie.

Jesus Christ felt deep pain. He grieved. He struggled. Christian women also struggle. They experience pain. They feel it deeply, just as every other human being. They ask questions when they are in pain. The questions, in fact, are sometimes the most difficult part of the pain.

THE QUESTION ABOUT PAIN

"The yellow and blue pills were laid out on the dresser in the bedroom. There must have been 100 of them, 'more than enough to do the job,' I moaned to myself. As I paced the floor, all I could think of was stopping the excruciating pain I felt. I thought of my four children. What of their pain on finding Mommy's lifeless body on the floor?... I knew I could not go through with it. Replacing the pills in the bottle, I angrily spat out the word that had gotten me into this mess: divorce!

"This was supposed to happen to other people. My husband of nineteen years had just declared he was leaving me. Even now it seemed impossible. This wasn't in the plan. After all, we were missionaries. Didn't that automatically protect us from horrors such as this?"[2]

This mother on the verge of committing suicide had just been dealt a hard, unexpected, unfair blow. She had given God her life, and it appeared He was returning the favor with dashed dreams and total rejection. What had she done to deserve this? Hadn't she loved her husband and been faithful to him? Hadn't she sacrificed the comforts of life to serve Christ in a foreign land? And what about her children? Did they deserve to carry such pain through life?

My mind goes back to a recent banquet. At our table were several Christian couples. I remember thinking as I sat down, "These people have it together. They are sharp and attractive. They must have everything going for them." As it turned out, every person at that table had gone through deep waters.

To my right was the bright, articulate wife of a lawyer. She was a teaching leader for several hundred women in Bible Study Fellowship, a nationwide women's ministry. He was an influential community leader at the state and local level. Although she had come from a troubled home, God had blessed her with success and a good marriage. But now in her mid forties, she had come to grips with the hard truth that she and her husband would never have children. They had tried every avenue for almost twenty years, to no avail. She had prayed, just as Hannah did for Samuel. What hurt most was that they both loved children and longed to raise a godly family. But the answer had been no.

To my left sat a warm, attractive woman who was the wife of a well-known youth camp director. She and her husband had lost their first daughter to leukemia only a few years before. Her eyes grew moist as she described the pain of the day they learned of her disease, the hopeful days of remission, its recurrence months later, the exhausting and harrowing battle through experimental bone marrow transplants, and finally their daughter's death. She and her husband had given their lives to rescuing other children. But they could not rescue their own little girl.

Things like this are not supposed to happen to Christians. Especially those who have given their all to serve Christ. But it does happen. Everybody hurts. *Everybody.*

Bad people hurt. This makes sense. They are on a path of destruction and death. But good people hurt, too. Very good people. This doesn't make nearly as much sense.

Nor does it make sense that sometimes bad people *don't* hurt. Sometimes they dance and have fun and make money while the good person suffers *because* of his integrity. Sometimes bad people walk all over good people and never get caught. This makes no sense at all.

When we look at the sufferings of Jesus, we see that it was His obedience to God that actually led Him into His deepest pain. And so it has been for His followers down through the ages. The Scriptures tell us: "For to you it has been granted [or gifted] for Christ's sake, not only to believe in Him but also to suffer for His sake" (Philippians 1:29).

Since God promises to those of us who seek His kingdom that "all these things will be added unto you," (Luke 12:31) why does it sometimes seem that *none* of these things are ours? God doesn't lie. This we know. But sometimes the realities of life don't seem to mesh with the teachings of Scripture.

What are we to think? We cannot let these questions repel us from God's word. You and I have to search out His response. And there is indeed a response. God doesn't answer every question, but He tells us enough to walk us through the wilderness and to equip us to survive.

GOD'S FIRST RESPONSE: "LOVE-TRUTH"

God's truth is a very tender truth. It is kind. It is merciful. It is infinitely loving. In fact, often in a reference to God's "truth" we find His "love" linked with it, as if they were meant to go hand in hand. The passages are far too many to recount them all here, but look at a few of them:

The LORD, the LORD God, compassionate and gracious, slow to anger, and abounding in *lovingkindness and truth* (Exodus 34:6).

May the LORD show *lovingkindness and truth* to you (2 Samuel 2:6).

Thou, O LORD, wilt not withhold Thy compassion from me;
Thy *lovingkindness and Thy truth* will continually preserve me (Psalm 40:11).

He will send from heaven and save me....
God will send forth His *lovingkindness and His truth* (Psalm 57:3).

O God, in the greatness of *Thy lovingkindness,*
Answer me with *Thy saving truth* (Psalm 69:13).

Lovingkindness and truth have met together;
Righteousness and peace have kissed each other (Psalm 85:10).

Lovingkindness and truth go before Thee (Psalm 89:14).

For *Thy lovingkindness* is great above the heavens;
And *Thy truth* reaches to the sky (Psalm 108:4).

And give thanks to Thy name for *Thy lovingkindness and Thy truth* (Psalm 138:2).

It's difficult to miss, isn't it? God's truth and love are inseparable. What a God we worship, whose great truth is filled through and through with lovingkindness! The apostle Paul knew this. That's why he told us to speak the truth in love (Ephesians 4:15). When we communicate with one another, we are to mirror the "love-truth" of God.

What "love-truth" does God tell us about suffering? When we ask "Why?" what is His response?

THE LOWEST COMMON DENOMINATOR

Scores of excellent books have addressed this subject so well that I would urge you to take what we say here as a mere beginning point. Two books that have biblically and profoundly addressed this issue are Dr. James Dobson's *When God Doesn't Make Sense*,[3] and Martin Lloyd Jones's *Spiritual Depression*.[4] They are an absolute must for the library of every woman seeking to follow God's plan. But, for the sake of time, we will bring it all down to the lowest common denominator.

Very simply, *life is hard because of sin*. When sin entered the world, so did death, and disease, and difficulty. So did evil, and all of the forces of evil that seek to destroy what is good. All of life's hardships can be traced back to sin.

I recently saw the movie *Schindler's List*, which portrayed a true and remarkably redeeming story in the midst of the horror of the Jewish holocaust. As I sat there, I was not watching actors and the special effects of Hollywood. I was watching real human beings from history. I was watching man's inhumanity to man in its most abominable, heinous form. The reality of it was so overwhelming that I could not get up from my seat when the movie was over. I felt totally overcome with grief for those who died, for those who endured such unspeakable suffering, for all of mankind.

Dr. Dobson once referred to this kind of experience as the "Doctrine of Limited Tears." Sometimes we are incapable of crying enough tears for all of the pain we see in this world. And sometimes we go into overload. You and I are limited as to how much sadness we can bear to take in.

But we must recognize something in the midst of all of this. The suffering of those people was not a testimony of God's indifference. It was a testimony to the despicable nature of sin and to the utter depth of depravity in a world that has rejected God. We cannot begin to fathom the greatness and holiness of God until we begin to fathom the seriousness and depravity of sin.

When Adam and Eve sinned, God called them to Him for a sad parting conference in the Garden. And God told them what their sin had brought upon mankind. They would be sent out from the Garden and separated from Him. Not only so, but sin would extract a price. The serpent (Satan, who had merely taken the serpent's form) would crawl and eventually be bruised by the woman's Seed

(Jesus Christ). Adam and all men after him would struggle in their work of provision, and then after struggling with the soil of the earth all of their days, they would die and turn back into that very soil. Eve and all women after her would have pain in the bearing and nurturing of children, and they would struggle greatly in their relationship to their husbands. And, yes, they too would die.

The upshot of it all was that sin would now bring to every *work* and every *relationship* of mankind the unfortunate element of pain and difficulty. Work, marriage, parenting, and love in life would become hard. And after all of the struggle would come the unnatural end of death.

And so we all enter into a world cursed by sin. We carry within our own hearts the proclivity to sin. And, from our very first breath, we face the certainty of future struggle and pain in life. No exceptions.

THE REDEMPTIVE GOODNESS OF GOD

Do you remember the line from the country song, "I beg your pardon, I never promised you a rose garden"? Well, in the very first chapters of the Bible we see that God never promised us a Garden of Eden. Our sin has erased the possibility of such a life on this earth. Yet, built right into that very curse of our sin, we find the promise of redemption. From the very beginning, God let us know that He would make a way for redemption, as well as the eventual destruction of sin through the Seed of the woman. Jesus Christ was the fulfillment of that promise.

With the sacrifice of Christ came the way to forgiveness and a restored relationship with God. And with the coming of the Holy Spirit came the means to changed lives. While sin curses the work and relationships of man, God's Holy Spirit in the lives of believers restores relationships and blesses the work of mankind to God's glory.

This is the truth. And this gives us a perspective of great hope. Even in this fallen world, God is good to His children. He works in our marriages. He works through our parenting. He uses our gifts and abilities to bring honor to Him.

ROSE GARDENS

But there is something more. God has not promised us a Garden of Eden, but God has promised to His children a rose garden. For those of us who are His children, the rose garden is as much a certainty as His promise of redemption.

I've got eight rose bushes, and I can tell you firsthand that rose gardens are no picnic. Rose gardens have weeds. Their bushes have thorns that prick and draw blood. They have to be constantly sprayed for bugs and diseases. They are sensitive to severe weather. But in the middle of the pricks, the thorns, the weeds, the bugs, the diseases, and the constant care, there are the roses. Beautiful, exquisite, fragrant roses.

God has promised to take the suffering of our lives and bring forth beautiful roses.

I will never forget a T-shirt I saw fifteen years ago. It was worn by a teenager, dressed in black with spiked hair and a safety pin in his ear. The T-shirt said: "Life is hard. And then you die." His antisocial dress and his gaunt, expressionless face were shouting his T-shirt message to the world. Life had indeed been hard for him. All that he could see ahead was a long, hard road that would eventually end in death. What a tragic perspective. This young man didn't know about the roses.

Yes, life is hard, but God is a very good God.

This particular truth saved David countless times. In fact, David understood this truth so well that his psalms proclaim the goodness of God more than any other portion of Scripture. In the middle of the wilderness, when life was at its hardest, David found this truth about God to be the *greater* truth:

I would have despaired *unless I had believed that I would see the goodness of the* LORD in the land of the living (Psalm 27:13).

Again he tells us:

O taste and see that the Lord is *good;*
How blessed is the man who takes refuge in Him!
O fear the LORD, you His saints;
For to those who fear Him, there is no want.
The young lions do lack and suffer hunger;
But *they who seek the* LORD *shall not be in want of any good thing* (Psalm 34:8).

This is "Seek ye first" all over again! With perspective.

While God's holiness expelled man from His presence, God's goodness blesses and sustains his children in a fallen world.

What are the roses of His goodness to us in a suffering world? Let's look at three of them:

1. *Christians do not suffer the inherent suffering of the sinner's rebellion.*

Yes, we are lovingly disciplined by our heavenly Father when we sin and rebel as His children. But because we have chosen to follow after Him, we avoid so much suffering in this life. Though an unbeliever may dance and sing, his heart is empty. He cannot know real joy, real peace, or genuine happiness apart from God. And inevitably the curse of sin will make its mark on his life.

Once David looked at the apparent happiness of the evil ones around him. It so embittered him that he lost all perspective:

When my heart was embittered,
And I was pierced within,
Then I was senseless and ignorant;
I was like a beast before Thee (Psalm 73:21-22).

What refreshing and open honesty from a man. I think this is why I love David so much. In the midst of suffering, he was honest enough to question the wisdom of choosing the path of righteousness:

Surely in vain I have kept my heart pure,
And washed my hands in innocence;
For I have been stricken all day long,
And chastened every morning....
When I pondered to understand this,
It was troublesome in my sight
Until I came into the sanctuary of God;
Then I perceived their end.
Surely Thou dost set them in slippery places;
Thou dost cast them down to destruction (Psalm 73:13-18).

When David entered the presence of God, he began to get perspective. He saw that God was indeed a just God and that evil did eventually bring down those who pursued it.

2. *Christians are sustained and brought through their suffering by God Himself.*

When we do suffer, God promises to go through the suffering with us. He promises to give us all that we need to bear it and bring us out on the other side.

Most Americans are familiar with the Twenty-third Psalm. My husband calls it a very dangerous psalm. Dangerous only because we know it so well. I have taken the liberty to give this psalm a fresh wording, based on the original meanings of its words. Look at it this time in light of God's promises to us in our suffering:

Because the Lord is My Shepherd, He meets my every need.
He gives me rest when I cannot sleep, and peace when I feel a sense of panic.
He feeds and refreshes my soul when it becomes exhausted and wrung dry.
When I am confused and need direction, He shows me the next step.
Even if I suffer so deeply that it is like a living death,
I will not be afraid of the future.
Even in the times when I don't feel Your presence, You are still right here with me.
You vindicate me by Your abundant provision in the face of those who are against me.
You have even protected me from the unseen dangers around me.
I am more than cared for. My life overflows with Your goodness.
Your goodness and Your lovingkindness will not abandon me for even a moment this side of the grave.
And when I die, I will be with You forever.

Our Shepherd will walk us through the hard times, from beginning to end, all the while pouring out His goodness and lovingkindness.

3. *Christians suffer with a purpose.*

There is no ultimate purpose for suffering in the life of the unbeliever—other than, perhaps, to bring him to a sense of his need for God. But in the life of the believer, suffering has great purpose. Dr. Dobson calls this the Adversity Principle. I like that.

God uses adversity to forge character in his children. And character goes on to bless our lives and the lives of those around us.

What's more, adversity develops a tenderness, a compassion, an empathy and caring. *Most ministries of significance on this earth were first started out of the seed of adversity.*

Adversity also keeps us close to the Lord. It reminds us of our great need for God. It refuses to let us forget the fallen nature of the world. It causes us to look beyond the temporal to the eternal. When you and I go through deep adversity, we are reminded that we are pilgrims passing through. We lose our attachment to this world. Adversity gives us an anticipation for heaven, for seeing our Lord and spending eternity with Him.

This is why we must allow our children to suffer. How many times I have hurt so deeply for one of my children going through adversity. I have longed to take that pain away or suffer it myself instead. But adversity forges character in our children as well. We must not teach them to avoid it or deny it. Rather, we must teach them to let adversity do its great work in their lives. Do you want a mature child? Teach him the truth about life and about God. And teach him to see adversity's blessings in disguise.

James, the brother of Jesus, tells us: "Consider it all joy, my brethren, when you encounter various trials, knowing that the testing of your faith produces *endurance*. And let endurance have its perfect result, that you may be *perfect and complete, lacking in nothing*" (James 1:2-3).

As Dr. Dobson points out, we must consider what this sinful world would be like if Christians did not suffer. What do you think would happen?

First of all, most of the world would try to jump on board the Christian boat—just to escape suffering. Their motive would be a far cry from that of repentance and a desire to serve Christ.

Christians themselves would become flabby. There would be little impetus to reach out to others, little tenderness and empathy for the hurting, little need to rely upon God, little reason to go to the Word and feed upon it. In actuality, *the removal of adversity from our lives would eventually lead to the demise of Christianity on this earth.*

Something to ponder, don't you think? When all is said and done, in the face of hardships we must cling to this first greater truth: Life is hard…but *God is good.*

But what is the second greater truth?

LIFE IS UNPREDICTABLE…BUT GOD IS SOVEREIGN

One day we may be healthy. The next day we may be sick. One day we may have a business. The next day that business may fold. One day we may have a spouse or child. The next day we may be standing at his grave. Life is unpredictable. In the midst of such unpredictable hardships, we must keep perspective by remembering a *greater* truth. God has a sovereign plan. He has not lost control. He knew yesterday what would happen today.

> I am God, and there is no one like Me;
> Declaring the end from the beginning (Isaiah 46:9-10).

> The *counsel of the* LORD *stands forever.*
> The *plans of His heart* from generation to generation.
> Blessed is the nation whose God is the LORD,
> The people whom He has chosen for His own inheritance....
> Behold *the eye of the Lord is on those who fear Him,*
> *On those who hope for His lovingkindness* (Psalm 33: 11-12, 18).

Just as the truth of God is "love-truth," so is His sovereign plan a "love-plan."

I can remember standing out in the middle of an empty field one night and glaring up at the starry sky. I had been rejected by a man that I loved, and the rejection had knocked me over.

I remember crying out loud, "God, I know You are sovereign! But Your sovereignty doesn't seem good. Can you be both sovereign and good at the same time? I can't see it!"

There was no answer. The sky was silent. I couldn't see then what I see now. I didn't know that Steve existed. I didn't realize that God was working His great good so that I would eventually be brought to another man. Steve happened to be the rose in that unexpected hardship.

Sometimes we *never* see the whole picture on this earth. There are times when the events of this life are so hard, so unexplainable, we simply have no alternative but to trust. We are out on a limb, and our only hope rests in the character of God. In those times our faith becomes "the assurance of things hoped for, the conviction of things not seen" (Hebrews 11:1). This was the kind of faith that brought the early Christians through the reign of Nero.

Gregory Fisher tells a gripping story of an experience while teaching a group of young men in West Africa:

> "What will He say when He shouts?"
>
> The question took me by surprise. I had already found that West African Bible College students can ask some of the most penetrating questions about minute details of Scripture.

"Reverend, 1 Thessalonians 4:16 says that Christ will descend from heaven with a loud command. I would like to know what that command will be."

I wanted to leave the question unanswered.... My mind wandered to an encounter I had had earlier that day with a refugee from the Liberian civil war. The man had been apprehended by a two-man death squad that had threatened to torture and kill him. He had narrowly escaped with his family after hiding in the bush for two days, but two of his children had been killed in their escape.

I saw flashbacks of beggars I passed each morning on the way to class. I thought of the poverty that I had seen all around me, robbing human dignity. I had been haunted by the vacant eyes of people who had lost all hope.

"Reverend, you have not given me an answer. What will He say?"

Then the answer came to me.

"Enough," I said. "He will shout, 'Enough!' when He returns."

"What do you mean, enough?" he asked with open eyes.

"Enough suffering. Enough starvation. Enough terror. Enough death. Enough indignity. Enough lives trapped in hopelessness. Enough sickness and disease. Enough time. *Enough!*" [5]

The day will come when Christ will shout "Enough!" When He will bring an end to sin's devastation of this world. But until that day, even in the midst of the most unexpected, unexplainable sufferings, God brings precious roses into the lives of His children. If you are in one of those dark, unexplainable times, cling to this. Look for the roses, for they will come from His hand.

Which brings us to the third greater truth.

LIFE IS UNFAIR...BUT GOD IS JUST

Quite frankly most of the hardships you and I experience on this earth will be unfair. That is the nature of life in a fallen world. But Peter tells us that the injustices of life do not escape the eye of God. He is a just God. "If you should suffer for the sake of righteousness, you are blessed.... Humble yourselves, therefore, under the mighty hand of God, that He may exalt you at the proper time" (1 Peter 3:14; 5:6).

Peter is telling us that in the midst of great injustice, we must allow God to make our case. We must not grow bitter when there is nothing we can do. We must rest in the mighty hand of God, who "loves justice."

> *Do not fret because of evildoers,*
> *Be not envious toward wrongdoers.*
> For they will wither quickly like the grass,
> And fade like the green herb.
> Trust in the LORD, and do good;
> Dwell in the land and cultivate faithfulness.
> *Delight yourself in the LORD;*
> And He will give you the desires of your heart.
> Commit your way to the LORD;
> *Trust also in Him,* and He will do it.
> And *He will bring forth your righteousness as the light,*
> And *your judgment as the noonday* (Psalm 37:1-6).

You probably recognize these famous words, "Delight yourself in the Lord." But did you know it was written in the context of unjust treatment? Yet David tells us that in God's own good time He will bring your righteousness to light. You will be vindicated. In the meantime, says David: "Rest in the LORD and wait patiently for Him.... Do not fret, *it leads only to evildoing.*" (Psalm 37:7-8).

Nothing goes more against my nature than this. I really hate to wait for God to take my defense. In fact, I am so good at defending myself that perhaps I should have been a lawyer.

Now, there is nothing wrong with stating your case at an appropriate time in an appropriate way. And there is great virtue in pursuing integrity before mankind. Some of us would do well to learn more about boldness in confronting injustice and unrighteousness. We have been called to be God's representatives and defenders of the faith here on earth. Stephen defended his own case before the angry mob in Acts 7. And Luke tells us that Stephen looked up into heaven and saw Jesus. Although we are told in Hebrews that Jesus is usually seated at God's right hand, Stephen looked up and saw Jesus *standing*. What a powerful picture. Jesus was standing in honor of Stephen's bold stand on earth on behalf of God.

The problem comes when we have done what we can do in a right spirit, and then *we refuse to let go.* There comes a time when we simply must let go. We must simply be quiet. Jesus recognized that moment when He was grilled before the Sanhedrin. They knew precisely where He stood. It was now time to let them simply hear the echo of their own accusations.

Very few in Scripture were treated more unfairly than David. David was slandered and hunted down as a common criminal for years, all because of his impeccable heart. But David learned a great lesson as a young man: let God be your justice bearer. Don't let the injustice of others pull you into an embittered response. Bitterness is like a match—it only burns the one holding onto it.

It is impossible to "trust in the Lord" and to "delight yourself in the Lord" when a spirit of bitterness rules your soul. The two cannot reside together. You and I must simply rest. Let go. And trust in the character of our just God.

"Justice is mine," says the Lord.

LIFE IS SHORT...BUT GOD IS ETERNAL.

Finally, we come to the last, greater truth. It is perhaps the most stretching— *and uplifting. Life is* very short.

> LORD, make me to know my end,
> And what is the extent of my days,
> *Let me know how transient I am.*
> Behold, Thou hast made my days as handbreadths,
> And my lifetime as nothing in Thy sight,
> Surely *every man at his best is a mere breath* (Psalm 39:4-5).
>
> As for man, his days are like grass;
> As a flower of the field, so he flourishes.
> When the wind has passed over it, it is no more;
> And *its place acknowledges it no longer* (Psalm 103:15-16).

This would be disturbing news without a *greater* truth from Scripture. The greater truth is this:

> Of old Thou didst found the earth;
> And the heavens are the work of Thy hands.
> Even they will perish, *but Thou dost endure;*
> And all of them will wear out like a garment;
> Like clothing Thou wilt change them, and they will be changed.
> But *Thou art the same,*

And *Thy years will not come to an end.*
The *children of Thy servants will continue,*
And *their descendants* will be established before Thee (Psalm 102:25-28).

David was farsighted. So farsighted he could see to the end of time. He could see that even the earth would perish. And what would remain? God. And with God, His servants, and their children, and their children. David is talking about a legacy far beyond the legacy of tomorrow and the next century. He is talking about an *eternal legacy.*

I have often thought we should come up with another T-shirt, and on this T-shirt we should print in bold letters:

Life is short...And then there is Eternity.

That certainly brings perspective, doesn't it? God is good. God has a sovereign plan. God will see that justice is done. *And then...there will be eternity.*

A few years ago I took my daughter and a friend of hers to a movie. As we drove home, they were chattering in the backseat. About boyfriends, and boring classes at school, and spats among friends. Normal preteen talk. I was lost in my own more significant thoughts, like, "What in the world am I going to fix for dinner tonight?"

Then Rachel asked her friend, "What do you want to do when you grow up?"

"Oh," reflected her friend, "I've thought a lot about being a fashion designer."

"Really? Me, too!" said Rachel. "It would be so much fun to design clothes." She paused for a minute. "But I don't think that's really what I want to do."

"What do you want to do?" asked her friend.

"I'm not sure yet. If I had *two* lives to live, I might be a fashion designer in one of them. But, you know, all of those things are going to be burned up someday. I'd like to do something that will last."

"What?" exclaimed her friend in shock. "What do you mean—burned up?"

At this point, I was so tuned in it was all I could do to keep from climbing into the backseat with them.

"Yeah. You didn't know that?" Rachel went on, "When Jesus comes back at the end of time, the entire universe, including the earth and everything in it, is going to be totally burned up. The only thing that will be left is people. So, I'd like to spend my life making a difference in the lives of people."

We were in the driveway at this point. Both girls dashed out the door so that her friend could read this amazing passage in 2 Peter for herself.

A few years later God used Rachel again to remind me of this perspective. In one of her classes, she was asked to respond to this question: "What epitaph would you wish to have on your tombstone?" Her response was very simple: "Her life made a difference."

Out of the mouth of babes, as they say. Now Rachel may end up being a fashion designer. It would certainly utilize her artistic gifts. And God knows that we need salt and light in *every* walk of life. Such perspective, however, will impact the way she does whatever it is God calls her to do.

Have you ever thought about the fact that in a hundred years you will be a mere memory in the minds of a few people here on earth? Your great-grandchildren may be familiar with your name. But except for your reputation, very little of what you have done will remain. Corporations collapse. Records are broken. Trophies fade and crumble. Books have a life span.

Think a little further down the line. In two hundred years, your name will probably not even be remembered. All that will remain of you is the legacy you have invested through the lives of your children.

Now think about eternity. Eternity lasts for a fairly long time.

C. S. Lewis used to say, "When I get to heaven, I'm going to look around and say, 'Ah, now I see'!" See what? See the big picture. See the whole story. See why God said to look beyond the temporal when we are in the middle of the struggle.

When you've been in eternity for a mere thousand years, how important will the things that so consume your mind and heart today seem to you then?

These thoughts give astounding perspective. Perspective on the use of our gifts. Perspective on what drives us. Perspective on the decisions and choices we must make in the here and now. Perspective on hardship.

Our publisher, Don Jacobson, happens to be a great brother in Christ. Don is a man of vision who makes things happen. This means that he is also constantly battling with the demands and pressures that his vision creates. Don has four little children and a precious wife. And over the course of time, Steve and I have observed that they are the top priority in his life.

Several years ago Don was in a near fatal hunting accident that changed the course of his life. It was also a hardship that changed his perspective. Not long after learning of his experience, I asked him, "Don, how do you keep balance in your life? What enables you to keep your family a priority?"

He paused and then lifted his eyes, as if he was focusing on something in the distance. He said, "Well, Mary, I just think about the day I will stand before Jesus. And more than anything else in the world I want my children to be standing there with me."

Now that is perspective.

Chapter Ten

A Woman's VIPs

If you don't know where you are going, you'll probably end up somewhere else.

DAVID CAMPBELL

Does not wisdom call, and understanding lift up her voice?
On top of the heights beside the way,
Where the paths meet, she takes her stand.

PROVERBS 8:1-2

C heshire-Puss…" said Alice, "would you tell me, please, which way I ought to go?"

"That depends a good deal on where you want to get to," said the Cat.

"I don't much care where—so long as I get somewhere," Alice added as an explanation.

"Oh, you're sure to do that," said the Cat, "if you only walk long enough."

Alice's problem is the problem of our modern world. Moving fast and furiously toward…who knows where?

But we are not so. We know our destination. The question for us is *how do we get there?* Equipped as we may be for the journey, and blessed as we may be to have the Seasoned Survivalist with us, we still need a map. A map that will tell us how to get where we are going. A lifetime map that will keep us on track as we walk through this world. A plan that will give us discernment when the tough choices come along.

But how does one acquire such a lifetime plan?

GOALS VERSUS PRIORITIES

The world's idea of a good lifetime plan is to set goals. In other words, decide what you want, and then go for it. Remember Peggy Reid of Wellesley College? Peggy wanted a good marriage, happy children, and a successful job. In a capitalistic democracy this didn't seem like too much to ask. Recent surveys have shown that the number one goal of the majority of college students today is to make money. Money, they have decided, is the key to a good life.

What kinds of goals do you have? To raise godly children? To grow old with your husband in a happy marriage? To achieve success in a particular area of your life? To make a mark in this world?

There is nothing wrong with having goals. "Aim at nothing and you will hit it every time" is a saying that is as true as it is old. God is certainly not opposed to goals. In fact, Scripture is filled with them. For example, look at Matthew 28:19-20: "Go therefore and make disciples of all the nations...teaching them to observe all that I commanded you." That is no small goal. People have devoted entire lifetimes and fortunes to that end and it is yet to be completely fulfilled.

The Bible also recognizes the wisdom of planning to reach a goal. Jesus said, "Would a man build a building without first considering the cost and logistics? Or what king would go to battle without first seeking counsel for a wise plan?" (Luke 14:28-31).

Setting wise goals is a good thing. As is establishing a plan to reach those goals. But goals are dreams, wishes, desires, things to hope and aim for. I cannot *will* a goal into existence, no matter how brilliant my maneuvering and planning. I cannot *will* happiness into my marriage. I cannot *will* healthy, happy children. I cannot *will* success in a job or in maintaining a fortune. Goals are elusive, uncertain, and, in the end, shortsighted.

What we need beyond good goals is a lifetime map based on priorities—solid, ever-constant priorities. Priorities not only shape our goals, but they determine the big and small choices of our lives. While goals can evade us, priorities are as solid as cement. While goals are dependent on me, my hard work and planning, and "chance" circumstances, priorities are dependent on God's timeless values.

God has given us a lifetime plan based on eternal *priorities*. In fact, as we will see from the book of Titus, God has given women at least five clear priorities to guide us through each season of life and at each fork in the road. I call these the five VIPs—*Very Important Priorities*—of a woman's life.

But before we talk about what those priorities are, we need to establish a clear *doctrine of priorities.*

PRIORITIES: RANKING VERSUS RUBBER BANDS

What first comes to your mind when you hear the word "priority"? Do you know what pops into my mind? When I was a first grader in Sunday School, I learned the JOY formula. Perhaps you learned it too. *Jesus* first, *Others* second, and *You* last. It emphasized the importance of putting Christ and others before my own selfish concerns. This would bring true JOY into my life. There was a certain amount of truth in that little formula.

As I grew older, I was often in Bible studies in which we listed our priorities. Inevitably, they went something like this: First, God and my relationship to Him. Next, my family and friends and neighbors. And at the bottom, once again, were my own personal concerns and desires.

If you are a wife and mother you have probably been in a group that has come up with a similar concept. At this stage of your life, the list has probably become a bit broader and quite a bit longer. There is God first, your husband second (since your marriage needs to be more important than your children), and your children third, of course. Then come your friends, perhaps a ministry in the church, those you work with, your neighbors who need to know Christ, and so on down the line. Somewhere at the bottom of the list, again, you may find yourself.

The serious flaw in this approach, however, is that it ranks the priorities of one's life in a one-two-three order. And while it may help us to see the values of life from a biblical perspective, it can be an unrealistic approach to priorities and lead to a terrible imbalance.

I readily admit I spent the first twenty-six years of my life in a state of such imbalance. God was first in my life, number one, all-consuming. In fact, I was so heavenly minded I was of very little earthly good. My roommates and family will attest to it.

Not only that, but my personal needs always seemed to get lost somewhere at the bottom of the pile. In my rush to be a leader, to make a difference, to meet the needs of others, to fulfill ministry goals, to complete jobs that could never really be completed, I ended up totally "burned-out." Not just "tired-out" or "stressed-out," but a charred, smoking ruin.

I lost interest and motivation. My heart was no longer in the things I was doing. My ability to focus and organize myself grew worse each day. I continually forgot things. My burnout was so great I would go to bed and cry myself to sleep, without understanding why. A cloud of depression hung over my life. I had an increasing desire to escape, to make a change. All typical signs of burnout.

It didn't occur to me that I had just spent the better part of my life ignoring the "sabbath" principle of Scripture. I had not recognized that my own needs for sleep, for restoration, for sheer fun and relaxation, for input and peer fellowship were absolutely vital to my survival. There was a good reason why the "sabbath commandment" was one of the ten most important commandments ever given by God to man—right up there with "thou shalt not murder or commit adultery"!

Johann Huizinga once wrote a long and learned book, *Homo Ludens*, in which he demonstrated that the health of a culture is determined by its ability for *healthy play*. (Note the emphasis on *healthy*.) "When we repress or neglect play, we dehumanize culture," he said.[1] Very few people know that the great and "austere" theologian John Calvin would lead his congregation in worship on Sunday morning and then spend his Sunday afternoons among the people of Geneva playing skittles.[2] Calvin understood balance within godly priorities.

The upshot of it all was that I had no balance in my life. And as a result I was working out of a major personal deficit. I was a dry, hardened sponge, unable to squeeze out another ounce of anything for anyone anymore.

Since then I have met a host of women who have also burned out—burned out for their children, their church, their communities, their schools. All good causes. All important priorities that reflect their values. But without a real sense of balance.

What then is a biblical perspective of priorities? A biblical perspective looks at life from the "inside out." It begins where Jesus began, with our relationship with God. "The first and greatest commandment is this," said Christ. "You shall love the Lord your God with all your heart, and mind, and soul" (Matthew 22:37-38). That covers just about all the bases of life, doesn't it? In other words, our relationship to God permeates all that we are and all that we do.

As it turns out, the biblical approach to priorities is not so much that of a ranking system as it is a *rubber band*. A steel rubber band.

STEEL RUBBER BANDS

Have you ever been to one of those memory courses, where they teach you to remember people's names by making them into ridiculous pictures in your mind? It really works, and people are pleased and complimented when you remember them (if you can keep from snickering in their face at the picture you've conjured up in your mind).

Well, I'd like to give you a silly picture. And I want you to remember it for the rest of your life.

Ready? I want you to picture your life as a pie. Fundamental to your pie is your relationship to God. Like the ingredients of milk and eggs in a cream pie, your relationship to God flows into every part of your life. But what about the different slices? Your pie is divided up into the priorities of your life. If you are a wife and mother, part of the pie is your children. Part of it is your husband. Part, your interests, activities, work. Part, your friends. Then there is you, of course— your needs for sleep, sustenance, fellowship.

However, this pie is not surrounded by a rigid edge. Instead, it is held together by a huge, super-strength rubber band. Sometimes the rubber band is pulled one way, sometimes it is pulled another. For example, when the baby is crying, your husband must wait. When you are sick, you cannot care for your family, do the laundry, or the cooking. The important thing at the moment is to get well. (Then why feel guilty about what you cannot do?)

Or when the children are toddling about, your ability for "quiet time" alone with the Lord is often completely out of your control, and many times is impossible. Unless you can rise each day at five for a rich, quiet time in Scripture, or unless you can stay alert for a deep, thoughtful time in the Word during afternoon nap time (I usually sacked out!), those are just plain tough years for spending quiet, quality time alone with the Lord.

That doesn't change your need to be alone with God or to receive input from His Word. But there are all sorts of creative ways for you to gain the input you need at this stage of life (like listening to tapes while you are nursing, praying while you are cooking or driving, joining a mother's group, getting away for time with God on a Saturday when your husband is home). If you are not rising for a quiet time every morning, perhaps you really need the sleep! God understands your situation. He knows you're doing the best you can in this phase of life when the rubber band is pulled and stretched to the limit.

The worst thing we can do is to berate ourselves because of the realities of our lives. All the Lord asks of us is that we seek to live within the priorities He has given, and do the best that we can.

Priorities are like that. They pull and stretch. They give and take. They shift and reshift in terms of emphasis and time. When your children have left home, your time and energies will shift into a new direction. But your children will always be there in your priority pie.

Why, then do I call it a "steel rubber band"? Because the priorities of God remain firm and constant. These priorities are an *unchanging*, yet *flexible* marvel of God.

This is a marvelous, freeing, realistic, and biblical view of priorities. It never lets us off the hook. It keeps us on track. It keeps us from stretching too far one direction before coming back into balance. When the big choices and decisions come our way, the rubber band is there to guide us. It keeps us within God's overall design and plan for our lives.

When we begin to get a biblical picture of priorities, we can see several things:

- Priorities are the *unchanging* values to which God has called us.
- Priorities actually *determine* our goals and long-range plans.
- Priorities give a context for the *gifts* and *callings* of God in our lives.
- Priorities bring *balance* to one another.
- Priorities, though constant, are *fluid*, moving with the *seasons* and *circumstances* of our lives.
- Priorities *pull and stretch* but never break.

THE PRIORITY PASSAGE

Now we come to the heart of our discussion, in fact, the heart of the book. If you wondered why we took the previous chapter to talk about the hardships of life, the pieces of the puzzle are about to fit into place.

What was the greatest hardship for a woman two hundred years ago? Do you think she struggled with priorities? To be sure. But her problem was different than ours. Our preindustrial mother struggled with the physical hardships of her life. She struggled with hard physical labor, the physical pain and threat of death in childbirth, the frequent deaths of loved ones, the extreme loneliness and deprivation out on the frontier, the constant battle with the elements of nature.

Today the hardships of our foremothers have to a great degree been eliminated. But hardships, nonetheless, persist. As long as we live in a world of sin, life will be hard. What then is the greatest hardship of the modern woman? Without question it is the choices she must make.

Why choices? Because our world has been split in two. The world of "work" and society, and the world of home. Because of the great Flashflood, we must choose between the two. And that's tough.

For some of us, our choices are tough because opportunities abound. Options loom before us at every turn. What makes these choices even harder is the peer pressure we feel. Our entire upbringing and education have geared us toward making choices that—quite honestly—don't jive with the priorities of God.

For others of us, our choices are tough because they are so limited. Single mothers and unmarried women have no choice but to work. And if they work, they often have no choice but to leave their homes and children. Other women feel they have no choice but to stay at home while the children are young. Yet this choice is equally as tough.

The only way to solve the issue of choices in our lives is to first come to grips with God's priorities. Priorities that rise out of His plan for homes and marriages.

We can't do it all.

We can't choose everything.

And so we need a clear, God-driven sense of priorities for our lives. Women who come to grips with such priorities find a new sense of freedom and clear direction in their lives.

What are God's priorities? In Titus 2:3-5 we find a passage of Scripture that couldn't be more clear or direct regarding God's priorities for women: "Older women likewise are to be reverent in their behavior, not malicious gossips, nor enslaved to much wine, teaching what is good, that they may encourage the young women to love their husbands, to love their children, to be sensible, pure, workers at home, kind, being subject to their own husbands, that the word of God may not be dishonored."

This passage is a great one for many reasons. It deals with the issues modern women face. It is a passage for all seasons, speaking to women at every stage of life, from the very young all the way up to grandmothers. And even though it isn't God's complete word to women in Scripture, its principles are soundly based in eternal values presented throughout Scripture.

However, although this passage focuses on priorities, it is not intended to define womanhood. A woman is never defined by a role or responsibility. She is never defined by what she does but by who she is in Christ. Marriage or motherhood does not make a woman more of a woman. She is totally woman, whether she ever marries or bears children or not. Mother Teresa is every bit as much a woman as you or me. She still carries the mothering instinct and still relates as a woman to the men of this world. Every woman must recognize that in the eyes of God she is the unique person God designed her to be.

So while this passage does not define womanhood, it lays out the clear calling of God to a woman in each stage of life. For this reason, we will devote the rest of the book to examining God's priorities set forth in Titus 2, springboarding from there to the entirety of Scripture on the issues it raises.

What, then, are the VIPs we find in Titus 2:3-5?

FIVE VERY IMPORTANT PRIORITIES

The book of Titus was originally written in the Greek language—a wonderfully specific and clear language. Using a stilted, but direct, translation, we will be able to come close to the original Greek words and their meanings:

VIP #1—Maturity

The older women are to behave as becomes holiness, not gossips or drunkards, [exercising control over their tongues and their bodies]....

The young women are...to be sensible [to receive training in good sense regarding the issues of life], pure and chaste [innocent, unjaded, exercising restraint and control of sexual desire], good [or kind, upright, filled with inner beauty].

VIP #2—Mentoring

The older [more mature] women are to...teach [teach exegetically, role-model, encourage, guide, counsel] and train [tutor, coach, disciple—bring to their senses through wise advice] the young women.

VIP #3—Marriage

The young women are to love their husbands [be a one-man kind of woman, having deep, caring, strong feelings of affection and devotion, even passion and physical sexual affection, choose or prefer him, value him simply for his own sake]....

The young women are to be subject to their own husbands [to choose, encourage, and insure the godly leadership of their husbands in the marriage and home].

VIP #4—MOTHERHOOD

The young women are to love their children [prefer, fully embrace, have strong feelings of affection, care deeply, nurture and value].

VIP #5—MAKING A HOME

The young women are to be homeworkers [hard workers, working diligently and skillfully in the home]…or home guardians [caregivers and gatekeepers].

These are the VIPs for any wise woman. VIPs for a lifetime. The five top priorities of our lives are to be maturity (close attention to our innermost hearts and souls), mentoring (the passing on of feminine values), marriage (loving our husbands and encouraging them to be the leaders God has called them to be), motherhood (loving, embracing each child with open arms), and making a home (focusing our hearts on our homes). These are the steel rubber bands.

What about single women, you may ask? Single women are very much here. No matter what your state or calling in life, every woman must understand God's plan for men and women, God's plan for parenting relationships, God's plan for the home, and certainly, God's plan for your vertical walk with Him and your horizontal relationship to other women. Single women, these words are very much for you.

Where is career, you may ask? It is very much here. Biblical submission? It is certainly here. The issues on twentieth-century women's minds and hearts are all here.

EXCAVATING THE TRUTH: A FEW BASIC RULES

Before we jump into our study of the five VIPs, we must make sure we apply the basics of good interpretation. When you and I go to interpret a passage of Scripture, we cannot just blithely read it over, do a few cross references, look up a Greek word or two, and then make an application.

Think of it this way. If you were Paul writing this letter to Titus at Crete, you would want people several years hence (even several hundred years hence) to try to discover your intent. That is the job of the biblical interpreter—to get at the *author's intent*. Not my intent. Not your intent. Not the intent of a theologian or a writer's personal agenda. Just simply the author's intent. The closer we can get to the author's intent, the closer we will come to the intent of the One who inspired him to write this epistle.

A few basic rules will help us to get at Paul's intent.

•We must consider the author and his audience.

•We must consider the historical and cultural setting in which he wrote.

•We must understand the meaning of the original language in which it was written.

•We must understand the purpose of the book.

•We must consider the immediate context of the chapter and book of the passage we are studying.

•We must consider the context and teachings of Scripture as a whole on the subject at hand.

Let's quickly look, then, at the people, the problems, and the purpose of the book of Titus.

CHARISMATIC "BUBBALAS" AND "MAMMALAS"

Let your mental eyes move across the blue-green waters of the Mediterranean to the tiny island of Crete. The year is A.D. 64, only thirty years after Christ's ascension into heaven and the day of Pentecost in Jerusalem. This little island ruled by Rome is a thriving island, within sailing distance of the great continents of Africa, Asia, and Europe, and is known for its hundred cities and advanced civilization. It also abounds with Jewish wealth and influence.[3]

Yet on this little spot of land in the middle of this vast expanse of water is a group of faithful, struggling believers. How in the world did they get there? And why did Paul commission Titus to stay and assist this band of believers? We don't know the full answers, but we do know that some of its very first believers were in Jerusalem at Pentecost.

When you picture these women of the Cretan church, visualize a Jewish grandmother, a "bubbala" (the affectionate term in Yiddish for a Jewish grandmother). As a beautiful young woman only thirty years before, she had possibly made the holy trek to Jerusalem to celebrate Pentecost with her husband, along with a delegation of other wealthy Jews from Crete. It was one of those grand, exciting trips of a lifetime, the kind you later tell your children about.

Little did she know as she celebrated in the streets of Jerusalem that day that a rather ordinary Palestinian Jew by the name of Peter would get up before them all and, using the ancient Scriptures, declare that the long awaited Messiah had come! Little did she know that while Peter spoke, others would stand before her and her fellow Cretans and speak to them in their own language. How did they speak a language they had never learned? It was a miracle!

Acts 2:11 tells us these Cretans were among those who first heard and believed at Pentecost. And so, returning to Crete, these converted Jews began the first Cretan church. When Paul spoke to Titus of the older women, then, he was most likely speaking of the Jewish grandmothers who had become believers at the time of Pentecost. The younger women were their daughters, the "mammalas" (the affectionate Yiddish term for a Jewish mother). I like to call them charismatic Jewish grandmothers and mothers because they were "charismatically" converted to Christ in the true, biblical sense of the word.

Paul was telling these women to pass on to their daughters the story of that great day in Jerusalem and the gospel they had heard. He was urging them to teach the young women in their congregations to live the separate, changed lives that God had once called them out to live.

There are other insights about these special women. These believers had started on a shoestring of faith, with almost no help or assistance from outside. No doubt various brothers in Christ had come along at times to encourage them. But it wasn't until twenty years later that Paul finally made a trip to Crete to teach and help these brave new believers in the Lord. What he found there was a church that loved Christ yet had deep-seated problems. Problems from without and problems from within.

THE CULTURE, PEOPLE, PROBLEMS, AND PURPOSE OF THE BOOK

First, the outside problems. The Cretan culture was about as heathen as it gets. It was so bad that there was a saying known worldwide about these people. It had been written by the poet Epimenides, and Paul actually quotes it in Titus 1:12: "Cretans are always liars, evil beasts, lazy gluttons."

In fact, the term "cretinizing" originated in those days. If you were "cretinizing" someone, you were deceiving them. The Cretans had a reputation for ripping people off in bad business deals and telling bold-faced lies. They were also known as wild, cruel, and fierce. They placed little value on human life. They were known for their sensual, slothful, lazy lifestyle in which they would take the fruit of someone else's labors and eat it for themselves. This was the international reputation of the Cretans for at least six hundred years!

Now for the inside problems. Inside the church certain heresies had arisen. Religious Jews seeking to pull the people away from the gospel were trying to set up rules and regulations, using legalistic, Pharisaical teaching. These heretical dissenters were more than annoying pests. They were doing their best to ruin this church.

In the first chapter of Titus, Paul calls these men "deceivers," "rebellious men," "vain talkers." They were fluent in speech, superficial in their faith, and effective enough in their dexterous arguments to bring whole families to ruin by their teachings (1:11). The damage was so great that the survival of the church was at stake, not to mention the good name of the gospel of Christ on this island of Crete. These deceivers, said Paul, "must be silenced."

And now Paul was leaving Titus to "set things in order." My guess is that Titus had to be a pretty tough nut for Paul to leave him among such sharks. What these believers needed was a strong shot in the arm. They also needed someone of character to stand up and call them to accountability. "Reject a factious man after a first and second warning, knowing that such a man is perverted and is sinning, being self-condemned," said Paul to Titus (3:10). When was the last time you heard of any modern evangelical church doing such a thing?

Paul made it clear. This church needed good, bold leadership made up of men of true character—men who managed themselves and their homes well, men who were good fathers and committed to their wives, men who lived lives of integrity before the world, men who knew the Scriptures well and could teach them boldly and effectively (1:5-9)—men completely unlike the Cretans who lived around them.

Beyond the confrontation of sin and heresy, Paul stressed that these people needed a strong dose of the Scriptures—part of which was being written even as they lived. They needed to be reminded of the truth of the Old Testament as fulfilled in the New Testament. Such teaching would immediately reveal the wrong teachings of those who were bringing down the church through heresy.

I find it interesting that Paul did not urge the men to train the women. On the contrary. Paul urged the women to take the responsibility of training one another. He urged the more mature women to teach and train those who were younger in the faith, those who were in their toughest early years of wifehood and mother-hood.

And what about the women in this church? They were as much a part of the problem as they needed to become part of the solution. Clearly, some of the older women had let the gluttonous lifestyle of the Cretans influence their own. Why else would they have a drinking problem? Paul was calling them back to sound biblical thinking.

Finally, as we consider Paul's instructions, we must remember the culture in which these women lived. They were preindustrial women. Their lives revolved around their homes. No doubt their church even met in believers' homes. The home was the hub of their lives. It was the place of their work. It was their social, educational, and religious hub in the middle of their cultural wheel. Knowing this sheds light on Paul's words to these women.

In the end, Paul's primary concern in writing to Titus was the honor and integrity of the Word of God. It concerned Paul so deeply that he expressed it numerous times in these three tiny chapters (1:9, 13; 2:1, 5, 8, 10, 12; 3:8, 14).

We could say that the honor and integrity of God's Word is just as much at stake today. And Christian women play a significant part in giving credibility to that Word.

We have looked at the author, the cultural and historical setting, the general Greek meanings behind the words, as well as the purpose for which this book was written. We've even become acquainted with these infamous women of Titus 2.

CULTURE VERSUS PRINCIPLE:
EXCAVATING TRANSCULTURAL TRUTH

One final question must be addressed in our excavation of this passage. Is this passage cultural? Is it part cultural and part noncultural in its emphasis? Or are we to take it all as God's timeless word to us today?

This is a most critical question. If the passage is primarily cultural, we can dismiss what doesn't seem to fit into our present-day culture. Indeed, there are certain passages of Scripture that do have strong cultural overtones—and need to be recognized as such. But if this passage is transcultural and soundly theological in nature, then we must take it in its entirety.

One of the clearest principles of good interpretation is this. Take a verse in its entirety. Take it in context. Take the clearest intent that comes out in the author's words and context. Ripping out a phrase here and there that doesn't fit our liking would be poor excavation.

Let's look at the passage one more time from this angle:

Is it cultural that older women are to teach younger women?

Is it cultural that older women should behave as becomes holiness?

Is it cultural that older women are not to gossip or be drunkards?

Is it cultural that younger women are to be sensible, sexually pure, kind, good, unjaded?

Is it cultural that women are to encourage and support one another?

Is it cultural that a woman is to love her husband?

Is it cultural that a woman is to love her children?

No, none of these things are cultural. They are timeless principles, wise priorities and precepts for living. They span culture and time.

Then why should it be cultural for a woman to submit to her husband's leadership? Why should it be cultural for her to work hard, focusing on her home? These mandates are no more cultural and no less critical in God's eternal plan. Not only so, but they appear elsewhere in passages of Scripture that are equally noncultural.

The principles we find in these verses are timeless. And because they are, they are amazingly applicable in the twenty-first century.

It is now time to get down to the real stuff of life: God's plan for modern women as they blaze a biblical trail.

Chapter Eleven

VIP #1: Maturity

The strongest man in the world is the man who stands alone.

HENRIK IBSEN

The older women are to behave as becomes holiness, not gossips or drunkards,
[exercising control over their tongues and their bodies]....
The young women are...to be sensible
[to receive training in good sense regarding the issues of life],
pure and chaste [innocent, unjaded, exercising restraint and control of sexual
desire], good [or kind, upright, filled with inner beauty].

TITUS 2:3-5

*O*utside my window at this very minute I hear a game of one-on-one basketball between my forty-five-year-old husband and our ten-year-old son, Josh.

Hardly a fair game, would you say? Josh is beating the pants off of him. But if my guess is right, Steve's probably giving him a break or two.

Of all the things our boys love to do with their dad, playing one-on-one basketball is by far their favorite. There's something about getting in there and mixing it up with the number one man in their lives, trying to outdo him, pushing the limit, laughing and yelling, and basking in his undivided attention.

One-on-one relationships make a great deal of difference in life, don't they? Indeed, the one-on-one parent-child relationship is the single most important relationship in a child's life. A child who never experiences that kind of intimate focus is a child in need.

The same is true of women. The single most important relationship of our lives is our one-on-one walk with God. Yet, while children clamor to be with their parents, we often find ourselves dragging into God's presence. While our children treasure those moments, we often find ourselves merely enduring our moments with the Lord.

The Westminster Confession tells us that, "The chief end of man is to glorify God and enjoy him forever." In other words, nothing will fulfill our purpose in living so much as our pure happiness in God.

Writer and theologian John Piper is a self-proclaimed "Christian hedonist." Says Piper, "The longing to be happy is a universal human experience, and it is good, not sinful. We should never try to deny or resist our longing to be happy." The key to happiness, however, is where we seek it. "The deepest and most enduring happiness is found only in God.... [Therefore it could be said that] the chief end of man is to glorify God *by* enjoying him forever."[1]

What a refreshing thought! Short of heaven, my greatest happiness in this life will flow out of a one-on-one relationship with God.

What does this have to do with maturity? Everything. A mature woman has developed a one-on-one relationship with the Lord. And it is out of this intimate relationship that the fruit of maturity will grow.

Do you wish to bear the marks of maturity in your life? Like the Titus 2 women, do you wish to have a tongue that builds up those around you? An innocent and unjaded spirit? An inner beauty that draws the world to you like a magnet? Wisdom to think clearly in the choices of your life? When people look at you, do you want them to think, "This woman knows God"?

Such fruit will be impossible outside of a one-on-one walk with God. "Abide in me...," said Jesus. "As the branch cannot bear fruit of itself, unless it abides in the vine, so neither can you, unless you abide in Me" (John 15:4).

But there is one more thing that needs to be said.

STANDING UP, STANDING OUT, STANDING ALONE

We need God. We need to be happy in God. We need to draw close to Him and abide in His words. And when we do, His fruit will be evident in our lives. But the evidence of such fruit will require something of us. Jesus goes on to tell us in John 15:18-21 that "if the world hates you, you know that it has hated Me before it hated you.... Because you are not of the world, but I chose you out of the world, therefore the world hates you.... If they persecuted Me, they will also persecute you.... But all these things they will do to you for My name's sake, because they do not know the One who sent Me."

If we walk close to Christ, we will have to *stand alone*.

This is the cost of maturity.

Maturity means that when everyone else is floating downstream with the crowd, we will be moving against that flow. But remember this. Any old dead fish can float downstream.

But how do you and I become strong enough to stand alone in this world? We do it one step at a time. And the very first step is to *stand up* for what is right. You may find that your first step is a baby step. It may mean something as small as not laughing at a sick joke or removing yourself from a destructive conversation. It may mean refusing to go to a movie filled with dirt when everyone else you know is going. It may mean gently saying "good night" when your date would like to do much more.

Eventually, as you stand up, you will discover that you are growing. And as you grow, you will find yourself standing up in big ways, such as making the VIP choices in life, even though no one else around you is making those choices.

A mature woman has discovered two important things. She has discovered that respect always outlives popularity, and that there is just too much potential for joy in this life to destroy it by making foolish, immoral choices.

And so in this fallen world, there will be times when we will be "different." There will be times when we must stand up for what is right. Not in a self-righteous, alienating way (I call this "standing weird"), but with a gracious, unpretentious, nonjudgmental spirit. This is the attitude of "kindness and goodness" we see in Titus 2.

When you and I stand up, the inevitable result will be that we will also *stand out*. A person who stands out is often misunderstood, sometimes ridiculed, occasionally falsely accused. As we stand out, we are a light in the darkness. Our lives are exposing the darkness of the world. And people do not like to have their dark deeds exposed. Therefore, to feel more secure, the crowd will put us down and even reject us.

But that's okay. It will be good for us. It will test us. And in the end, it will increase our maturity and our closeness to God. We can be certain that in the midst of rejection, God will not reject us. He will delight in us and honor us. Just as Steve does with Josh in the one-on-one game, He will give us the edge.

Finally, standing up and standing out means we will also find ourselves *standing alone*.

Perhaps all alone.

Barring a major revival, I believe we can expect our culture to continue moving farther and farther away from God. A woman who is close to God will find herself standing alone, more and more each day. Expect this. We are the wheat. And as the wheat and tares grow side by side, each becomes more apparent (see Matthew 13:24-30).

There may not be another woman where you work who embraces the values of God. There may not be another soul who stands with you in your neighborhood, in your dorm, in your classes at school. But, once again, that's okay.

Do you know what will happen to you when you reach this point of maturity? Unbelievable blessing. Kindred friendships. Honors. Perhaps a spouse who has been looking for a person of such character, or children who adore you and respect you. God will bless you a thousand times over for your willingness to stand alone.

But perhaps best of all, you will realize that you are not standing alone at all. He is standing right there with you—beside, behind, and before you.

You are not alone at all.

Chapter Twelve

VIP#2: Mentoring

~～⌒

Example is the school of learning, and they will learn it at no other.

EDMUND BURKE

The older [more mature] women are to...teach
[teach exegetically, role-model, encourage, guide, counsel] and
train [tutor, coach, disciple—bring to their senses through wise advice]
the young women.

TITUS 2:3-4

Were you surprised that this would be in the top five priorities? I was shocked. *Mentoring?* But Paul obviously had a good reason. In fact, he chose to book-end this Titus 2 passage with the idea of mentoring.

Mentoring in this passage is simply another way of saying "discipleship." And this means several things.

First, the command "to teach" here includes the idea of *exegetical teaching* of the Word of God. In recent church history women have been led away from this idea. We have felt that men were to do the tough, exegetical, profound, theological study.

Not so, says Paul.

Next time you go to a women's retreat or conference think about this command. We are to teach the Scriptures to one another, and teach them well.

What does this mean to us as a body of women in the church? It means that we need to become more proficient in our study and knowledge of the Scriptures. Some women need to see this as their calling. Some need to be willing to do the homework. And God will call some women to seminaries and to theological study, simply for the purpose of excellently teaching other women.

But this command of Paul also involves the idea of *training* and *coaching*. It means *counseling*. It means constantly supporting and *coming alongside* the young women in the body of Christ. God knows they need it in a day in which support for the VIPs of Titus 2 comes from almost nowhere else in society.

Paul also knew that mentoring—men to men (as he instructed Timothy to do) and women to women—was part of insuring a legacy of biblical manhood and biblical womanhood. There are certain things that only a woman can teach another woman and, likewise, certain things that only a man can teach another man. Paul is reiterating the "to the fourth generation" idea in yet another form.

Yet mentoring has become a lost art in our time for several reasons:

- the mobility of society, causing lost friendships and few long-term relationships.
- the devaluation of age and experience and the exaltation of youth.
- a spirit of independence and individuality that says "I don't need anyone else."
- a marked generation gap, due to rapid change in our culture and a resulting feeling of inadequacy in so many older women.
- a retirement mentality among older women once the children have left the nest.
- mothers absent from the home.

THE PRIME MENTORING RELATIONSHIP

I am convinced that God intended the primary mentoring relationship among women, by far, to be the mother-daughter relationship. I was blessed with a mom who took this VIP seriously, so I can speak firsthand on the unsurpassed value of such a relationship.

Mom graduated as valedictorian of her high school and then went on to become salutatorian of her college with a degree in pre-med. (I didn't get an ounce of her left-brained intelligence or her natural bent in science.) Many who meet this quiet-natured, sweet woman today would be shocked to learn she was one of the best on her high school debate team. Or that she knows the current batting average of the entire Braves' baseball team. Beyond that, she also is an excellent musician. In brief, my mom is a woman of many colors, multigifted, and consistently wise.

How did my mom mentor me? She did so by making the choices of Titus 2:3-5.

My mother made me a priority.

We often talked for hours, debating and discussing the issues of life. She was always honest, open, and willing to listen at the drop of a hat. She mentored me by listening as often to my heart as to my words. I never went through a struggle that Mom did not sense it and offer wise input and encouragement. Most importantly, Mom mentored me by living in the Scriptures herself. The pages of her Bible are well worn, and she always had a notebook going on a subject she was studying in the Scripture. When life was unclear, Mom always seemed to know where to go in Scripture to meet and address my needs. She had a firm grip on the teachings of Scripture when I most needed to hear them.

Yes, we went through the typical teenage years of tension and arguing, but she never gave up listening and caring for me. She hung in there with me through my most turbulent stages so that we came out the other side of those years stronger than before.

As a result, she has become one of my dearest friends. I can pick up the phone, and she will always be there, listening with her whole heart and with the wisdom of her years spent walking with Christ. She will never know what her mentoring model has done to make me the woman I am today.

When mothers and daughters lose their ability to communicate, when they become distanced and unable to enjoy one another, when they grow to resent one another or feel the need to control each other, when they cannot endure the faults and weaknesses of each other—the most valuable mentoring relationship of their lives has been lost. Without a doubt, this is the top reason for the mentoring crisis among the women of our nation. Daughters are no longer mentored by their mothers.

Mothers, we need to make it a high priority to stay close to our daughters. To understand them. To be part of their lives. To lie in bed late at night and talk together heart to heart. To be constantly encouraging and listening—ever listening. To do special things that let them know we are thinking special thoughts of them. To ask the tough questions. To refuse to let conflict slide by. We cannot afford to let the natural distances turn into miles, and then years. There will never be a more valuable mentoring relationship in your daughter's life than the one she has in you.

QUALIFICATIONS FOR MENTORING

Who is the "older woman" that is to be the mentor? The qualifications of being an "older woman" lie in two areas: experience and maturity. When you get right down to it, the only difference between an older woman and a younger woman is that an older woman has had a few more years to blow it and make mistakes. She has the edge when it comes to sheer experience.

And so, in the Titus passage, age is not so much the issue as is experience and maturity. "The older women are to behave as becomes holiness," said Paul. How then is maturity exemplified? In a woman's *choices* and resulting *lifestyle*. Not in her togetherness or perfection, but in her heart of pursuing hard after God. She needs to let those she is mentoring see that she too has struggles. She is growing, just like the rest of us.

As a once-younger woman who has talked to hosts of other younger women frustrated in their mentoring relationships, let me give you the best tip. *The more vulnerable a woman is about her weaknesses and shortcomings, the more effective she will be as a mentor.* Just be real. Ask any young woman, and she will tell you this is so.

Perhaps you are a junior in college, mentoring a group of high school girls. Or maybe you are a mother of teenagers, mentoring a group of women whose children are preadolescents. You may be a friend mentoring another friend by your mature walk with Christ. In the end, the experience of having failed a few times and the willingness to make choices based on God's priorities—those are the qualifications of a mentor.

OLDER WOMEN: JUST DO IT!

One last word to older women. (I now officially qualify as one.) Older women, *don't be intimidated by younger women.* Young women may know how to manage multimillion dollar accounts, build successful businesses, and market successful products. They may carry briefcases and wear thousand dollar suits. They may have an education from Harvard or Yale. But many younger women don't have a clue about how to be a Christian woman, wife, or mother in this society.

These skills of life are among the most important skills you and I can teach and learn from one another in the body of Christ. Where else in this world are we going to learn these things? Just as survivalists need each other in the wilderness, so we desperately need the input and support of one another on the trail of biblical womanhood.

Older women, you have so much to offer. You are called by God to boldly teach and live before these young women the timeless principles from the Scriptures. Teach them about being a woman who follows close after God. Model before them a lifestyle of loving a husband, meeting his needs, nurturing and training up their children, caring for a home. Teach them about developing godly wisdom and maturity. This is what they so desperately need to know. This is what they want you to show them.

So just do it! Reach out to a younger sister in Christ. Be a friend, and let her know you care.

Even if you don't feel adept at teaching Scripture, teach out of your life, your experience. Teach the lessons God has taught you along the path in becoming a seasoned survivalist.

WE ARE ALL IN THIS TOGETHER

Perhaps there are no seasoned survivalists, no available mentors in your life. Don't let that stop you. Pull together as sisters in Christ. Mentor one another as you move along in life together.

Do you know why geese fly farther than eagles? Because they fly together. As the stronger of the geese leads the V form, the updraft of wind from the coordinated flapping of the entire group gives each member an extra pull and lift. When the head goose grows weary, he drops back and another steps in. That's how they undertake their transcontinental journeys.

Mentoring can happen through books, through Bible studies, through friendships, or through simply watching another woman live out her life—a picture of godly living in action. Watching a couple fight and work it out. Watching a mother lovingly discipline her child. Watching a woman handle adversity with peace. In fact, I am convinced that the real life model is by far the most effective form of mentoring.

A PICTURE OF A MENTOR

A few years back I came across an amazing little article tucked away in the back of *Newsweek* magazine. It was written by author and artist Linda Barry, who was relating the remarkable impact of one woman's real life model upon her life.

I grew up on the last street before a garbage ravine where people from other places drove up to dump old refrigerators and mattresses and bodies of dogs and other trash.... You can bet that, like most kids in a disintegrating situation, we needed a guardian angel. She came knocking on our back door.... I knew right away there was something different about her. It was a look she had when you talked to her that we had hardly ever seen on an adult. She looked like she was actually paying attention.

Barry describes often stealing wild flowers from another yard, and taking them to Mrs. Taylor, this "guardian angel," hoping to be invited in. Mrs. Taylor always acted like this little clump of yanked up plants with dirt clods was the most beautiful thing she had ever seen.

She would laugh and put her arms around you and hold you tight. Almost all of us had parents so deep in various sorts of trouble that they just couldn't remember how to do this anymore. Mrs. Taylor was about the only remaining evidence of purely affectionate contact for no good reason between adult and child, and I have no doubt that a lot of credit for the sanity of the kids who grew up in my neighborhood is due to her.... We invented a game called 'church' in Mrs. Taylor's front room. We dragged her huge Bible out and took turns playing the preacher, the lead singer, and the lady whose wig was on crooked by the end of the song. And the greatest part was Mrs. Taylor leaning out of the kitchen to tell us that our sins had been washed off us and they were laying all over the rug, so would one of us please vacuum.

I loved going over to her house so much that one day I sneaked over at dawn. I stood on her porch knocking and knocking and knocking, weighing how much of a bother I was becoming against how badly I needed to see her. Finally the door opened and Mr. Taylor looked down at me in his bathrobe and said, 'Now, girl, what are you doing here?'

'Who is it, John?' Mrs. Taylor stepped out from behind him with her robe on, and for the first time I saw her long hair down. The whole picture of it made me unable to speak.... When I told her my mom said I could eat with them, she laughed and pushed open the screen door. Mr. Taylor was getting up for work and Mrs. Taylor was making him breakfast. I remember her son, Sammy, walking in and crawling up onto his father's lap, leaning his head into his dad's green coveralls, like doing that was the most ordinary thing in the world.

Even if it wasn't happening in my house, I knew that just being near it counted for something. I'll never forget that morning, sitting at their table eating eggs and toast, watching them talk to each other and smile. How Mr. Taylor made a joke and Mrs. Taylor laughed. How she put her hand on his shoulder as she poured coffee and how he leaned his face down to kiss it.

And that was all I needed to see. I only needed to see it once to be able to believe for the rest of my life that happiness between two people can exist.

I vowed that I was going to grow up and be…just like Mrs. Taylor.[1]

Blessed be all of the Mrs. Taylors of this world.

Chapter Thirteen

VIP #3: Marriage, Part One

Today it's ludicrous to expect that two people stay connected for their lifetime.

MARGARET MEADE, FOLLOWING HER THIRD DIVORCE

What God has joined together, let not man put asunder.

JESUS (MATTHEW 19:6)

Steve took the phone call in his office.

When he hung up moments later, he called me inside. "You better sit down," he said, shutting the door.

I could tell by the look on his face that this had been no ordinary phone call. A longtime friend and pastor of a well-known evangelical church had called to ask if Steve could fill in at a conference the upcoming weekend. The original speaker had canceled at the last minute.

"Is everything okay?" Steve had asked.

It wasn't like this guy to cancel. He, too, was a longtime friend. In fact, he and his wife had mentored us in our early years. In recent times, God had blessed them with a successful national ministry.

"You haven't *heard?*" our friend asked.

"Heard what?"

"Well, Steve, he and his wife have separated. He was forced to resign this week and cancel all upcoming conferences. His ministry is over."

The news left Steve stunned. Another tragic casualty on the front lines of battle.

Such casualties among highly visible men and women in ministry had mushroomed in recent years. How would this affect those who had recently sat under his ministry? What kind of impact would this have on their resolve to fulfill their own marriage commitments?

Checking his calendar, Steve apologized to our friend. There was no way he could come the next weekend. "But please call me next time you guys decide to do a conference," Steve said.

There was silence for a moment on the other end of the line.

"Well...unfortunately I won't be here, Steve," he said. "I felt sure by now you would have heard. Darlene left me over a month ago. I tried to work things out with her, but she's divorcing me. It's been pretty rough. I finally resigned from the church last week."

I felt as sick in my heart as Steve looked. Two ministries. Two families. Gone. Demolished. We stared at each other, overwhelmed with incredulity and sadness. Sadness for them and their children. Sadness for the ministries and the people their lives had touched. Sadness for lost integrity to the faith.

And sobered.

Sobered by the thought that if this happened to them after more than thirty years of marriage, it could happen to anyone. It could happen to *us*.

Questions burned in our minds. *How did this happen? How could we keep it from happening in our marriage?*

Even our children have felt the uncertainty of the times. Too many of their friends have come home to find their dads leaving. Too many families around them are reeling in the aftermath of marital breakup. In our children's early years when Steve and I argued (yes, we did and still do!), they would sometimes ask, "Are you getting a divorce?" We would sit down with them and hug them and assure them that never, *ever* would we divorce. We would always work things out. We were committed for life. It grieved us that they would even think of such a thing.

Amazing, isn't it, that when we were kids almost forty years ago, it was a rare child who entertained such thoughts. Steve remembers the first time he even heard the word *divorce*. He was shooting basketball hoops with a new kid in the neighborhood and asked him what his dad did. The boy replied that his parents were divorced.

"What's divorce?" Steve had to ask.

Times have changed. Not that marriage hasn't always had its troubles. The battle between the sexes has raged since the beginning of time.

AND IN THIS CORNER...

"Marriage is like life in that it is a battlefield, not a bed of roses," Robert Louis Stevenson once said. He joins the ranks of countless writers who have observed the dark side of marriage. "If I ever marry it will be on sudden impulse, as a man shoots himself," said H. L. Mencken. Shelley couldn't come up with anything more positive to say. He wrote, "A system could not well have been devised more studiously hostile to human happiness than marriage." You get the feeling these guys were maimed in the line of duty.

Even a great man like Abraham Lincoln found marriage to be hard. "Marriage is neither heaven or hell; it is simply purgatory," he once said. Is there any way to avoid all this travail? Nietzsche came up with one possible solution: "If married couples didn't live together, there would be far more happy marriages."

An interesting thought, but somehow I don't think it will ever catch on.

What is our society's response to the never-ending struggle? The battle isn't worth it. It's unrealistic these days to think that love should last for a lifetime. No one can be expected to remain in an unhappy relationship anymore. People change. Life is full of unexpected turns. Relationships sour. A man and woman are plain lucky if their love makes it through an entire lifetime.

World-famous sociologist Margaret Meade related in a recent interview: "Not long ago, on TV, I was discussing the family, and someone in the audience asked, 'Since your three marriages were failures, what right do you have to comment on the family?' Well, I don't consider my marriages as failures!... Today it's ludicrous to expect that two people stay connected for their lifetime."[1]

Perhaps Jane Fonda best summed up the modern perspective: "For two people to be able to live together for the rest of their lives is almost unnatural!"

Her point is well-taken. And surprisingly biblical.

In a fallen world love for a lifetime *is* unnatural. Anyone who has been involved in a love relationship can vouch for this. Why is it unnatural? Because of sin. When sin entered the world, pain and difficulty entered every marriage relationship. The plain truth is that one sinful man plus one sinful woman equals conflict. There is no way to get around it, and anyone who says otherwise is lying.

Jesus came into this fallen world. He watched the couples around Him. He saw the conflict and pain. Yet He stood by God's words spoken to the first married couple in Genesis 2: "For this cause a man shall leave his father and mother, and shall cleave to his wife, and the two shall become one flesh.... What therefore God has joined together, let no man separate" (Mark 10:7-9).

Marriage, said Jesus, is for life.

As unbending as these words are, we need to hear them. This is the plan of God, and He has not changed His mind in the last half-century. The only exception, said our Lord in Matthew 5:32 and 19:9, is in the case of adultery. And even then, it is a last resort.

There are certainly times, as we will see in the next chapter, when separation is appropriate. In the case of abuse, it may become a necessity. But aside from these situations, *biblical reconciliation* is at the heart of God's plan for resolving conflict in marriage. Biblical reconciliation begins with genuine repentance and change in the one who has wronged, and genuine forgiveness and restoration by the one who has been wronged.

Is God unfair to ask us to pursue such restoration? Is He unrealistic to expect us to be committed for life? Does He not care about failures, hurts, broken commitments, and betrayals?

Yes, God cares deeply. He understands the often excruciating pain involved in making a marriage work. He knows the seemingly unbridgeable chasms that can come between a man and woman. But God also knows that the survival of marriage is foundational to the health and survival of individuals, families, and nations. He knows what happens to children when marriage ties are broken. He knows the pain in the partner that is betrayed. He knows the deterioration that occurs in the partner who betrays. And He knows what happens to society when it is filled with all these broken lives.

How many couples have said to us, "We just can't work it out. We're all wrong for each other. Our boat is going down, and the only way to survive is to jump ship." When you are drowning, all you can think about is escape. That's why God gave us a clear and timeless standard. He knew we would need it when things got tough.

It is true that it takes two to make a marriage work...and only one to tear it apart. God knows that you and I live in times that promote the one-person marital breakup. Since the "liberation" of woman through no-fault divorce, the marriage contract has become a mere piece of paper to be torn up and trashed at will.

A man or woman can simply walk away, and no one can stop them. God knows this. And He hates it.

But don't believe all that you hear.

Margaret Meade is dead wrong. Love for a lifetime is more than possible. It is *necessary*. Two people can stay connected for life—if they pursue the plan of God.

What is His plan? That is the subject of the next few chapters, beginning in this chapter with the *ideal*—the unchanging blueprint drawn up by God. We will move on in the next chapter to address the *real*—the tough issues of marriage that modern women face in a less-than-ideal world.

THE GREAT MYSTERY OF ONENESS

Have you ever wondered what in the world God was thinking when He created marriage?

A few years back one of my sons came to me with eyes as big as silver dollars. "Mom, Dad told me all about sex," he said in a hushed tone. "That's the wildest thing I've ever heard! Can you believe God actually came up with that? I wouldn't have thought of that one in a million years!"

I have to agree. Sexual intercourse *is* a wild idea. Steve's first thought when he learned about sex was, "My *pastor* does this? No way!" But then everything about marriage is highly irregular.

Think about it. Two people—who are different hormonally, anatomically, and psychologically, who are from different backgrounds, have different personalities and expectations, and carry different baggage—united before God and humanity to live together for a lifetime. It is an incredibly creative thought.

What *was* God thinking?

In a nutshell, God was thinking "oneness." One man for one woman, growing into oneness for one life. That was His great plan.

PHYSICAL ONENESS

The first book of the Bible states it simply: "a man shall leave his father and his mother, and shall cleave to his wife; and they shall become one flesh" (Genesis 2:24). Ephesians 5:31-32 repeats those words, with an additional phrase: "This mystery is great." (You're not kidding!)

What do you think of first when you hear the words "one flesh"?

People usually think of sexual intercourse. The "flesh" part gives it away. But sexual intercourse doesn't make two people "one." This is another of the great lies of our times. In the heat of passion a couple may imagine there is oneness, but it's an illusion.

I once heard it described this way. Sex is not a thermostat, changing the state of affairs in a relationship. It is a thermometer, reporting the state of affairs. In other words, sex is more than a physical act. It is "intercourse" or *communication*. God designed sex to express a "oneness" already present, to seal a oneness already experienced emotionally and spiritually. Indeed, sex is the most precious and intimate communication known to human beings.

This means the better the relationship, the better the sex. It's as simple as that.

Has our world ever missed the boat when it comes to great sex! Outside of a marital commitment, sex actually ends up stealing from us. It steals trust and respect. It takes a part of our souls that every person gives in the sex act. As a result, sex outside of marriage actually ends up eating us alive.

Why? Because God designed sex only for marriage. "You shall not commit adultery," said God (Exodus 20:14). "For this is the will of God…that you abstain from sexual immorality," reiterates Paul (1 Thessalonians 4:3).

The Scriptures are clear. Sex outside of marriage is sin. Period.

I find it amazing that our society persists in viewing God as the great Prude in the sky, when He was the One who created sex in the first place. The Bible tells us that, on the contrary, God is the source of complete and unending pleasure: "In thy presence is fulness of joy; In thy right hand there are pleasures forever" (Psalm 16:11). God wants us to find fullness of joy. He wants us to experience pleasure in what He has created.

A year ago Steve went a little crazy and bought the boys a go-cart. I think it was the fulfillment of a boyhood dream. The cart was a two seater, and when the boys put on their helmets and sat in it side by side, I thought it was about the cutest thing I had ever seen. But when they put their feet to the pedal and began swerving at top speed down the road, I turned into a nervous wreck.

So Steve sat them down for a few instructions. First, there was to be no driving in the street. The reason was that there were vehicles on the street which could smash them to smithereens. Plus, it was illegal and they could go to jail. Both boys were equally horrified and disappointed.

Second, there was to be no driving in the back alley between four and seven in the evening. Too many people were coming home from work and whipping in and out of their driveways. But these are the hours right after school, the boys protested! The rules were starting to become a drag.

"I suppose we will have to wear these helmets all the time," the oldest said with a sigh. Of course. That was a given.

We could have thrown out the rules and just told them to go have their fun. But what kind of parents would we have been?

Likewise, what kind of God would condone sex outside of marriage when He knows it destroys, and even causes death? Sex outside of marriage is just as dangerous as our boys flying down the street in the middle of rush-hour traffic with no helmets.

"I have no pleasure in the death of anyone...declares the Lord GOD" (Ezekiel 18:32). Again, these are narrow words, but they are words we need to hear.

Perhaps you don't think you could ever be drawn into immorality. But let me urge you to think again. It has happened to better women than you and me. Men are not the only creatures who must guard their hearts. Women must guard their hearts, too! In fact, when we think we are safe, then we are most vulnerable of all.

AFFAIR PROOFING YOUR HEART

How does a woman become drawn into an affair? Steve wrote about the process in his book *Point Man*, and even though he wrote it to men, the process for a woman is not really much different. How does an affair begin?

> It usually begins with discontent. Things have changed. It's not the way it used to be between the two of you.... You don't seem to have the same good times you had when you were dating. You rarely enjoy good conversation. You're just not close. You eat at the same table, share the same bathroom, sleep in the same bed, but you might as well be hundreds of miles apart. If there's one word that describes your marriage, it's "distance."[2]

Let me pause for a moment. Men are most often tempted when they are unfulfilled sexually. (As we've seen, this is simply a reflection of something much deeper.) Women, however, are most tempted when they are unfulfilled emotionally. If a woman feels empty, unloved, misunderstood, unappreciated, or simply shut out of her husband's life, she is wide open to the lure of an emotional affair.

How, then, can you know when you are being drawn into an affair? Take a look through a man's eyes:

Perhaps you had never noticed her. But as you walked by her desk today, she looked up and smiled. Or maybe she's the new receptionist for a client you've been calling on for several years. Or perhaps a new project involves two different departments working together, and suddenly you're spending large amounts of time with a woman you didn't even know two weeks ago. Or maybe she's in the church and has come to you for counsel.

Whatever the reason or the circumstances, you now find yourself relating to another woman. She's attractive and a lot of fun to be around.... [Or, he is interested in you, and seems to know how to make you feel special.] If you were single, you would definitely ask her out.

This is how an affair gets started. You're frustrated and disappointed with your wife. Your needs aren't being met. And then *she* comes along.

Here's where it gets tricky. It is what you do in these innocent situations that will either make or break you. If you don't make the right choices here, within a matter of weeks or even days you are going to be emotionally hooked. And once you've swallowed a hook, it's almost impossible to spit it out.

The central issue here is how to avoid taking the hook.... Every marriage has its "down" times, and if a man doesn't recognize his increased vulnerability during these phases, he is sure to get himself in the deep weeds.

Randy Alcorn suggests that you ask some important questions to determine if there is a hook lodged in your emotional jaw.

• Do I look forward in a special way to my appointments with this person?
• Do I seek to meet with her away from the office in a more casual environment?
• Do I prefer that my co-workers not know I'm meeting with her again?"[3]

Let me add a few questions for women:

• Are you acutely aware of his presence over the presence of other men?
• When you dress, do you find yourself dressing to please him?

- Do you hope to see him at a function or feel disappointed if he is not there?
- Do you feel a surge of excitement when he comes by your desk, or when you are talking together?

If you answered yes to any of these questions, you are on the verge of becoming emotionally hooked. Whether you mean to or not, it will only be a matter of time before you will be comparing this man with your husband. When that happens, says Steve, "Look out, friend. You're about to step on a land mine."

It's amazing how subtle the enemy can be, isn't it? Randy Alcorn has some great insight. "A relationship can be sexual long before it becomes erotic," he says. "Just because you are not touching or thinking of a sexual encounter doesn't mean you aren't becoming sexually involved."[4] Indeed, for women, emotional involvement usually comes first, pulling us along into sexual sin.

What is a woman to do when she realizes she is approaching a land mine? She can rationalize it as no big deal and keep going. Or she can turn and run in the opposite direction. There is no standing still.

"Flee from youthful lusts," said Paul to young Timothy, "and pursue righteousness" (2 Timothy 2:22). How does a woman "flee" and "pursue"?

HOW DOES A WOMAN FLEE?

If the man you're attracted to is unmarried, think of the wife he will one day have. Paul told the young guys at Thessalonica not to deprive their brothers by defiling their future wives (1 Thessalonians 4:6). The same is true for you.

If he's married, think of his wife. Pray for his marriage. Pray for him as your brother in Christ. Commit his needs to God and leave them there. It is very hard to lust and pray for someone in the same breath.

Fleeing also means you must free yourself from the relationship. Immediately. Sometimes this will require some hard steps.

Perhaps freeing yourself will mean dropping out of certain involvements or functions. You may even need to find another job. Does this seem severe? Hardly, in light of the consequences of an affair. If you have become entangled with a married man who is counseling you, don't go back. Find another counselor. If you are being pursued by a married man, be clear and decisive. Withdraw, set the boundaries, and don't waver one inch. And if you have already become physically involved, determine to end the relationship. Tell him so and refuse to see him ever again. Period. No exceptions.

Satan is out to destroy marriage, and He knows how to hit us at our weakest points. You cannot afford to toy with even the start of an unhealthy emotional tie.

Fleeing lust isn't easy, but Paul also advised Timothy do something more, to be proactive. "Pursue righteousness," he said.

HOW DOES A WOMAN PURSUE RIGHTEOUSNESS?

First, turn your heart to God and ask Him to meet your need. A woman who finds her needs met through a relationship with God and discovers that He is completely able is on her way to finding true happiness. Jesus understood the needs of the woman who was caught in adultery and brought to Him (John 8). He did not condemn her. He could see into her heart. All she had ever known was sexual betrayal through the men of the world. What she needed was the perfect, unwavering, forgiving love of Christ.

And so Jesus protected her and treated her with respect. And then He spoke to her gently, saying, "I forgive you. Go now and leave your life of sin." Do you think her life was changed? I am certain of it. Why pursue false, perverted "love" when real love can be freely found in Christ?

Secondly, turn your mind and heart upon your husband. Pray for him. Seek to meet his needs. Even if you don't feel great love, do these things for Christ's sake.

If you flee and pursue, do you know what you will have become? A virtuous woman. You will be the woman of Titus 2 who is a "one-man-kind-of-woman," a woman who is sensible and pure, one who seizes control of her heart and emotions when the world around her is going haywire, a woman who is filled with inner, unfading beauty.

God delights in such a woman. He honors and blesses her. If you have obeyed Him in the face of great difficulty in marriage, get ready for the onslaught of God's blessing. Eventually it will come. God will see to it.

ONENESS THROUGH COMMITMENT

If sexual unity doesn't make two people "one flesh," how do we become "one"?

Consider Ephesians 5:29: "No one ever hated his own body, but he feeds and cares for it, just as Christ does the church" (NIV). When I become one flesh with my husband, his flesh becomes mine. If I care for my own body and flesh, *then I will care for his as well*. If I am committed to my own well-being, *then I will be committed to his well-being also*. I will never abandon myself. *I will never abandon him*. That is loving commitment.

We can measure our oneness by the loving commitment we have for each other—emotionally, intellectually, spiritually, and physically. Loving commitment is the glue that cements us into "one flesh."

How long does this take? Oneness doesn't happen in a year, or ten years, or even twenty years. At twenty years we are just getting started! Oneness takes a lifetime.

Oneness means we will take the unexpected curves on the road of life *together*. If the business fails, we will bear the brunt of it *together*. If emotional depression strikes, we will stick *together* and hold up the one who is hurting. If addictions consume, we will take the tough steps to address the need. If harsh words or hurtful actions are hurled, we will still pursue oneness through honest, loving communication.

How many times will we need to forgive? "Seventy times seven" was our Lord's response to that question. While His disciples were getting out their calculators, Jesus was going beyond their finite mentality. It takes a lifetime, he was saying, to use up our forgiveness quotient.

Talk about ideals. Left to our own devices, none of us could pull off such a standard of committed love. We need help.

A TRIANGLE OF ONENESS

"Two are better than one because they have a good return for their labor. For if either of them falls, the one will lift up his companion.... Furthermore, if two lie down together they keep warm.... And if one can overpower him who is alone, two can resist him. A cord of three strands is not quickly torn apart" (Ecclesiastes 4:9-12).

Two people can help each other. One falls, the other picks him up. One works, the other comes along and works by his side. One is cold, the other keeps him warm. (In some cases one is warm, and the other keeps her cold!) One is attacked, the other protects and comes to his aid. But notice Solomon's last line. He switches gears on us. "A cord of *three* strands is not quickly torn apart." Why would he say three?

A marriage of two committed people is a very good thing. But a marriage of two people who are both tied to Jesus Christ—the third strand—will not be easily torn apart. That marriage will have a strength otherwise unattainable. What a tremendous truth! God's ultimate plan is that He be at the very center of your marriage. Two people, one flesh, come together in Him.

I realize some women reading these pages have husbands who are far from God. God can not be central to your marriage. And that is tough. First Peter 3 gives some direction.

Peter encourages such women to live out the standard anyway so that "even if any of them [husbands] do not believe the word, they may be won over without words by the behavior of their wives, when they see the purity and reverence of your lives" (1 Peter 3:1-2). This is what I call "silent persuasion." Speak through your actions, says Peter.

Does Peter have any idea how hard this is for a woman? (Probably so, since he was married.) Is he telling us not to talk about the very thing that is most important in our lives? (Yes, he is.) There it is in black and white: Don't badger and nag him. Don't drag him to this or that, or talk incessantly about his need for the church or God. Don't shove people or books down his throat. Once your husband knows the source of your hope and strength—Jesus Christ—then be quiet. Believe God when He says He can work best in your husband's life through your silent actions of committed love.

Rest in God, Peter continues. Be at peace. "Let it be the hidden person of the heart, with the imperishable quality of a gentle and quiet spirit, which is precious in the sight of God" (1 Peter 3:4).

In the end, God must hold your marriage together.

ONENESS THROUGH DIFFERENCE

The last piece of the "oneness" puzzle can be found in an apparent paradox—oneness through difference. God's great plan in creating us differently, as male and female, is that our very differences will actually complement and complete us.

What a far cry this is from the thinking of our world. Difference in our world is a threat. Difference suggests inequality and inferiority. But nothing could be further from the truth.

MALE AND FEMALE

Twenty years ago the civilized world became swayed by the idea of androgyny—the belief that men and women are essentially the same. Research since has blown that idea out of the water. The evidence is conclusive. We are different—anatomically, biologically, and psychologically.

Most of us don't need to read the works of a Harvard psychologist to be convinced of this truth. All we have to do is open our eyes and observe the men we live and work with. May I give you a few of my own observations?

Have you ever noticed that men don't typically sit around and sip coffee and share their "guts"? When men sit around, they usually are settling business. But if a man wants to get with the guys, he much prefers the camaraderie of fly fishing, for example—cracking jokes and chewing the fat or just sitting there, throwing out the line and reeling it in again for hours at a time, waiting for the big catch. Other men like to get out on the basketball court and jab each other to death, racing up and down the court, sweating buckets, competing for the big swish or slam, spraining their ankles, pulling their groins—all for the sake of competition and hanging out with the guys. Men actually enjoy this.

They may at times get down to discussing the real heart issues of life. In fact, healthy men do. But this camaraderie of competition and togetherness is a man's form of fellowship.

Women normally don't do this when they get together with each other. Sure, women can become expert fisherwomen, and some women are incredible athletes. But when women get together, they really prefer to do something that allows them to talk.

This same difference occurs with couples in bed at night. Men love to be physical. Women love to talk. Men can't, for the life of them, figure out why a woman would want to talk—even if there was conflict in the kitchen an hour before. This is a mystery to a man and a frustration to a woman.

Why the difference? The difference is due in large part to testosterone, the male hormone released by the mother into the baby's system when he is just a few days old in the womb. Testosterone brings out the aggressive, competitive, warrior side of a man and is given by God to a man to enable him to rise up in the face of life's struggles, to provide, protect, and care for his family. It equips a man to go out and conquer or to stand up in the heat of the battle for righteousness in this world. Testosterone is God's gift to man in a fallen, sinful world. In the wrong hands, it becomes ugly, but in the hands of God, it is absolutely glorious!

I am convinced that testosterone is why my boys spit, why they constantly jump to reach the top of every doorway in the house, why they love snakes and live on Nintendo. They didn't learn it from watching Steve because he quit spitting before we married. And I have never known him to jump in doorways or to so much as look at a snake.

Now, my daughter can do all of these things and do them well. She can beat any male within miles at Nintendo and will even hold a snake. In fact, she is probably the most competitive one in the whole bunch. But she can live without that gross, fighting stuff. It's just not the driving force of her life.

When testosterone is released into a little boy's system, it washes through his body. And in the process it destroys many of the connectors between the right and left sides of his brain. And so a man's brain tends to function either in one side or the other. A woman's connectors, however, remain strong, giving us a more holistic way of thinking.

Testosterone and the male development yield many other differences. Studies show that, generally speaking, men are by nature conquerors, protectors, and penetrators. They tend to be more tactile and physical, to see more in black and white, to be solution oriented and to gravitate to the bottom line in their relationship conflicts. Even in their sexual makeup, men tend to be triggered differently, stimulated by the outer senses of sight and smell.

Generally speaking, women are more fine tuned in their sensitivity to people, more nurturing, more connected, more process oriented. They tend to be geared to relationships and inner needs. Women are usually triggered sexually by their internal sense of well-being in the relationship.

And we haven't even mentioned differences in body metabolism, pain thresholds, life spans, work capacities, or skeletal, muscular, and blood systems.

As a result we can expect that the needs of women will be different from the needs of men. Our ways of communicating will tend to be different. Our focus in conflict will tend to be different. Our perspectives in parenting, decision making, and problem solving will tend to be different.

We are different. *By design.*

Why did God make us so utterly different? So that we could complete one another. So that we could learn to appreciate our God-given differences, and receive the blessing those differences provide. So that we could fulfill the callings of God for men and women in the home. So that our children would have the benefit of both kinds of parenting. So that we could experience the joy of becoming *one*.

Your husband needs your pespective. And you need his. Difference, when embraced, is a great gift to men and women.

STRONG RELATERS

Dr. Stu Weber has written a moving analysis of the biblical male as the *Tender Warrior*.[5] He speaks of a four-pillared man, who has within his chest the heart of a king, warrior, mentor, and friend. I've often wondered what would be the complementary description of the biblical female. The best one that I have been able to come up with isn't nearly as poetic. But at least it does convey the idea. We could call her the *Strong Relater*.

Go back to Genesis 2 for a moment. "Then the LORD God said, 'It is not good for the man to be alone; I will make him a helper suitable [or corresponding] for him'" (Genesis 2:18).

There was something unique about our creation. Woman was the only being created by God to fill a specific need.

Adam had the need—he was lonely. Although God was there with him, along with all the animals, Adam was still intensely lonely. Even though he had work that was pleasurable and could fill all his days, he was incomplete. There was no one *like* him. No one with whom to share his human experience. No one to work by his side, think with him, talk together with him, enjoy this world with him. For the first time God stood back and said, "It is *not* good" (Genesis 2:18).

And so God made woman out of man. She was not exactly like him but *corresponded* to him, fitting him perfectly as a companion and helpmate. The Hebrew term used here for *helper* denotes inherent strength. It is the same term used in the Old Testament for God Almighty, our Helper. Eve was more than a companion. She was designed to be a strong helper to her husband.

In other words, as women we are not quiet-mates, play-mates, or slave-mates.

We are helpmates.

Think about that word for just a moment. Help implies care. It also implies action. In fact there are many strong and tender words connected with *help*— words like *collaborating, contributing, supporting, sustaining, redeeming, advocating, inspiring, teaming up with, lightening the load, bringing through, rejuvenating, nurturing, counterbalancing, quieting one's fears.*

What a word. What a concept. What a great call.

Woman is designed to be the single most important person in a man's life—a strong, undergirding support and a help to man all of her life. All the while she communicates. And communicates. And communicates.

God's plan is that we become one. And part of that plan is that we find oneness through completion—completion through our *differences* and completion through the *roles* that rise out of our differences.

Which leads us to Titus 2. And the exploding potato.

Chapter Fourteen

VIP #3: Marriage, Part Two

～⌒〜

All the baggage of a patriarchal society will have to be thrown overboard.
Women must explore the dark ages alone.

GERMAINE GREER

Encourage the young women to love their husbands...and be subject to them.
[to choose, encourage, and insure the godly leadership of their husbands
in the marriage and home].

TITUS 2:4 - 5

*L*ove your husband...and be subject to him.

Talk about standing alone. If you believe in these teachings, you are probably standing out on a deserted island right about now.

Who in their right mind really holds to such ideas anymore? Isn't this the kind of teaching that turns women into victims and losers?

Next to the issue of career, there is probably not a more volatile issue in the church today. And understandably so. "Traditional roles" have fallen short of the biblical plan. And in the wake of lost fathers and a feminist revolution, Christian men and women have suffered an identity crisis.

What are we to do with such biblical mandates? Despite the cry that they are outdated, they quietly remain. They stand in noncultural settings, wholly theological in nature. We simply cannot ignore them or throw them out.

But many Christian women who wish to embrace them are asking deep, penetrating questions. How do we translate this biblical model into a marriage in which a man doesn't value his wife, abuses leadership, is driven by destructive addictions or worldly pursuits, or simply doesn't seem able to lead? What about a woman who turns out to be wiser, more gifted in leadership, or more spiritually mature than her husband? How are we to translate the ideal standard into an ever-deteriorating culture—without compromising womanhood *or* God's Word? These are difficult questions that demand a biblical response.

Our society has made its position clear. Women can no longer allow themselves to be the victims of "patriarchal rule." We must overthrow the "vast array of external hierarchies that depend for *their* authority on weakening *our* authority—especially women's," as Gloria Steinem put it.[1] Society says we must get tough and stand up for ourselves. Whatever we do, we must never allow a man to think he is the boss in the relationship. Personal power is the key to a woman's happiness and security.

The real woman these days is independent, aggressive, competitive, physically fit, sharp-tongued, and intimidating. She has control of her own destiny and is a formidable foe in the battle for success. She is *better* than man…but difficult to love.

She is the Amazon woman.

THE RISE AND FALL OF THE AMAZON WOMAN

Every woman has a little of the Amazon woman within her. Every woman has the instinct to fight for her own survival. *And if she is to be a healthy woman, she will fight for survival.*

A healthy woman recognizes her individuality and separateness. She is created a *person* first, in the image of God. And as a person of infinite value in the eyes of God, she draws her self-esteem primarily from Him. She thinks for herself, develops her God-given skills, and expresses her uniqueness. In every relationship of life she draws the lines of healthy self-respect. Discovering such *personhood* is the beginning of healthy *womanhood*.

But modern women have pushed these ideas to an unhealthy extreme. Today's Amazon woman is the feminist reaction to the failure of *both* men and women in fulfilling the biblical plan. But she is also the feminist response to Darwin. Yes, she is concerned with personhood. But in her effort to recover her personhood, she has discarded her womanhood. She has heeded Darwin's suggestion that femininity means "less."

And so in the battle between the sexes, the Amazon woman is out to win, to prove herself the fittest in the great fight for survival. She has become a "man-woman."

Her marriage may not survive her hard, competitive nature, and the strong men around her may not be particularly drawn to her. But they will simply have to "deal with it." The important thing is that she intends to emerge the winner, personally unscathed.

After all the degradation and oppression, the great thing about being an Amazon woman is that she can never really be hurt. Or so she may think.

THE WOMAN BEHIND THE MAN

Let me recount the story of the first great Amazon woman. According to Greek legend, she was Queen Hippolyta, who reigned on the island of Amazon over a nation of warriorlike women. These women were taut, athletic, and gold from the sun. They swam the open sea and rode bareback upon their horses.

Once, while on a long journey, King Theseus of Athens happened upon their island. Astonished at what he saw, he mused, "If these are the women, what are the men like?" Theseus was struck instantly by Hippolyta. He had never seen a woman of such pride and beauty, and he fell madly in love with her. He wished to win her, but there was no man of the tribe to fight for her. Then it dawned upon him. The warrior with whom he would have to do battle was Hippolyta herself. He sensed she would fight to the death, but he desired to take her alive, for he had seen the woman behind the man.

The day came when Hippolyta challenged him to battle. Theseus agreed to the fight on one condition. If he won and she lived, she was to take him as her king and follow after him. Vowing to die in combat rather than to lose, Hippolyta readily agreed. She asked only that if she died, he would leave her Amazon maidens in peace. Choosing first javelins and then swords, she fought a fierce battle. But then in a reckless lunge at her, King Theseus pinned her to the ground. "The fight is over," he said, "and you are not dead. Will you keep your vow?" She lay stunned in disbelief. "So be it," she agreed, as if in a dream. Gathering her in his arms, he carried her from the field of battle. Theseus was convinced their fates were joined forever.

But Hippolyta had only known a life of self-sufficiency and independence. Bonding to a man was forbidden by Amazon law. She could not face the loss of her own identity, and so she determined to take his life or die. That night, as

Theseus lay sleeping with his back to her, an Amazon maiden slipped her a dagger. She quietly approached his bed and raised the dagger to slay him.

Unknown to her, Theseus had awakened and lay silent, awaiting his fate. But the dagger never came.

He turned to see her bent over in tears, preparing to thrust the dagger into her own body. Theseus leaped from his bed, wrested the dagger, and flung it into the corner. Looking into her eyes, he said, "One often stakes one's life on a little thing. So why not on a great one?"[2]

Theseus was challenging Hippolyta to *risk love*. Until that moment, giving up her armor had meant giving up her identity. But now, something within her awakened—something that responded, that trusted. She hadn't known such feelings could exist. She fell into his arms and accepted his love.

The tale does not end there. Hippolyta accompanied Theseus to Athens and became his wife. In the ensuing years she discovered a fullness of life she had never known on the Amazon island. She did not lose herself at all. Becoming a woman only served to broaden her identity and enrich her world.

Happily-ever-afters are for fairy tales and legends. And certainly love and marriage are far from being the solution to the "woman question." But the real lesson of Hippolyta is a lesson of finding love. An Amazon woman cannot know real love because real love involves the lowering of defenses and the giving of ourselves as women and men. If a woman is to give and receive love, she must embrace more than her personhood. She must embrace her womanhood.

Few men are as strong as Theseus or as willing to fight for the "woman behind the man." And because the Amazon woman insists on battling, it is difficult for her to be feminine or to respond openly or supportively with men, especially strong men. That is why, oftentimes, the man who marries an Amazon woman is confused in his masculinity and lacks an aggressive edge. Although she maintains control, eventually she is bound to disdain his lack. It is hard for an Amazon woman to truly love a weak man.

Amazon women and feminized men are the worst of both worlds. In her book *Knowing Woman*, Irene Claremont de Castillejo points out, "When women become masculine and men become feminine, each takes on the worst traits of the other. Men take on a woman's softness without her strength; women take on a man's toughness without his kindness."[3]

I am convinced that many a modern Amazon woman has learned somewhere *not* to trust, not to give, not to relinquish absolute control. Somewhere a man has violated her trust. Perhaps her father abused her position of weakness as a child. Perhaps he violated her mother. Perhaps a husband or lover proclaimed love, all the while expressing destructive unlove. Perhaps he violated the sacred bond, throwing away her gift of trust and stripping her of self-worth and dignity. Perhaps she has taken on Amazon traits out of the sheer effort to survive. Perhaps she has never met Jesus Christ, felt His great love, and found her womanhood in Him. Whatever the specifics, make no mistake about it. The disfigurement of manhood and womanhood through sin has brought us to where we are.

But is the Amazon woman the solution? No. She has only stepped up the battle and heightened the problem. If we are to become all that God created us to be as women, we must embrace our womanhood. And if we are to experience God's great plan for us in marriage, we must embrace *biblical* manhood and womanhood.

In light of these things, let's pose an alternate answer.

STEPPING INSIDE THE ROPES

Picture a husband and wife. Two boxers, stepping inside the ropes of the boxing ring of marriage. Sin has created this scenario, but nonetheless, it is real life. The battle for oneness is every couple's lot.

The world has determined that the battle is not worth fighting. God tells us, however, that it is. It is more than worth the fight. It is absolutely essential for our survival. That is why when things get difficult, we cannot run away. We've got to stay in the ring and fight the battle for oneness.

But there are good fights and bad fights. "Fight the *good* fight," said Paul to Timothy. The Amazon woman is not fighting a good fight. She is fighting to win, but in so doing she loses. The only way to win is if *both* the husband and wife win. And the only way for both to win is through oneness. The good fight is never the fight to win. The only good fight is the fight for oneness.

What happens to even the healthiest of Christian couples who enter the ring? We find ourselves literally barraged with temptations and philosophies that would destroy our union. And so we find ourselves fighting two battles: the internal battle for oneness, and the external battle against the forces that would cause our marriages to go down in defeat.

"For our struggle is not against flesh and blood, but against the rulers, against the powers, against the world forces of this darkness, against the spiritual forces of wickedness in the heavenly places" (Ephesians 6:12). Ephesians 6 is the experience of every committed couple.

In the face of such forces Paul goes on to tell us how we must fight: "Take up the full armor of God, that you may be able to resist in the evil day, and having done everything, to stand firm" (6: 13).

What is this armor? Paul describes the things that save us in battle—truth, righteousness, the gospel of peace, faith, salvation, and the Word of God. But we must notice something. Every piece of this armor is defensive—breastplates, shoes, helmets, shields—except the Word of God. The Word of God, says Paul, is our sword—our one *offensive* weapon against the onslaught.

We cannot abandon God's Word in the battle. We must take it up and use it rightly. The fight for oneness in marriage is an excellent and worthy fight, but it must be fought according to God's plan.

OUR GREATEST OFFENSIVE

In the sheath of womanhood are two powerful weapons given to us by God in His wisdom—*philandros* and *hupotasso*. *Philandros* is the sword of biblical love, and *hupotosso* is the sword of biblical submission. If we are to use them rightly and well, we must know exactly what God means by these two powerful words.

"Make love, not war" we used to say in the sixties. But our idea of love was a far cry from God's.

PULLING PHILANDROS FROM THE SHEATH

"Encourage [teach, train] the young women to *love* their husbands," said Paul. The term *philandros*, or "husband-love," used by Paul here only appears this one time in Scripture. It is a combination of the Greek word for *husband* and the Greek word *phileo*, meaning *love*.

The Greek language has several words for love. We have only one. We can "love" cotton candy, spy novels, horses, and people—all with the same word. Not so in Greek. Greek distinguishes one love from another. We are most familiar with the Greek word *eros*. We use its derivatives, such as *erotic* and *erogenous*, quite often today. *Eros* is the sexual, physical attraction that excites and enamors our world. But there are two other Greek words for love that are important to women.

The first is *agape*. *Agape* is unselfish, unchanging, committed love. It is unearned, undeserved, and is given with no thought of return. *Agape* is love of the highest order—God's perfect love for us. It is the love we are urged to pursue in Paul's great love passage of 1 Corinthians 13.

The second is *phileo*, and this is the word we see here in Titus. *Phileo* is often used to describe the love between very close friends. It is an affectionate, personal, deep, and even passionate love. The *phileo* lover chooses the one he loves. He sets his heart on this one above others. Oftentimes *phileo* is used synonymously with *agape*, emphasizing strong feeling and attachment. For example, *phileo* is used in John 5:20, when John speaks of the love God the Father has for His Son. In other words, at the heart of God's holy love for His Son is *phileo*. It is used in John 16:27, speaking of the love the disciples had for Jesus, and in John 13:23, referring to the beloved disciple. When Jesus wept over the death of Lazarus in John 11, the Jews said, "See how He loved *[phileo]* him!"

What does this mean for us as wives? God has called us to fix our hearts upon our husbands in a special "one-man-kind-of-woman" love. *Philandros* means that we prefer him over all others, that we accept him simply as he is, that we understand and value his manhood, that we seek to meet his unique needs as a man living in a postflood world, that we regard our husband and treat him with respect, and that we express our feelings of affection to him.

A woman who takes up the sword of *philandros* will fight the battle on every turn by giving love. The weapon of love is powerful. It is difficult to refuse. Every man, whether he realizes it or not, needs and longs for *philandros*.

But for our *phileo* to be its best, it must be put into the context of all of Scripture. Biblical love is not a syrupy, weak-kneed love. Biblical love is both tender and tough. It does what is best for the one who is loved. And this requires great wisdom. Let me illustrate.

FORGIVENESS AND ACCOUNTABILITY

First Peter 4:8 says, "Love covers a multitude of sins." Peter was speaking firsthand. Peter had blown it big-time. He had betrayed Christ. And Christ forgave his betrayal. Not only so, but Christ permitted Peter to be restored. Do you remember when he asked, "Peter, do you love *[phileo]* me?" and Peter responded, "Yes, Lord, I do." Christ then called Peter to "feed My sheep." Peter went on to become a bold yet tender leader of the early church. It is a moving picture of what forgiving love will do in the life of a man.

Our husbands will disappoint us and hurt us time and again. Some of them will blow it big-time like Peter. A relationship cannot survive without this kind of "covering" through love.

But there is another passage that balances this teaching from Peter: "My brethren, if any among you strays from the truth, and one turns him back, let him know that he who turns a sinner from the error of his way will save his soul from death, and will cover a multitude of sins" (James 5:19-20).

James gives us remarkable perspective. "Covering a multitude of sins" does not mean that we look the other way and let immorality or wrongdoing just slide right on by. This is not love at all. No, our responsibility in love is to do what is best for our husband. It involves holding a man accountable when he "strays from truth" and enters a lifestyle of sin. We are to draw the lines of loving accountability by calling sin what it is and seeking his restoration. In so doing, we are covering a multitude of sins.

In other words, accountability is just as much a part of true love as is forgiveness. Forgiveness is the tender side. Accountability is the tough side.

The bottom line is this. Oneness involves accountability. I must be accountable to my husband, and he must be accountable to me. If we throw out accountability, we will strengthen sin's hold on our lives and insure its eventual victory in our relationship. A healthy marriage is impossible without accountability.

Paul throws more light on the subject. Holding someone accountable must be done right. Look at Galatians 6:1: "Brethren, even if a man is caught in any trespass, you who are spiritual, restore such a one in a spirit of gentleness; each one looking to yourself, lest you too be tempted."

We are to hold one another accountable in a spirit of humility and gentleness—rather than anger and vengeance. Do you respond to confrontation that comes at you as a jagged dagger? Neither does your husband.

SINLESS ANGER

We see this kind of balance throughout Scripture. Ephesians 4 puts it in a phrase, "speaking the *truth* in *love.*" What a great phrase. Truth preserves us and love preserves us. We need both. Paul is saying we need to love one another with this "truth-love" if we are to grow up: "Speaking the truth in love, we are to grow up in all aspects into Him" (4:15).

Scripture is so sound and practical, isn't it? And so realistic! It not only tells us "what," but "how." A few verses later, in Ephesians 4:25-27, Paul tells us how to express this "truth-love" in the nitty-gritty of life—when we are knee deep in arguing in the bedroom or when conflict sparks in the car on the way to the restaurant. "Speak truth, each one of you, with his neighbor.... Be angry and yet do not sin," he says, quoting the Old Testament. He explains, "Do not let the sun go down on your anger, and do not give the devil an opportunity."

But Paul isn't finished. "Let no unwholesome word proceed from your mouth, but only such a word as is good for edification, according to the need of the moment, that it may give grace to those who hear." Wow! Not *one* unwholesome word. Words that *edify*. Words that give *grace*. Words that address the real *need* of the speaker and listener. This is a tall order, this "truth-love."

Have you been struck, as I have, by the foul and bitter language that seems to coolly flow from the mouths of modern-day feminists? Sometimes it is so biting and revolting that it is a wonder any man would ever actually "hear" what is being said. This is the age-old strategy of fighting ugliness with ugliness, filth with filth, and perversion with perversion. Who wins here? What is resolved? The answer is: no one and nothing. Sure they have rattled a few cages and received some attention. But attention and attentiveness are two very different things.

"Be angry, and sin not," says Paul.

THE THIRD EAR

One final note on the subject of "truth-love." "Truth-love" is to be received as well as given. When swords and javelins of anger are being hurled at us, it is especially hard to receive the truth. Have you ever heard of "listening with the third ear"? The third ear is the ear of the heart, which listens beyond and beneath the words. The third ear listens to what the person is really saying, however poorly it is expressed. Oftentimes a man will say, "I don't care!" when the very anger in his words says he does. Other times he may say, "Leave me alone," when he is really crying out for help.

Once our son Josh was distraught because he felt Steve was being unduly impatient with him. I explained to him that his dad had had a rough day and that his problem was not really Josh. It was "displaced anger."

"What's that?" Josh asked.

"Well," I explained, "a person can't yell at somebody out there in the world.

You can't yell at the airline stewardess, or your secretary, or a member of the board. And so when something upsets you, anger builds up inside. Then when you come home, you let down. Sometimes the least little thing will set you off. And boom! You suddenly let all that anger out on someone you love."

A few minutes later Steve came into the room. "Dad, I know what your problem is," said Josh. "It's dyslexic anger."

The third ear listens for displaced anger. It seeks to discover the pain behind the hurtful words.

Just the other night Steve and I got into an argument. He seemed agitated with me before I even opened my mouth. I was tired and didn't really feel like listening with my third ear. The thing we were arguing over was really foolish, but aren't a lot of arguments foolish? And so Steve hurled and I hurled back. In my hurling I was ever so faithful to hold him accountable to *his* hurling! (Take my word for it, hurled confrontation never works.)

About five minutes into this thing I stopped and looked at him. His eyes were dark, with heavy bags under them. The hour was midnight. And it dawned on me. This man was tired. He was exhausted. Midnight was no time to be working out a foolish dispute. Then I remembered something else. He had had a stressful day. His nerves were shot. These things affect anyone's ability to resolve conflict.

"You're dead," I said grimly.

"Yes," he said, a little testily.

"I'm dead, too."

"Why don't we figure this out in the morning?" he offered. And so we went to bed.

"Wait a minute," you may be saying. "Doesn't the Bible say not to let the sun go down on your anger? And what about accountability?"

This is where the third ear has to come in. The only thing I could hold Steve accountable for that night was to get some rest. He needed sleep. And so did I. *Phileo* considers the need of the moment. Interestingly enough, after seven hours of sleep the first words out of both of our mouths the next day were, "I'm sorry. That was totally inane of me. Will you forgive me?"

Can you see why we must employ wisdom when applying Scripture? When Paul said, "Do not let the sun go down on your anger," he was giving us the principle of short accounts. He was saying, don't sweep conflict under the rug. Don't ignore attitudes of disrespect. Don't let misunderstanding accumulate. Deal with these things openly and swiftly.

We have taken that idea to heart in our marriage. I wish I had a quarter for every time Steve and I have stayed up until all hours of the night, refusing to move on with life until we had come to resolution and understanding. And we have worked through some pretty tough things that could have easily derailed us. That's what I love so much about Steve. He is committed to oneness. And he knows that the only way to get there is to communicate. I am convinced this is why we love each other more today than the day we married.

THE WAY OF PHILANDROS

When you begin using the powerful sword of *philandros*, you may find yourself a little clumsy at first. You may even unwittingly draw a little blood. But you will also grow. And the more you use it, the more adept you will become.

There are hosts of other teachings from Scripture that have implications for *philandros*. *Philandros* means meeting his needs sexually, and in so doing, building and confirming his maleness. It also means being honest in your sexual expression—insisting on integrity in your sex life together. Intercourse must reflect a relationship of love and communication if it is to work.

Philandros also means guarding your critical tongue in public and at home. It means not being picky or insisting that everything be right. It means praying for him "without ceasing." It means appreciating him, thinking of him, and doing special things to let him know you care.

Sometimes it means silence, allowing him to hear the echo of his own words. Sometimes it means standing back, letting go, and letting him fail, rather than rushing in to save him and thereby encouraging his immaturity and preventing him from growth.

Always it means confronting addiction and abuse. And, at times, that may require leaving and living apart. Certainly it means protecting your children, whose emotional and physical health are all-important to God. Finally, it means you will go on caring even if the feelings are gone.

Josh McDowell speaks to thousands of teenagers every year. On one occasion he handed out sheets of paper and asked all the young people in the audience to write an unsigned letter to their parents, answering this question: "If there is one thing you would want to say to your parents, but can't say, what would it be?"

As you can imagine, the responses were eye-opening. One letter I have never forgotten was from a young, teenage girl. The front page was covered from top to bottom with the words "Mom and Dad, I love you. I love you. I love you. I love you. I love you." On the back she continued this same message—"I love you. I love you. I love you. I love you"—until she reached the bottom of the page.

Then she stopped and wrote one line: "Mom and Dad, *please* love each other."

Women, our children desperately need for us to *phileo* our husbands.

PULLING HUPOTASSO FROM THE SHEATH

There is one final way we are to love our husbands. It can be found in the second weapon in the fight for oneness—submission.

Submission, a weapon?

Somebody once called the idea of submission in marriage the Christian "hot potato." This is not a hot potato. It is an exploding potato!

The Greek word for *submission* is so far from our English meaning that it is no wonder it draws such reaction in our day. Webster's definition of submission is—

Noun: yielding, giving in, subservience, abasement.

Adjective: non-resisting, unassertive, docile, timid, passive, subdued. (Anyone getting excited yet?)

Verb: to surrender, bite the dust, lay down arms, raise the flag, cry or say uncle, resign oneself, throw in the towel, give up the ship, (and my personal favorite) grin and bear it.

Given this definition, a woman choosing godly submission in the time of Paul would have done just as well to sign up as a galley slave in the Roman navy. But biblical submission is light years from Webster's description. It is not a mandate for an "owner-slave," militaristic, "command-obey" relationship. Far from it. Not only does this idea of submission not exist in God's plan for marriage, but it is outright anathema to Him.

The demeaning overtones for submission have so permeated our culture that I am reluctant to use this word when we teach the biblical concept. It's a shame we have no better word to express the meaning of the Greek. But since we're stuck with it, we must do some careful excavating of this dinosaur word.

Hupotasso is a Greek word meaning to "voluntarily place oneself under." A little bit different from Webster, wouldn't you say? But we must dig a little deeper if we wish to get the full meaning of this key New Testament term.

Let's begin with Jesus and his "male chauvinist" follower, Paul.

JESUS AND PAUL ON WOMEN

The ancient societies of Mesopotamia, Asia Minor, and Egypt held demeaning views of women. The Greeks were only a little better. By the time of the Roman Empire a feminist revolution was on, and women on the whole fared a bit better. Around the time of Christ ancient Judaism reacted to the Roman feminist movement by constricting their women more tightly than ever.[4]

It was into this world that Christ entered, breaking all the rules. He took women along as followers. He used them in His parables (Matthew 13:33; 25:1-13; Luke 15:8-10; 18:1-8). He did not hesitate to teach women (Luke 10:39). He offered tender forgiveness (Luke 7:47-48). He initiated a conversation with the outcast Samaritan woman (John 4: 7-26). While Christ called for chastity, forbidding even to look with lust upon a woman, he moved freely and with great integrity among women. As a result, women wholeheartedly responded by following Him and honoring Him in what has been called "an unprecedented happening in the history of time."[5]

Those who followed Jesus treated women likewise, granting them full membership in the church, declaring them equal heirs to salvation and joint heirs of the grace of life (1 Peter 3:7). Women converts were mentioned often, their ministries praised at every turn, and their impact felt powerfully in the early church. A large number of prominent women of the Roman Empire became Christians and were involved in missionary ventures, as well as martyrdom for the faith.

Unless you do an in-depth study of how women were treated in the known world until the time of Christianity, you cannot comprehend the unprecedented, barrier-breaking position and value Christianity brought to women in the world.

The *only* restriction on Christian women we see reiterated throughout the New Testament relates to God's call to men to be the leaders in the church and home. Passages such as 1 Corinthians 14 and 1 Timothy 2 make it clear that although men and women are equals, men are to lead in the church and home. In the church, men have been called by God to teach authoritatively and to lead. They are to do it not by lording over, but with serving hearts (1 Peter 5:2-3).

Likewise, in the home, men are to provide sacrificial leadership, loving their wives as their very own bodies (Ephesians 5:22-28).

God has also given our husbands two weapons to use in the fight for oneness—sacrificial leadership and, yes, love. Do you know what I have observed? I have never met a bitter or unfulfilled woman whose husband has implemented biblical leadership and love.

New Testament writers explain that God created man first, designing him for this primary role of provision and leadership, while woman was created out of man and designed for the primary role in marriage of helpmate and nurturer. Yet man continues to be born from woman, and this cycle is part of the continuing *interdependency* God intended for man and woman.

Says Paul in 1 Corinthians: "In the Lord, however, woman is not independent of man, nor is man independent of woman. For as woman came from man, so also man is born of woman. But everything comes from God" (11:11, NIV). A man who understands this interdependency will recognize the strengths and gifts of his wife. And as the leader of the home, he will wisely delegate to her strengths. Good leaders know how to maximize their team. And so should a man of God.

Therefore, while God's call for man's leadership is clear, it is to be carried out with the utmost integrity and care. Biblical leadership is never a right, which a man can demand. It is a privilege, which a man must earn. Every passage on marriage emphasizes leadership through character. Ephesians says a man is to lead and love his wife as Christ does the church. First Peter 3:7 says a man is to treat her with respect and honor, or he will find that God will not honor him!

Some have pointed to women like Deborah and Priscilla as the exception to the New Testament model of male leadership. But when we look closely at Deborah, we find she lived in a period when Israel was in shambles. There was an utter vacuum of leadership. And so God spoke through Deborah as she sat under the shade of a palm tree near her home. Men can certainly gain from the insight and instruction of women, as they did in the time of Deborah. But God did not put her up as a high priest or authoritative leader. And she encouraged the assertive and godly leadership of Barak in Israel. Deborah was a godly woman, used by God to prick the conscience of Israel, and not once did she violate biblical leadership.

Priscilla was also a gifted woman, used by God in New Testament times. But Priscilla also insisted on working with a man. Apollos learned the way of God through Priscilla and Aquilla, a husband and wife team (Acts 18:26). Much has been made over the fact that her name comes first. My guess is that Priscilla had a dynamic, impressive personality. But in no way was Priscilla exercising authority here. She was simply sharing out of the wealth of knowledge and wisdom God had given to her. Noteworthy too is that Apollos was clearly not feminized. He was a man strong enough to learn from a woman, and eventually he became one of the strongest of the early church leaders.

On this Scripture is clear. While men are to lead sacrificially in the home and church, they are to honor, respect, and value women. And just as women were crucial to the life and ministry of the early church, so they are today. The church desperately needs the influence of its godly women. It needs the intelligence, the talents, and the insights God has so impartially given to them.

MUTUAL SUBMISSION

For the rest of our discussion on submission in marriage, we are going to springboard from Ephesians 5:22-33. Paul begins the whole discussion of submission with the idea of mutual submission.

Earlier in Ephesians 5, Paul says husbands and wives are to put the concerns of their mates over their own concerns. "Walk in love, just as Christ also loved you, and gave Himself up for us" (5: 2). "And *be subject to one another* in the fear of Christ" (5:21). This idea of *mutual submission* sets the tone for the rest of the chapter. It is not an afterthought. Mutual submission comes first.

MUTUAL SUBMISSION + HUPOTASSO

But when we come to the next three verses specifically addressed to women, we see a different kind of submission—that of *hupotasso*: "Wives, be subject to your own husbands, as to the Lord. For the husband is the head of the wife as Christ also is the head of the church, He himself being the Savior of the body. But as the church is subject to Christ, so also the wives ought to be to their husbands in everything" (5:22-24).

And at the close of this passage Paul adds these final words to wives: "And let the wife see to it that she respect her husband" (5:33b). Here God is saying that the wife is to acknowledge her husband's authority to lead—voluntarily and with sincere respect for his calling by God.

Then Paul explains a husband's calling to leadership. Yes, it is servant leadership, but it is nonetheless leadership. As with leadership in any organization, it's the "buck stops here" idea. It's a take the lead, set the pace, accept final responsibility kind of leadership. God has issued your husband a very high, and tough, calling.

While Paul spends three and a half verses in this passage speaking to wives regarding their calling, he spends eight and a half verses speaking to husbands about their calling. The sheer space given to this discussion on godly leadership shows God's clear emphasis on the importance of a man's role. God places the ultimate responsibility on his shoulders. Three times in this passage alone a husband is commanded to love his wife *as his very own flesh.*

Whom is God being tough on here? If the feminist wants to take issue, she must first take a good hard look at these verses.

If a man is serious about being a godly leader, it will require an all-out effort. It is, indeed, a call of a lifetime. He will blow it at times. He will have setbacks, especially when you recognize that he probably did not grow up with a role model. Even for the best of men, who have had the greatest father relationships and role models in their lives, it is no small thing to be a biblical leader in this world in which we live. Making you and your children top priority is going to extract a huge price from him. A man, therefore, will need the time and freedom to grow and fail and improve as a leader, just as you will have to grow in your skills of *philandros* and *hupotasso.*

God knows this is a high calling for a man. But that is what He has called your husband to do. It is to be one of the top VIPs of his life.

HUPOTASSO, IN A PHRASE

The definition for biblical submission I'm about to give you comes as close as I can get. In a nutshell, biblical submission means *giving the best of myself to enable my husband to become the godly leader God has called him to be.*

This is the kind of submission a woman can embrace eagerly. It dispenses with the doormat, passive, command-obey model that so many women have embraced to the detriment of their marriages.

True biblical submission is freeing, but it is also demanding, challenging, and surprising. It forces us to grow up, along with our husbands.

VOLCANOES AND UNDERGROUND CAVES

Let's pull biblical submission down to where we live. There is something we must learn about *ourselves* in using the weapon of submission.

To make things simple we will say there are two kinds of women in this world—volcanoes and underground caves. We may fall anywhere in between, but before life is through, our desire will be to hit the middle—to find a balance in life.

Volcano:	Underground cave:
Expressive.	Less expressive.
Explosive.	Hides; uses silence as a weapon.
Experiences anger in conflict.	Experiences fear in conflict.
Obvious where she stands.	Not obvious where she stands.
Unafraid of conflict; faces it head-on.	Avoids conflict; wants peace.
Communicates freely, but also nags.	Has difficulty freely saying what she feels.
Tends to react first, think later.	Tends to become paralyzed and hold hurts inside.
Tends to want to take over.	Tends to want to please; easily manipulated.

These two kinds of women have two quite different things to learn in *hupotasso*. The volcano needs to learn to cool down rather than explode, to be quiet and think carefully before blurting out her strong feelings and emotions. She needs to learn when communication has ceased and nagging has begun. A volcano needs to be willing to enter into conflict by listening first, thinking next, and speaking last. She needs to admit her own faults during the conflict.

A volcano also needs to learn how to stand back and trust God. A volcano doesn't tend to pray a lot. (I know because I am one.) She needs to force herself to wait prayerfully for God to work, before she jumps in. Amazing things will happen once she learns this. In short, a volcano needs to gain confidence in God's ability to lead through her husband, even though he blows it. In a word, a volcano needs to *relax*.

But what about the underground cave? She has to be willing to speak out rather than to run. To express her thoughts and feelings. To risk rejection and conflict. She can't hide behind silence; she has to gain the courage to say what is on her heart, what hurts her, what grieves her. She needs to be willing to express her needs and the needs of her children. How can her husband grow in his leadership if he doesn't know her needs and feelings? She needs to believe in her value to her husband. She needs to be convinced that her husband needs her perspective. She must be willing to forego momentary peace for the long-term sake of communication and growth. She has to stand her ground, draw the line of respect, and never—never—allow abuse.

In the end, she too must learn to trust God. She has to give her heart first and foremost to the Lord and draw her self-respect and value from Him. And in a very real sense, she must be strong in the Lord, trusting Him in those hard moments of conflict and vulnerability. In a word, an underground cave needs to *risk*.

While the volcano must learn to trust God to work *through her husband*, an underground cave needs to trust God to *work through her*.

But whether a woman is a volcano or an underground cave, she must understand three fundamental elements of biblical submission:

LOOKING—to her husband for leadership.

LOVING—giving him the best of herself so that he may become the man God has called him to be.

LEANING—on God, when all is said and done.

As Corrie Ten Boom once said, "Never be afraid to trust an unknown future to a known God."

As with *philandros*, *hupotasso* does not eliminate the rest of Scripture. It wisely incorporates all those principles of accountability, communication, edification, loving confrontation, forgiveness, and tough love in the face of sin.

Women, the whole counsel of God was intended for us, too. And we cannot ignore it or throw it aside on the altar of passive, unbiblical submission. Using the weapon of submission requires great wisdom, great boldness, great humility. But when it is used right, by God's grace, it can make the difference in whether a man reaches his full potential as the leader in his home.

What would happen in our world if it began to see biblical roles lived out?

For starters, Gloria Steinem would be looking for a job.

Chapter Fifteen

VIP# 4:

Motherhood

~~~

Can a woman forget her nursing child,
And have no compassion on the son of her womb?
Even these may forget....

ISAIAH 49:15

Encourage the young women to... love their children,
[prefer, fully embrace, have strong feelings of affection,
care deeply, nurture and value].

TITUS 2:4-5

I t was October 1983 and the first warm day since fall the year before. San Francisco is kind of crazy that way.

Mark Twain once said that the coldest winter he ever spent was a summer in San Francisco. In San Francisco you basically freeze all summer and then lie back to enjoy the overdue coziness of an "Indian summer" fall. Today the sun was high in God's heaven, bathing the countryside with welcome warmth.

I was driving up the peninsula on I-280, one of the most scenic freeways in the world. Giant redwoods were stretching into the stark, crystal blue sky as far as the eye could see, filling the mountainside with their plush evergreen hues. It should have been a day for overflowing joy.

I certainly had every reason for such joy. A few days before I had heard the strong heartbeat of the three-month-old baby in my already bulging tummy. And now I was heading to the hospital to pick up Steve.

He had been hospitalized with meningitis, and we had been waiting for three days to find out if he had the viral or bacterial form. Had it been bacterial, his condition would have been serious, and the children and I would have been brought in for spinal taps. This morning we had learned it was viral. Steve could come home, and I would not have to undergo a test which is particularly risky in pregnancy.

In light of all this, I should have been basking in the beauty and warmth of an October sun as fine and rare as vintage wine. Instead, I was in a mess of tears. They were streaming down my face, spilling over into my lap, blurring my vision. I couldn't seem to stop them. It was as if an emotional dam had broken somewhere inside my soul, and nothing could hold it back. I was desperately trying to sort out the last few hours I had just spent in a specialist's office. To assimilate his words. To absorb their impact and think clearly. I needed to pull myself together before I reached Steve at the hospital.

To fill in the picture, let me take you back ten months. A blood clot had formed in my left leg and was heading towards my heart when, by the grace of God, it lodged in my upper thoracic region, bloating my leg to twice its normal size. After the hospitalization and immediate crisis were over, I was put on a medication to further break down the clot. I was told that any pregnancy thereafter could endanger my health and was particularly advised not to become pregnant within the year. The great chance of developing a new clot could put the baby and myself in a life-threatening position.

Needless to say, Steve and I were extremely careful, "to the point of irritation" as he would say. We prayed over whether we should even risk having more children in the future. Steve was concerned for my safety, understandably. Yet somehow we both felt that our family was not complete. How can you explain these things? Having no clarity on the matter, we decided just to take life one step at a time and put it into the hands of the Lord.

Seven months later we were given our answer. I became pregnant by what Steve declared to be the second immaculate conception in history. And since an angel hadn't appeared to either one of us, we were both completely shocked. We had been *so* very careful.

From this point on, things moved very quickly. In a matter of days I had seen three top experts. Expert #1 was a top gynecologist on the West Coast. He was concerned for my well-being and promptly set me up to see Expert #2. Expert #2 was a circulation specialist, who immediately took me off the blood de-clotting medication and put me on a careful plan. He explained that the medication could have harmed the baby and warned us that I could end up spending a good portion of this pregnancy in the hospital. At one point he asked how we felt about the possibility of "interrupting the pregnancy."

Knowing that such an "interruption" would make it impossible to pick the pregnancy back up again, Steve responded, "Well, sir, we don't want to interfere in any way with the plans of God. We are committed to seeing this pregnancy through." At this the doctor warmly assured us of his full support and the best care throughout the pregnancy. Then he set me up to see Expert #3.

Expert #3 was *the* expert on the subject. He had done extensive research in the area, having recently delivered a paper on his findings before a national physician's conference. He had studied the effects of the de-clotting medication on the developing infant in the first few weeks of life. And he had treated women all over the country in my exact condition. If I needed to know anything about the situation, this was the man to talk to. Since Steve was in the hospital, I had gone to the appointment alone.

It didn't take him long to get down to brass tacks.

"Mrs. Farrar," he began, "you have a serious situation on you hands." This we knew.

"I'll put it to you clearly. The medication you were on when you became pregnant has most likely done serious damage to the fetus."

"What do you mean?" I asked.

"Well, the primary organs and body structure of the fetus were forming during those first few weeks. I've seen some very tragic, horrible results. There can be physical as well as serious organic abnormalities. The damage can be very severe."

"I see," I said, feeling the weight of his words. "Is this damage a certainty?"

"We can't know anything for certain, of course, Mrs. Farrar."

He paused, looking at my records. "You have two other children, I see. A boy and a girl. Is that right?"

"Yes," I said, wondering where this was going.

"How fortunate to have one of each. I have a son and daughter myself." He hesitated. "Mrs. Farrar, you're so fortunate to have such a wonderful, healthy family. You should be very grateful. My suggestion to you would be not to carry through with this pregnancy—for your sake and for the sake of your family."

"Well, you see, I do not feel that is my decision to make," I replied.

"Then whose decision is it?"

"My husband and I both feel that such a decision rests with God," I said.

He looked somewhat surprised, so I went on to explain. "What I mean is that we believe that God formed this little life, and so it's really not our call to step in and make such a decision. My husband and I both feel our responsibility is to provide the best care we can for this child and let God make those decisions. Do you see what I mean?"

He looked down at the floor and sighed.

"Mrs. Farrar," he said, "I respect your religious feelings. But, despite those feelings, I must be very blunt with you. You must realize that it is very likely you have a little monster in your womb. Do you think that would be fair to the child? Would it be fair to bring a child into a life of such possible torture and pain?"

This was an argument I had not anticipated. Quite frankly, it blew me away. It was the first time he had used the word "child" in our conversation, rather than "fetus." I sat there for a moment thinking about what he had just said. He was placing the burden of responsibility on me, the mother. This doctor was suggesting that I would be responsible for allowing this child to endure a life of possible difficulty and pain, that I was actually doing this child a disservice by considering letting him live. No mother would ever wish to be held responsible for her child's pain.

This was pressure from the medical profession at a level I didn't know existed. Steve and I had long before made our decision to go through with this pregnancy and trust God with the results. We were resolute. But what about the woman who is not so clear, not so resolute? What if there isn't support from the father of the child, or from friends, or parents? This doctor was a concerned professional, a father with two children, an expert who genuinely viewed abortion as "preventative treatment." I began to wonder how many other mothers had been put in the position of feeling that it was actually their *loving duty* to take their child's life, as I had been made to feel. How could a woman ever hold up under such pressure?

"Let me see if I understand," I finally said. "You say there's a chance of abnormality. But you don't know for certain. You don't even know what kind of abnormality there may be. Is it possible that there is none at all?"

He shrugged his shoulders. "That's always a possibility, Mrs. Farrar. But why take the chance?"

Why take the chance?

It took me a moment to respond. He had been very straightforward and up-front. Why was I feeling so reluctant to do so? I needed to simply come out and make our position perfectly clear.

"I guess we all take chances every day of our lives," I replied. "I took a chance just getting into my car and driving down here to your office." He smiled, acknowledging the fact. Then I continued, "But I don't see this so much a matter of taking a chance as it is a matter of...*taking a life.*"

After a moment of silence, he replied, "Well, in the end, of course, that's your decision."

That is your decision. Those words would not go away. They hung in the air and followed my footsteps to the car. This child's future rested solely upon me. It was *my* decision.

But if my decision was so resolute, why was I crying from the depths of my soul as I drove down the freeway? As terrifying as was the prospect of caring for a child with serious health problems, this was a burden that went deeper. I was overwhelmed by the thought that *I*, the mother, might be responsible for allow-ing my child to live a difficult life. This doctor had reached down inside of me and touched the tenderest nerve of any woman's heart, the mothering nerve.

My eyes were suddenly opened to a completely different side of the abortion issue. Mothers don't just *decide* not to have a baby. Most mothers are persuaded, and in many cases *pressured*, into ending a pregnancy. In the ten years since that day my experience has borne this realization out.

Sometimes mothers are pressured by their husbands who do not consider the baby part of the "plan."

Sometimes they are pressured by an embarrassed boyfriend or by well-intended parents and friends.

Sometimes a woman is overwhelmed by her own sense of survival—her cir-cumstances, her inability to mother this child, her lack of resources.

Too often a woman caught in a difficult spot has *no* support or encouragement to complete her pregnancy. While her strong mothering instinct is calling out to her on the one hand, she finds herself surrounded by voices telling her otherwise.

PRO-MOTHERHOOD

This is not a chapter about abortion. It is a chapter about mothering. I will be honest with you. I wanted to skip over the issue of life in the womb. I fought dealing with it in black and white print. The issue is so personal, so deep, so tender. But in the end I have realized there is no way to honestly separate childbearing from motherhood. It goes to the heart of our womanhood. Childbearing has been part of the struggle for woman since the Garden of Eden. It is part and parcel of biblical motherhood. It surrounds us on every hand in our culture today. Indeed, it is one of the most deeply felt issues women struggle with today.

A woman finds herself asking, "Can an entire Supreme Court of caring, intelligent human beings make a wrong call on such an all-important issue? Can this many people who really care about me be so wrong? Can those in the medical profession who have such expertise and stature really be so off-base?"

Recently I heard President Clinton interviewed on his position. In just his third day in office, he lifted the ban on fetal tissue research, the gag rule stopping clinics that receive federal money from counseling about abortion, the "Mexico City policy" that kept federal money from international family planning groups that allow abortions, the ban on privately financed abortions at military hospitals, and the prohibition against importation of the RU-486 abortion pill. He also sought to repeal the Hyde Amendment, which bars federal money for abortions for poor women, though his effort was defeated after bitter debate in the House.[1] And he has remained firm in seeking to make the Freedom of Choice Act a law, which would legalize any and all abortions beyond the first trimester all the way up to the point of childbirth.

The interviewer asked how he could reconcile these actions with his professed Christian faith. His response was that as a member of the church he believed that adoption was what we all would like to see. But he also expressed that he did not believe that in every case abortion was the actual taking of a child's life. He was appealing to the "necessary evil" perspective which has been endorsed by so many within the church.

A careful examination, however, would tell the listener that the Freedom of Choice Act, which he so strongly supports, flies squarely in the face of even those who embrace the "necessary evil" view. As my husband has so aptly pointed out to me, the only difference between a little child ten minutes before birth and ten minutes after he is born is about twenty minutes. At least Joycelyn Elders, surgeon general appointed by Clinton, was openly frank about her opinions when she said that "the American public, particularly the Christian Right, needs to get over their love affair with the fetus."[2] The feminist cry is that without the legalization of a woman's freedom of choice, the cause of womanhood will perish.

In the face of all of this, I would be remiss to simply walk on by the subject.

But I would like to approach it from a different angle.

The question continually before us has been, "When does human life begin? When does the life of a child begin?" The high courts have determined that *viability* is the test, although science continues to push this test to the limit. In the not so distant future, technology will enable an embryo to survive from the point of conception forward without the need of the mother's womb. The point of viability will then be moot.

But the question I would like to consider here is different.

"When does *motherhood* begin?"

This, I believe, is actually the emphasis of Scripture. When do you and I become mothers? If we can answer this question, we will have focused on the need within society. Touch the mother, and you have touched the child. Teach the mother, and you have taught the child. Care for the mother, and you have cared for the child. Help the mother work her way through her deep need, and you have met the great need of the child. The needs of mothers inherently affect the needs of children.

THE EXAMPLE OF MARY

Let me take you to a passage of Scripture often used by those who hold the pro-life position—the gospel of Luke, chapter one. In this remarkable account of the only genuine immaculate conception, an angel appears to Mary announcing that she is going to conceive and bear a son, the Messiah. The angel also tells her that her close relative and friend, Elizabeth, who has been barren for years, has conceived a son in her old age and is in her sixth month of pregnancy (Luke 1:36).

We are all familiar with Mary's great prayer response to the Lord at the close of the angel's visit, in which she prays in essence, "Thy will be done."

Luke tells us that Mary then took a trip in "great haste" to visit Elizabeth in Judah. Mary was in a tight spot—one that few would understand. She was a virgin, "with child"! And God had provided an older woman to encourage her through those tough early months of her pregnancy.

The moment Mary walked into the room, Elizabeth cried out, "Blessed among women are you, and blessed is the fruit of your womb! And how has it happened to me, that the *mother* of my Lord should come to me? For behold, when the sound of your greeting reached my ears, the *baby* leaped in my womb for joy. And blessed is she who believed that there would be a fulfillment of what had been spoken to her by the Lord" (Luke 1:42-45).

I want you to notice something. This text has often been used as a powerful case against abortion because the word here for Elizabeth's sixth-month-old fetus is the Greek word *brephos*, the word for "child, infant, baby." It is the same word used to refer to the baby Jesus lying in the manger (Luke 2:12, 16). This idea is consistent with the Old Testament pattern of referring to the unborn with the Hebrew word *yeled*, which typically indicated young children and sometimes was even used for teens or young adults. In Scripture there is no separate word, as we have in our English language, for "fetus"—the "almost child" concept.

But there is something else we cannot miss here. Mary's visit occurred within days after her conception. And what did Elizabeth call her? Elizabeth called Mary a "mother."

Within days of her conception, Mary was a mother.

There were *two* mothers in the room that day in the city of Judah. One had been a mother for six months. The other had been a mother for only a matter of days.

Motherhood begins at conception. And when pregnancy ends, motherhood ends. That is why a mother grieves so deeply after a miscarriage. That is why in so many cases abortion is followed by deep emotional wounds and scars.

What would happen if we began a pro-motherhood campaign in this country? What would happen if we raised the value of mothers? We would raise the value of life within the womb. What would happen if we cared for mothers who are in trouble? We would care for the troubled child within the womb. What would happen if we embraced a biblical perspective of adoption? We would see homes provided when a mother cannot give this to her child.

In Scripture adoption is a beautiful, powerful concept. In fact, if you know Jesus Christ, *you* are adopted. You have been adopted into the family of God, Paul says in Galatians 4:5. And adoption into the family of God is a permanent affair. You will never be released or taken away from your heavenly Father. Your adoption is eternal. And it is also a gift. It is a gift of God's loving grace to us. He simply receives us into His family, handicapped and messed up as we are. He takes us and makes us His very own sons and daughters. Adoption is a great thing when viewed through the biblical lens.

Scripture also tells us that children are a gift from the Lord (Psalm 127:3-5). As a gift, they are "on loan," a trust placed into our hands. There are times when adoption can be the greatest act of love a mother can ever do for her child—placing this little one into the trust and care of two people who have been unable to conceive such a gift.

Not only so, but *every* child is a gift, says the psalmist. Whether he is frail or strong, impaired or perfect, blind and lame or beautiful and athletic.

"For He has not despised nor abhorred the affliction of the afflicted;
Neither has He hidden His face from him;
But when he cried to Him for help, He heard" (Psalm 22:24).

In another psalm, David urges us:

"Vindicate the weak and the fatherless;
Do justice to the afflicted and destitute.
Rescue the weak and needy" (Psalm 82:3-4).

And then he gives us this great promise in Psalm 41:

"How blessed is he who considers the *helpless*;
The LORD will deliver him in a day of trouble.
The LORD will protect him, and keep him alive,
And he shall be called blessed upon the earth" (Psalm 41:1-2).

Whether afflicted or whole, children are a gift. They are a blessing. They teach the world to embrace the weaker brother, to sacrifice for those who are needy, to care for those who require care. They remind us all that we are needy, helpless, and weak before God. They cause us to trust God; they force us to depend upon Him in order to meet their needs. Children are weak and needy human beings, the most helpless among us.

The issue of Scripture is never the value of the unborn, the value of the helpless, the value of the needy. Their value is assumed. Rather the issue we find addressed over and over again is *our responsibility* to the helpless one. That is why Titus 2:4 says to teach the young women "to love their children."

We don't need a ruling from a high human court. We don't need legislation. What we need most is to retool the thinking of America towards its *mothers*. What our nation needs most is a healthy dose of "phileoteknos."

PHILEOTEKNOS

This Greek word *phileoteknos* in Titus 2:4 doesn't appear anywhere else in Scripture. It is a special kind of "mother-love" just as *philandros* is a special kind of "husband-love." The idea that flows out of this word is that of "preferring" our children, "caring" for them, "nurturing" them, "affectionately embracing" them, "meeting their needs," "tenderly befriending" each one as unique from the hand of God.

What we see is that not only *has God endowed* us as women with the ability to mother, not only has He *equipped* us uniquely both physiologically and psychologically, but He has also *commanded* us to see "mother-love" as our responsibility.

The problem with biblical motherhood is that it does not fit into the feminist world-view. Feminism and biblical motherhood are at odds with one another. As a result over the last half-century a terrific battle has been waged to win the hearts of mothers, to numb their mothering instinct. And a fearsome battle it has been.

Such a powerful drive as the mother's instinct is not easily thwarted. It takes a tremendous amount of Novocain to deaden such a tender, finely tuned nerve.

NERVE NOVOCAIN

If you were Satan and you wanted to destroy the nerve of *phileoteknos*, how would you do it? You might consider four shots of anesthetic, one on top of the other:

Shot #1: Diminish the role of the father in the home.
Shot #2: Diminish the value of the mother in the home.
Shot #3: Diminish the needs of children in the home.
Shot #4: Diminish the value of life itself.

And this has indeed been his successful strategy in deadening the mothering nerve.

How then do we re-sensitize that nerve? We do it by injecting a good dose of God's word.

FATHERS ARE TO LEAD

A few years ago I decided to do a biblical study of what God had to say to mothers, and I came away amazed. I hardly had enough verses to fill a few lines on a page! I was stunned to discover that every significant passage on parenting is addressed to fathers. Titus 2:4 is one of the rare exceptions where we see mothers addressed.

It isn't that mothers aren't to be found in the Scriptures. We see the mothering role modeled and greatly valued. And we constantly see allusions to the mother's role in teaching and nurturing children. God even describes *Himself* to be like a nurturing mother protecting her little ones when referring to His great compassion, care, and love for us. Motherhood is clearly there, woven throughout Scripture. But the ultimate responsibility of leadership in parenting is consistently laid at one place.

At the feet of the father.

The evidence is overwhelming:

• The entire book of Proverbs is actually the advice of a father to his son. There is a ton of parenting advice in Proverbs, yet given from father to son. The son, however, is admonished to honor his mother, to respect her, and to adhere to her teaching.

• Deuteronomy 6:6-7 is a key parenting passage. Yet, in this passage *fathers* are addressed. *Fathers* are told to teach their sons, model for their sons, spend significant time with their sons: "And these words, which I am commanding you today, shall be on your heart; and you shall teach them diligently *to your sons* and shall talk of them when you sit in your house and when you walk by the way and when you lie down and when you rise up."

Even when a legacy is mentioned just a few verses before, it is mentioned in the masculine: "so that *you and your son and your grandson* might fear the LORD your God, to keep all His statutes and His commandments, which I command you, all the days of your life, and that your days may be prolonged" (Deuteronomy 6:2).

• Ephesians 6:4, another key parenting verse of Scripture, is also addressed to fathers: "And *fathers,* do not provoke your children to anger; but bring them up in the discipline and instruction of the Lord."

• And in Hebrews, the image is once again that of fathers and sons: "and you have forgotten the exhortation which is addressed to you as *sons,* My son, do not regard lightly the discipline of the LORD.... It is for discipline that you endure; God deals with you as with *sons;* for *what son is there whom his father does not discipline?"* (Hebrews 12:5-7).

This is the pattern we see in passage after passage. What then does this mean to us as women? Does it mean that daughters are insignificant? Or that the role of the mother is minor? No. What this does tell us is that men are to lead. Men are ultimately held responsible for the training of a generation, for the leading of a family and nation. God designed it to be so.

In the process, men are to value their wives, the mother of their children, and they are to see them as helpmates in the parenting process.

What occurred in the Great Flash Flood, however, is that the role of parenting was flip-flopped. Women were handed the leadership in parenting, and so it has continued. As a result our nation is paying a steep price. Not because women cannot parent well. Women have gifts that are desperately needed in the parenting process. Women are tuned in as Strong Relaters. They are holistic in their thinking and tend to be remarkably sensitive to the needs and development of their children. In fact, as we will see in the next chapter, the home—the environment in which children are raised—is to be the special focus and forte of the woman. God also designed this to be so.

But in the end God commanded fathers to be responsible for taking the lead in parenting. In a nation where almost half of our homes are fatherless, this vital concept of biblical parenting has been tragically forsaken.

Mothers are having to take up the slack, carrying a burden far beyond anything envisioned a century ago. Such a dearth in male leadership and responsibility for parenting has inevitably led to the damaging and eventual devaluing of motherhood—thus beginning the numbing process of the mothering nerve.

Parenting was designed by God to be a partnership. And when the partnership is neglected or broken, everyone suffers, including mothers.

All the more reason, mothers, that we become Strong Relaters with our husbands. That we encourage their leadership. That we pray for them. That we use great wisdom as their wives and sisters in Christ. And all the more reason that *we* take seriously the responsibility of *phileoteknos*—of loving our children. For the sake of these little ones, *someone* must do what our heavenly Father has asked.

The foremost principle in biblical parenting, therefore, is that God intended parenting to be a partnership, with fathers taking the lead.

MOTHERS ARE VALUABLE

As we saw earlier, no role has lost more value in the twentieth century than has the role of the mother. In the 1800s the "stock market value" of motherhood was at its all-time high, largely due to the loss of fathers in the home. But in the 1900s the motherhood stock plummeted.

Mothers have been told for almost fifty years now that they are unnecessary, that they are really nothing special.

They have been told that professionals can do the job better in many cases.

They have been told that a man can nurture and care for a child, just like a woman.

They have been told that children simply need a loving, qualified caretaker, and they will be fine.

What we have witnessed is the sabotaging of the role of the most valuable person in a child's early life—his mother. And along with it the child loses the mother-child relationship—a relationship which, if firmly established, endures through adolescence, early adulthood, and throughout life.

Children *do* need their mothers. No one can *phileoteknos* a child in the way a mother can. A hired hand simply cannot love a child in the same way. Nor can a father. Mothers are the glue in a little child's life. They are the lens through which a child sees the world. They are the emotional tank-filler, the touch point of security, the one who can listen, observe, and appreciate in a special way that no one else can.

Fathers are absolutely vital, but there is a difference in how mothers and fathers meet the needs of their children. And, as we have said before, God designed it to be so.

G. K. Chesterton once spoke of the value of a mother's time with her children in the early years of their lives: "[A mother of young children is] with a human being at the time when he asks all the questions that there are, and some that there aren't.... How can it be an [important] career to tell other people's children about mathematics, and a small career to tell one's own children about the universe?... [A mother's] function is laborious...not because it is minute, but because it is gigantic."[3]

A mother's value in the early years of a little child's life is incalculable.

The bottom line of Scripture is that fathers and mothers are *both* valuable, and they are both responsible in the parenting of their children. Certainly there was a sense of strong community in the Old Testament nation of Israel, but *parents* were commanded to parent their own children over and over again. Likewise, in the early church, *parents* were issued the responsibility of raising and training their children. Parenting, according to the Bible, is the job of parents. Which leads us to the third shot of Novocain to the mothering nerve.

THE NEEDS OF CHILDREN

The third step has been to significantly diminish and understate the needs of children. Parenting in our society has been reduced to the basic feeding, clothing, and educating of a child. Good parenting has been scrunched into so-called "quality time." And when parenting is so reduced, it becomes a job that others can do. Others can feed and clothe a child. Others can treat the scrapes and bruises. Others can certainly educate a child. If good parenting can be accomplished in a few moments of quality time here and there, why should the presence of a parent in a child's life be an issue? As a result, adults today spend 40 percent less time with their kids than their parents spent with them.[4]

But even the strongest concepts of parenting we find in our nation today tend to fall far short of what we find in Scripture. What Scripture has to say to parents could fill a book. In fact, when I got into this portion of study, that's exactly what I did. I actually ended up writing another book! (It wasn't funny at the time, since I was supposed to be writing *this* book.) There is so much rich truth on the subject that I was overwhelmed.

I can only give you the tip of the iceberg here. Even so, the tip is enough to take your breath away. But that's okay. We can all use a good shot of sensitization to the Bible's astounding call to parents.

OUTCOME-BASED PARENTING

The big deal in American education today is "Outcome-Based Education," a philosophy which seeks to reach to the whole child, teaching values, perspectives, ways of thinking, and a world-view.

But this is what you and I are to be doing for our children! God has commanded *us* to parent the whole child. We are not to hand our children over to society to do this for us. "Values clarification" is the job of the parent. The development of thinking skills, the process of learning to make good decisions, and the establishing of a world-view are supposed to be learned *at home. We* are to teach, train, and inculcate values. And such a job simply cannot happen in a few moments of "quality time." Such a job requires tremendous focus, thought, energy, sacrifice, and time—lots and lots of time.

God has issued countless commandments—not suggestions—to parents. Commandments which take us far beyond the mentality of feeding, clothing, and educating a child. They involve the whole person—emotionally, physically, mentally, and spiritually. When we see God's idea of parenting, we see that biblical parenting is a VIP of the first order. It is, put simply, the *shaping of a human being.*

Not only has God given us clear commandments, but He has asked us to implement them consistently, habitually, day and night. God's desire is that biblical parenting become a way of life in our homes. And when such biblical parenting is habitually practiced, God has promised great blessing and success.

What are some of these habits He has asked us to implement?

• Availability—morning, noon, and night (Deuteronomy 6:6-7).

• Involvement—interacting, discussing, thinking together, processing life together (Deuteronomy 6:6-7; Ephesians 6:4).

• Teaching—teaching the Scriptures, teaching a biblical world-view (Psalm 78:5-6; Deuteronomy 4:10; Ephesians 6:4).

• Training—helping a child develop skills and discover his strengths (Proverbs 22:6).

• Discipline—teaching the fear of the Lord, drawing the line consistently, firmly, and lovingly (Ephesians 6:4; Hebrews 12:5-11; Proverbs 13:24; 19:18; 22:15; 23:13-14; 29:15, 17).

• Nurture—providing an environment of constant verbal support, freedom to fail, acceptance, affection, unconditional love (Ephesians 6:4, Titus 2:4; 2 Timothy 1:7; Ephesians 4:29-32; 5: 1-2; Galatians 5:22; 1 Peter 3:8-9).

• Modeling with integrity—living what you say, being a model from which a child can learn by "catching" the essence of godly living (Deuteronomy 4:9, 15, 23; Proverbs 10:9; 11:3; Psalm 37:18, 37).

Do you feel overwhelmed? Join the club. It is an awesome task, a high but worthy calling. A nation that abandons these habits, says God, will go down. This is where it all happens. Children desperately need to be taught, trained, disciplined, and nurtured consistently by their parents. And we simply cannot do this if we are not present, involved, and available.

The concept of consistent parental presence pervades the Scriptures.

Deuteronomy 6 tells us to teach our children when we rise, when we walk along the way throughout the day, when we sit (watching TV), when we lie down at night. And Jesus Christ modeled it in His life. Jesus did not drop in on His disciples, meet with them occasionally, grab a meal with them here and there. He was *with* them, purposefully *with* them, morning, noon, and night. Jesus Christ understood that godly living is "caught" in the process of living together with our young "disciples," being there at the teachable times, focusing on their development and needs, taking the time to stop and teach them, being tuned into the influences around them, constantly helping them to shape and think through a biblical world-view, enjoying life together with them, establishing a communication that lasts a lifetime.

The world in biblical times was conducive to "presence." Our world, on the other hand, is totally unconducive. Fathers have to sacrifice in order to make presence with their children a priority. And mothers are faced with some very tough choices.

Yet if we are to find success in our parenting, we must somehow come to grips with this great need in the lives of our children. Single mothers, God understands that your time and energy are limited. God knows that you carry the burden of parenting alone. You mothers whose husbands are uninvolved, God understands that you also have struggles that come with the lack of support. God knows that there are times when mothers have no choice but to help provide food and shelter for their families. He is more aware of your needs and dreams and longings and frustrations than you could ever imagine.

Life is never a neat little package, with a bow on top.

But *no matter what our situation*, God honors those who pursue the path of biblical parenting. He blesses those who sacrifice in order to make it happen. He takes care of those who are willing to make tough choices on behalf of their children.

There is no challenge like this challenge from Scripture—no greater sacrifice, no more critical calling with which we must struggle.

Dr. James Dobson once compared parenting to the "passing of the baton" in the relay race of life. When is the baton most often dropped in a relay race? It is rarely dropped at the starting line, on the stretch down the lane, or even at the finish. The critical point of the race, the point where the baton is usually dropped, is at the point of the hand-off, when one runner passes the baton to the next.

I don't want to drop the baton of Christian faith in the hand-off to my children. And neither do you.

Biblical parenting is God's way of insuring the passing of the baton from one generation to the next.

No wonder the call to parenting is such a high, demanding call.

THE VALUE OF LIFE

Once the needs of families and those who live within them begin to be ignored throughout an entire nation, the de-sensitization of a society is nearing completion. And devaluation of life itself is the next natural step.

Recently a book was put in my hands that has marked me for life. It is the memoirs of Levi Coffin, the deeply principled, wise Christian businessman who became the reputed president of the Underground Railroad.[5] He, along with his wife, risked life and fortune to aid thousands of slaves in reaching freedom before the Emancipation Proclamation. At the same time I was reading it, I was reading a biography of Lincoln. I found myself stunned by the remarkable similarities between the pro-slavery movement of Coffin's and Lincoln's day, and the pro-choice movement of our own time.

Proponents of slavery:

• spoke for freedom of choice, claiming the right to choose to have slaves or not.

• saw slavery as a "necessary evil" to prevent hardship and total economic collapse in the South.

• sought to justify slavery from Scripture.

• secured a Supreme Court ruling that slaves were not legal persons and therefore unprotected under the Constitution (Dred-Scott Decision, 1857), and secured legislation on their behalf (Fugitive Slave Act).

• argued that slavery was in the best interest of blacks, that they could not make it on their own, and that they were at least in a better place than the uncivilized country of Africa from which they had been brought.

• insisted on innate Negro inferiority, as did most people in our nation in the nineteenth century.

• considered slaves to be the property of their owner to do with as they wished.

But what amazed me even more was the role that the sensitization to families, and particularly motherhood, played in freeing the slaves.

When Coffin described his conversion to the anti-slavery movement, he described two incidents. The first occurred when, as a child walking down the road one day with his dad, he met a group of beaten slaves. His father pleasantly asked the slaves, "Well, boys, why do they chain you?" Says Coffin: "One of the men, whose countenance betrayed unusual intelligence and whose expression denoted the deepest sadness, replied: 'They have taken us away from our wives and children, and they chain us lest we should make our escape and go back to them.' My childish sympathy and interest were aroused, and when the dejected procession had passed on, I turned to my father and asked many questions concerning them, why they were taken away from their families. In simple words, suited to my comprehension, my father explained to me the meaning of slavery, and, as I listened, the thought arose in my mind—'How terribly we should feel if father were taken away from us.'"[6]

Coffin's sensitivity to losing a parent was his first awakening to the true plight of those whose skin happened to be black and who had the misfortune of being born on another continent. But then Coffin relates a story of an experience as a young man that became etched in his mind forever. He was on a business trip and happened to stop in front of a court house where a slave auction was taking place.

> The slaves who were to be sold...appeared intelligent, but their countenances betrayed deep dejection and anxiety. The men who intended to purchase, passed from one to another of the group, examining them just as I would examine a horse which I wished to buy. These men seemed devoid of any feeling of humanity, and treated the negroes as if they were brutes. They examined their limbs and teeth to see if they were sound and healthy, and looked at their backs and heads, to see if they were scarred by whips, or other instruments of punishment. It was disgusting to witness their actions, and to hear their vulgar and profane language....
>
> When the examination was over, the auctioneer mounted the platform, taking one of the slave men with him. He described the good qualities of that valuable piece of property—then bidding commenced. The slave

looked anxiously and eagerly from one bidder to another, as if trying to read in their countenances their qualities as masters, and his fate. The crier's hammer soon came down, then another slave was placed upon the stand, and bid off. After several men had been sold in this way, a woman was placed upon the stand, with a child in her arms apparently a year old. She was a fine looking woman, in the prime of life, with an intelligent countenance, clouded with the deepest sadness. The auctioneer recommended her as a good cook, house servant, and field hand—indeed, according to his representation, she could turn her hand to anything, and was an unusually valuable piece of property. She was industrious, honest and trustworthy, and above all, she was a Christian, a member of the church—as if the grace of God would add to her price! The bidding was quite lively, and she sold for a high price. I supposed that the child was included in the sale, of course, but soon saw that it was to be sold separately. The mother begged her new master to buy her child, but he did not want it, and would not listen to her pleading.

The child was sold to another man, but when he came to take it from her, she clasped her arms around it tighter than ever and clung to it. Her master came up and tore it from her arms amid her piercing shrieks and cries, and dragged her away, cursing and abusing her as he went. The scene moved my heart to its depths; I could endure it no longer. I left the ground, returned to my tavern, called for my horses, and left the town without attempting to do any business. As I mounted my horse, I heard the voice of the slave mother as she screamed: "My child, my child!" I rode away as fast as I could, to get beyond the sound of her cries. But that night I could not sleep; her screams rang in my ears, and haunted me for weeks afterward.

This incident increased my abhorrence of slavery and strengthened my determination to labor for the cruelly oppressed slaves. I resolved to labor in the cause until the end of my days, not expecting that I would live to see the fetters broken and the bondmen free, yet hoping that the time of redemption was not far distant. [7]

The Quaker couple upon whom Harriet Beecher Stowe based her story of *Uncle Tom's Cabin* was Levi Coffin and his wife, Catherine. And the young girl

Eliza? She was a real young slave woman helped by the Coffins. Guns firing all about her, she did indeed risk her life by crossing the Ohio River, quickly jumping from one chunk of ice to the next as each sank beneath her weight. Why would she do something so crazy? She had her tiny child in her arms.

And what about Stowe? She had lost a child to infant death the year before she wrote *Uncle Tom's Cabin*. It was her motherly grief that caused her to grieve for all the black mothers who had lost children through slavery and that motivated her to write such a book. Amazingly Stowe was the first American writer to break the silence on the issue.

It took a woman. A mother.

Her book made waves worldwide, to such an extent that Longfellow said of her: "How she is shaking the world with her *Uncle Tom's Cabin*! At one step she has reached the top of the stair-case up which the rest of us climb on our knees year after year. Never was there such a literary *coup-de-main* as this."[8]

Upon meeting her during the Civil War, Lincoln remarked, "So this is the little woman who made this big war."[9]

The embracing of biblical motherhood can bring an entire nation to its knees. Sensitize the mothers, and you have sensitized a nation.

There are mothers reading these pages who have had abortions. Others have abandoned the call to parent. Let me speak to you from my heart. *There is nothing you can ever do to keep God from loving you.*

Nothing.

God's greatness lies in His unconditional grace and His astounding ability to turn even our deepest failures into redeeming fruit for His kingdom. The only thing that would keep any woman from ever experiencing His grace would be her unwillingness to accept His forgiveness. The only thing that would keep any woman from expressing such fruit in her life would be her reluctance to believe that God can still bless and use her.

I must conclude with the story of one such woman who crossed my path a few years ago. Ellen told me the story of how, as a young teenager in trouble, she had undergone an abortion. But she did not grasp what she had done until some twenty years later. The revelation occurred when she was present during the stillborn delivery of her daughter's first child. This little child was at the same stage of development that her own child had been at the time of the abortion. Seeing this tiny baby's completely formed body, she was suddenly struck by the reality of what she had done some twenty years before. And so in the midst of grieving for her grandchild, she found herself grieving for her first child and for what she had done. The weight of her grief was so great that it threw her into a deep depression.

Then a Christian woman entered her life and sought to help her out of her depression. She told Ellen about God's unconditional forgiveness, His desire to restore her joy, and His promise in Scripture that each little child who perishes goes to be with Him in heaven.

Ellen found herself longing to respond, but she was not willing to allow God to forgive her. She felt it was her fault that her daughter was now suffering and that she was not worthy of forgiveness.

It wasn't until six years later on her birthday that Ellen's life turned around. On that day her daughter delivered a healthy child, and she, the grandmother, was once again present. To her, it was an unmistakable demonstration of God's grace. And so in her heart that day Ellen laid flowers at the tomb of her first child. Then she turned to fully embrace the forgiveness of God. The weight was lifted and she was set free, never to be the same. Since that day Ellen has given her life to working with young mothers in trouble.

And what about our third child? What about the baby my doctor said should never be born?

Our third child, Josh, happened to be born in perfect condition, and I never spent a day in the hospital. Yes, he could have been born with disabilities, but God had another plan. He was also the toddler that Steve pulled out of the pool that evening several years ago. Josh has been the spark of our family; he is a thinker, a reader, and a competitive gymnast.

One night a few years back he called me into his room. He was crying from way down deep, just as I had sobbed that day on I-280. The truth surrounding the circumstances of his birth had sunk in for the first time, and he was grieving that he might not have ever been permitted to live. I just held him very tight. I told him that God had a special plan for his life, that only when God was ready for him to be with Him could he ever go. After a few moments he asked to see his birth certificate.

We got it out, and he looked at it for a very long time.

Then he said, "I'd like to go see the doctor who wanted you to have an abortion, Mom. I want to tell him that he could have made a serious mistake."

"Perhaps one day we'll have an opportunity to do just that," I said.

"Mom?" he said quietly, putting his arms around me as I tucked him in.

"Yes?"

"Thank you for loving me."

This evening I walked by Joshua's room. To my surprise his Michael Jordan poster was gone and taped to his door in its place was a verse, copied in his own handwriting. Josh has recently become attached to *The Living Bible*, and this, he later explained, has become his favorite verse: "In everything you do, put God first, and he will direct you and crown your efforts with success" (Proverbs 3:5-6).

"Eat your heart out, Michael Jordan," I thought.

And then it hit me.

What a fitting promise for any mom who chooses to sacrificially "love her children."

Chapter Sixteen

VIP #5:
Making a Home

There's no place like home. There's no place like home...

DOROTHY , AFTER DISCOVERING WHAT WAS "OVER THE RAINBOW"

Encourage the young women to be homeworkers
[hard workers, working diligently and skillfully in the home]
...or home guardians [caregivers and gatekeepers].

TITUS 2:4-5

*M*eanwhile, back at home...

Strange, isn't it, that we should start with the home in the very first chapter and end up here as well? Maybe it isn't so strange, after all. When we consider that home is *central* to life, the extra emphasis should come as no surprise.

Despite the blows it has taken over the last decades, the home persists. It lives on as the heart of our nation. It stands ever-central, as the pivotal environment in which lives are shaped.

Homes R still Us.

Yesterday as I was headed up the stairs to begin work on this chapter, the doorbell rang. There on our front step was a teenage friend in a state of hysterics. She had run away from home and had found her way to our house. On her body were scratches and bruises resulting from an argument with her parents. Before the day was through, we were in the middle of problems that could be traced back to several generations of homes, homes in which the biblical plan of God had not been followed.

This teenager lives in a beautiful, upper middle-class house. Both of her parents have great jobs and can provide the best life has to offer materially. But the tragedy is that this family has never learned to express love to each other, to work through problems, to meet one another's needs. How can they, since they are never present or available to one another? Home, for them, has been an afterthought.

Recently the news broke that Kurt Cobain, lead singer of the hugely successful '90s "grunge" band Nirvana, had killed himself. What led to the rebellion and fury in his music, and eventually his self-destruction? According to his mother, it was his parents' divorce when he was eight.

"The divorce just destroyed his life," she said. "He changed completely. I think he was ashamed. And he became very inward."

Sadly Cobain's tragedy was the key to his huge success. Said *Newsweek* magazine, Generation X identified so strongly with Cobain because "they'd grown up more or less the same way. Which is to say: grunge is what happens when children of divorce get their hands on guitars."[1]

Broken homes lead to broken lives lead to broken nations. We look at the state of affairs, and we ask, "What kind of hope does a nation have when its future lies in the hands of so many wrecked lives?" May I say it once again? Your home and my home—that is our hope. In the midst of the inferno, we must secure our homes, because homes are the workshops of human construction and destruction.

You've heard the old saying, "All roads lead to Rome." That was once true. It used to be that if you wanted to get to Rome, all you had to do was find a road, point yourself in the right direction, and start walking. But there is another truth that endures every great civilization. It says that "all roads lead home." Step onto the highway of any man or woman's heart, start walking, and you will eventually arrive back at the home of their childhood.

When I think about the "atmosphere" of home, I have a mental picture of two tall candles on the kitchen table.

Our children have always loved eating dinner by candlelight. There is something about the dimly lit room, the hot meal, and the family gathered around that makes them feel special. Our youngest son used to beg me to break out the candles. He called it a "family." "Can we have a family tonight?" he would ask. It didn't matter if all we had to eat was macaroni and cheese. If candles were on the table, his eyes would light up and he would exclaim, "Hey, guys, we're having a *family* tonight!"

If only the world could see things through the perceptive eyes of a four-year-old. Meals *are* where we "have families." Family rooms are where we "have families." Kitchens and bedrooms are where we "have families." And in the midst of living life—dressing, eating, sleeping, working, changing diapers, doing homework, teasing, fighting, watching television, tucking children into bed—far more is happening than meets the eye.

Children see it. Why don't we?

Our homes will never become valuable to us until we see a *family* seeking to survive there. And so, despite where the home stands in terms of position and value in this culture, it remains absolutely central to the health of our culture. It remains central to the needs of all who dwell in our land. It remains central to our problems and to our survival. God designed it to be so, and until He returns and the stars fall from the sky, it will always be so. Look closely with me at God's words regarding the home.

PRIMARY PLACE—PRIMARY ROLES

The first four priorities God has called us to as women revolve around the most important *people* in our lives. But this priority focuses on the most important *place* in our lives. In fact, this place is so important that God decided it should be cared for by two people in a partnership. Just as parenting is a partnership, the preservation of the home is a partnership. For this reason, in an act of wisdom God set down different responsibilities for husbands and wives in the home. And in an act of grace He equipped us uniquely to fulfill those responsibilities.

What are these responsibilities?

A Man's Responsibility: Provision

Paul tells us that men are to *provide* for those in the home. Men are born with the propensity to provide and protect. Their aggressive drive to conquer and their strong, protective spirits were given by God to enable them to make physical provision for their families. In fact, when men don't provide, says Paul, it's a very serious thing: "But if anyone does not provide for his own, and especially for those of his household, he has denied the faith, and is worse than an unbeliever" (1 Timothy 5:8).

Do these words sound a bit strong? They *are* strong because God feels passionately about provision for the family. This, says our Lord, is a man's responsibility and high calling. Nowhere in Scripture do we see women commanded to provide financially in this way. Rather, we see women using their gifts to assist in provision, as helpmates. Certainly in times of unusual need or bereavement we see women stepping into the role of primary providers, but this is the exception, not the rule. God's divine plan is for the husband to "till the soil," laboring hard to provide for his family. His physical and psychological makeup reflect such a plan. Even man's curse found in Genesis 2 reflects his constant, unending struggle in the work of provision.

But men are to provide more than material goods for their families. As we saw in our study on marriage, they are also to provide healthy leadership in the home. In fact, the New Testament writers tell us that if a man wishes to serve in any capacity in the church, he must first model his commitment to leadership at home: "He must be one who manages his own household well, keeping his children under control with all dignity (but if a man does not know how to manage his own household, how will he take care of the church of God?)" (1 Timothy 3:4-5). "Let deacons be husbands of only one wife (a one-woman kind of man), and good managers of their children and their own households" (1 Timothy 3:12).

The word for *manage* here actually means "rule well." What does it mean for a man to rule his family well? Scripture tells us that a man is to discipline and train up his children (Ephesians 6:4), he is to love and serve his wife as Christ loves and serves the church (Ephesians 5:25), and he is to meet the emotional needs that only he can meet in the lives of his wife and children (1 Peter 3:7-9). The ultimate test, then, for a man's leadership in the church is the health of his marriage and the character of his children.

A Woman's Responsibility: Care

Women have been entrusted with the care and guardianship of the home environment. What does it mean to "care"? Biblical "care" means being concerned first and foremost with the needs of our husbands and children. It means nurturing family life and relationships. It means insuring the strong and healthy environment of the home. This is the thrust of Titus 2, as well as the whole of Scripture.

Not only has God called us to care, but He has also equipped us with the propensity to care. Some have called this "the nesting instinct." But call it what you will, this inclination to care for our homes is endemic to femininity. To deny this is to deny our very womanhood.

In fact, there is a great similarity between our call to motherhood and our call to care for the home. Have you ever considered that the home is, in essence, the "womb of the family"? Women have been given guardianship over two wombs—the womb of the unborn child and the womb of the family. Gladys Hunt once defined a home as "a safe place, a place where one is free from attack, a place where one experiences secure relationships and affirmation."

A safe place. A place free from attack. This sounds just like a womb. Inside the mother's womb, the unborn child is protected from the outside world and nourished from within. Inside the womb of the home, the family is sheltered from the outside world and nourished from within. We have been charged with the high calling of caring for both wombs.

CARELESS HOMES

Does this mean that a man need not be involved in care or that a woman need not be involved in provision? Absolutely not. Provision often includes some degree of care, and care often includes a certain degree of provision. What it does mean is that men and women have been called to a different focus when it comes to the home. Husbands are primarily to provide, and wives are primarily to care. This is the bottom line in building a healthy home.

But what is happening today in American homes? Husbands and wives across America are both focusing on financial provision, leaving the home virtually uncared for. The result is that we have become a nation filled with "care-less" homes. In the words of my husband, this is the great Continental Provide, which is becoming our great Continental Divide, dividing family peace and unity.[2]

If we women don't focus on the care of our homes, who will? The answer is, no one. Which is exactly what Satan wants. Satan knows that God's calling to a woman is far from confining or squelching and that a woman who embraces this calling will discover God's best. He also knows that the woman's inclination towards the home is very strong. And so the nesting instinct has been added to Satan's hit list. If he can minimize the value of the home and turn a woman's heart toward personal achievement at the expense of her home, he will have succeeded. For the home, uncared for, is like a castle with no walls. The enemy can walk right in.

The battle for the home is a huge one, and Satan is not about to give up. How can we fight him? In the same way Jesus fought Satan's attacks in the desert—with God's Word (Matthew 4). What, then, does God say in His Word regarding women and the home?

THE POWER OF A WOMAN

Two key passages in Scripture speak directly about our call in the home. In 1 Timothy 5:14 Paul encourages young widows to remarry and focus their energies in the direction of their homes. Here he uses the term *oikodespoteo*, which means to "guide the home" or to "provide management as the mistress of the home." This gives us the partnership picture of the husband as ruler of the home and the wife as the associate ruler of the home.

While the man is held ultimately responsible for the health of his home, his wife works in conjunction with him. Proverbs tells us time and again that a woman can make or break her home: "The wise woman builds her house, But the foolish tears it down with her own hands" (Proverbs 14:1). How does she tear it down? "A constant dripping on a day of steady rain and a contentious woman are alike; He who would restrain her restrains the wind, And grasps oil with his right hand" (Proverbs 27:15-16). What kind of wife and mother is so self-willed that she is like oil in the hand—impossible to communicate with, impossible to lead, impossible to love? A family who lives with such a woman will long to escape. As if to drive the point home, Solomon tells us twice: "It is better to live in a corner of a roof, Than in a house shared with a contentious woman" (Proverbs 21:9; 25:24). But, if you thought that was bad, what about this? "It is better to live in a desert land, Than with a contentious and vexing woman" (Proverbs 21:19).

Do you get the sense that Solomon knows this from experience? Out of a few thousand wives, I would imagine he ran across an irritating, discontented, vexing woman or two. It's tough enough on a man to come home to such a woman, but think of a child growing up in such a house.

We determine the health of our homes as much as our husbands do. A bitter heart, discontented spirit, and an out-of-control tongue can do serious damage. Do you know what James says about an uncontrolled tongue? "Behold, how great a forest is set aflame by such a small fire!" (James 3:5). A woman's tongue can be the spark that sets her home ablaze. An awesome thought, isn't it? How many fires I have had to squelch—all because I lost control of my tongue!

One afternoon not long ago Josh decided to bake cookies. He pulled out the frozen dough and placed it in chunks on an extra oven rack—without a cookie sheet. In a few moments cookie dough was oozing over the bars and exploding all over the oven. Trying to save himself, he pulled out the rack and tracked dough all over the kitchen. By the time I got there, it was a fiasco.

Do you know what I did?

I lost it. Plain and simple.

First I lit into him for baking without permission. Then I lit into him for doing something so "stupid" as baking without a cookie sheet. The rest of the family witnessed this volcanic eruption and quickly split the scene. Meanwhile Josh was trying to apologize.

"I'm sorry, Mom. I wasn't thinking," he said.

"Next time, *think!*" I shot back.

Later that afternoon I decided to blow up a float with our air pump. I hooked our pump to the car battery, attached it to the float, and went inside for a while. When I finally thought of it again, the car battery had gone dead, and the air pump motor was fried. It was a stupid thing to do, but, you know…I just wasn't thinking. Talk about humble pie. I had to go to Josh and tell him what a foolish thing I had done. Then I had to ask his forgiveness. Then I had to get the rest of the family together and ask their forgiveness. We all had a laugh that God had certainly shut my mouth!

In the end our homes are just as much the measure of *our* character as they are of our husbands' character. A woman of character opens her mind before she opens her mouth. She listens to her husband and children, and she draws the lines of respect. The more character a woman has at home, the more character her children will have, and the more respect she will receive without having to draw lines. Such a woman of character will be praised by her children and husband (Proverbs 31:28).

Let me ask you a question. How many teenagers have you heard praise their mother recently? How many husbands do you know that speak highly of their wives to their friends in the workplace? A wife and mother who is worthy of such praise is hard to find, says Solomon.

EXCAVATING TITUS 2:5

Now we come to Titus 2:5 in which we find a tiny little phrase, packed with insight: "and teach the younger women…to be homeworkers (or, home guardians)."

Unfortunately this brief command has created all kinds of confusion among Christian women. Some teachers have dismissed it altogether. Some have simply minimized its importance. And some have gone to the opposite extreme, drawing stringent ideas regarding a woman's work.

We have here one of those dinosaur word combinations, like the word for "submission," which must be carefully excavated and interpreted, based on its original meaning, its context, and the entire teaching of Scripture. If we don't handle it carefully, we can find ourselves making decisions based on unbalanced teaching or half-truths. You and I simply cannot afford to do sloppy work when it comes to the home.

On my shelf are two books that illustrate how easily confusion can set in. One book, published by a major Christian publisher, supports the idea of the "dual-income, dual-career, hired-help-raising-the-children" approach to the home. This writer wanted to show that such a lifestyle choice is legitimate and biblical. But unfortunately what we find throughout this book is a quick reading of passages and leaping applications to support theories the author has already put forward. When she comes to this Titus 2 passage, she never mentions context or original language. Instead, she opts to take the term "domestic," which is used in some translations, and to surmise that a woman simply needs to make sure her house is clean and that, when she is able, she should certainly enjoy being "domestic." When children are mentioned, it is in the context of being reared by caring substitutes. The roles of men and women are seen as interchangeable and negotiable—both can be primary providers if they wish, and both should be adept nurturers. Didn't God command fathers to raise their children in the nurture of the Lord? Ultimately the husband's and wife's careers are the key factors in family decisions. To sum up, this writer does not see any serious implications in this particular command given by Paul.

Another book on my shelf goes to the opposite extreme. This second book, widely read by Christian women a few years ago, emphasizes the *place* of work, insisting that Titus 2:5 teaches that a woman is to work only "at home." If a woman works outside the home, says this writer, she is violating the passage. While this writer is to be commended for her study of the Greek words, she succumbs to "interpretational narrowness"—zooming in on a single idea in Scripture to the exclusion of its context and the thrust and teaching found throughout Scripture.

But when Paul uses the term "homeworker," he is not confining a woman to her house. Even the virtuous woman of Proverbs 31 worked in other settings than the home. She worked among the poor. She traveled. She spent time overseeing her vineyards. Other godly women in Scripture functioned in many capacities unrelated to their homes.

The point of this passage is not to hem a woman into a certain square footage of space. It's something quite different and far more important.

Both of these writers are, without question, sincere. These two books only show how easy it is for any one of us unknowingly to carry ideas to Scripture and allow them to shape our interpretation. While we cannot completely purge ourselves of personal bias, the more ways we come at a passage with good hermeneutics, the less the possibility of swinging to extreme conclusions.

So for the next few pages we must try to walk in Paul's shoes, speak his language, and see the world through the eyes of the women to whom he was speaking. But once we discover the principles here, we can expect that when they are applied to different lives, different homes, by different women of differing skills, personalities, and resources, they will look...different! That is the great beauty of Scripture—it is so flexible as to be applicable wherever we are in life.

A CALL TO "MINISTRY"

The rarer word that appears here is *oikourous*, which means "home-guardian" and carries the idea of the woman as the "home-keeper" or the "watchwoman" of the home. This New Testament word is strikingly similar to the Hebrew word in the Old Testament for the Levitical priest, the "keeper of the temple" or the "temple-guardian." And from these similarities we can gain wonderful insight.

In the early days of the nation of Israel, the tribe of Levi was given a unique calling among the twelve tribes. Their job was *the ministry of the temple*. It was a huge task, involving care of the temple, ministry in music, teaching of Scripture, and assistance of the people in daily worship. In those days the law of God touched every part of the people's lives, and the priests and Levites were to be there continually to teach them, remind them, assist them, and lead them.

God also instructed that the Levites *be free to focus* on this job. In order to do so, they were not required to labor in the same manner as other people but were supported by the tithes of the people.

The Levites were given special cities inside of each tribal territory, enabling them to live *among the people*. This was important to God since His primary concern was the people and their relationship to Him rather than the upkeep of a building. And so, although the priests and Levites had families, homes, and even fields for livestock and farms and vineyards, the primary focus of their work was ministry to the people, whose hearts were more important to God than a thousand sacrifices.[3]

HOMES, OUR PRIMARY FOCUS

How is this Levitical role similar to a woman's role in the home? We have been called to a ministry—the unique ministry of being the guardian and caretaker of the home. Your home and the people who live there are to be your primary focus, as well as the primary beneficiaries of your energies and gifts.

When I think about working at home, I tend to think about cleaning, cooking, doing laundry, and the endless other tasks required for maintaining a home. But the emphasis here is not so much on which jobs a woman does around the house or how she oversees the upkeep of her home. God doesn't care whether we are crafty or not. He doesn't care if we use hired help to clean house or do it ourselves, whether we bake cookies or buy them at the store, whether we iron our shirts or send them to the cleaners. Every woman has her own style, her own strengths and bents, her own situation.

No, the emphasis here is on *focus*.

God asks that we focus our gifts and energies on the ministry of the home. What do we mean by "focus"? It means "to fix your heart on," "to set your sights upon," "to think about first," "to direct your energies toward." God asks that we fix our hearts on our homes with diligence and love. Yes, a woman can and must be involved in the world outside of the home. But first He asks us to take very seriously the needs of those who dwell inside our homes. That is the call to the woman.

The Proverbs 31 woman is a great illustration of such focus. In fact, many theologians believe that this Old Testament woman was in the mind of Paul as he penned his words to these women of Crete. As busy as this woman was, her primary focus was her family: "She looks well to the ways of her household, And does not eat the bread of idleness" (Proverbs 31:27).

But notice something. Did this woman feel constrained to do all the work herself? Not at all. She delegated much of the work to a household of servants, "maidens" (31:15), working under her supervision. Our preflood mothers also often had a staff of workers to help them. Yet one job these mothers did not delegate was the parenting of their children. Mothers continued to nurture and live in a close, hands-on relationship with their children and taught them to be "home-workers" too.

Today we have all kinds of help available to us in the home. We have servants in the form of washers, dryers, ovens…and cookie sheets. And for those who can afford it, there are multitudes of services. But even if a family can't afford other services, it shouldn't prevent a woman from having help. A husband who understands servant leadership will certainly help his wife. (Steve can wash, iron, and grocery shop. Just don't ask him to cook!) And children are capable of all kinds of responsibilities at home. Even a four-year-old can sort clean silverware from the dishwasher, put away his toys, and pull up the covers on his bed.

God has no problem with help. The problem comes when we use help to escape the responsibility of being the primary guardian and caregiver of the home.

PEOPLE, OUR PRIMARY CONCERN

As we are weaving the nest, God asks us to focus on the people who live in it. In Scripture, a house is an edifice, a mere shell, a greenhouse in which young plants sprout and grow up. Nothing more. If a woman creates a beautiful museum in which her family cannot live, work, or play freely, she has lost the focus. Children need to be able to use paste and scissors. Husbands need to be able to romp on the floor with their kids. Teenagers need to be able to track in loads of other snacking, fun-loving, sloppy teenagers.

I have a good friend who amazes me with her attitude toward opening up her home. Not long ago I dropped my kids off there for a hayride, only to see nearly 150 other kids spread out on the front lawn, strung through the house, swishing hoops in the driveway, and hanging off the back porch. When I walked inside, I saw masses of food overflowing her kitchen counter, and I knew what her house would look like by the end of the night.

And I also knew something else those kids didn't know.

Just that day she had laid down brand new carpet. Now this woman has perspective!

However, if a woman pays little attention to her home environment, allowing it to become so filthy, cluttered, and uncomfortable that it is uninviting for people to live in, she has also lost the picture.

Birds have the right idea when it comes to such things. Birds know how to nest. They know how to work diligently with what they have, and they know exactly what their little family will need. An oriole doesn't look at a marsh bird's raft nest or a flamingo's impressive mud nest and opt for its design because it has status or looks better. No, an oriole builds a nest that is optimum for her babies' survival. She labors to make it strong and conducive to the protection and growth of her babies. A bird can make a nest out of a pile of old dry grass, and yet if it suits her babies, it is beautiful to her.

I know families who live in small, unimpressive homes whose members are thriving. I know other families who live in mansions, yet whose members are dying. The size and furnishings of a home are irrelevant to God. It's the constructive environment that matters to Him.

Likewise there are some women who work hard at home all day long, yet never look up to focus on their children or husband. Perhaps you have heard the old proverb, "A clean house is the sign of a life miss-spent." I will never forget reading a *Hints from Heloise* column in which someone asked what she thought of housekeeping. She replied, "There are a few people who really love housework. Those people are sick." Now that's my kind of woman. The next time a friend stops in, surprise yourself by resisting the urge to apologize for your dirty dishes or toys on the floor. Why apologize for something you don't have to apologize to God for? Instead, invite her in and let her absorb the warmth of your home and the joy of your children playing.

The central issue is never the house. Nor is it housework. Never let housework consume your life. And never let old furniture destroy your perspective. A new couch will only get dirty, and clean windows will soon have spots. Your children, however, will grow up and leave home.

People, says Scripture, are to be our concern, not buildings. A woman who focuses on people and their physical, emotional, psychological, and spiritual well-being will never grow bored or lose her sense of challenge!

DOUBLE HONOR, OUR PRIMARY NEED

There are other insights also to be gained from this idea of "guardianship." The early church leaders took up the Levitical priests' role of ministry. They kept watch over the souls of their flocks (Hebrews 13:17), shepherding them with a willing, servant spirit rather than in an effort to find power or wealth (1 Peter 5:2-4). We get the sense that this "guarding over" is a ministry of service in which a person cannot expect to make a great deal of money or receive a great deal of glory. Those who chose such a ministry in the early church and who "ruled well," said Paul to Timothy, were worthy of double honor and should be remunerated (1 Timothy 5:17-18).

What is "double honor"? It is honor through praise and recognition, as well as through provision. Paul was recognizing that shepherding the flock was a demanding, time-consuming role and that those who did this well would not have time for a second career.

The idea here is that when time-consuming ministry is done in the right spirit and done well, the one ministering is worthy of honor and should be taken care of financially. I find that interesting, don't you? We all know that the ministry of guarding over the home does not promise wealth or glory and that it is time-consuming. I find it interesting that God also commanded husbands to honor their wives and provide for them. Why? Because the job of guarding over the home is a huge task, particularly when the children are young. There is not a more demanding, exhausting, unending, or unappreciated job than that of caring for the needs of a family. And the woman who focuses her heart and energies on such a task is indeed worthy of double honor.

ISOLATION, OUR PRIMARY ENEMY

Finally, I find it interesting that God was careful not to isolate the Levites.

He commanded them to live together in cities so that through their own fellowship they might strengthen one another.[4] Today the minister of a local church is often the loneliest person in the church. But isolation in ministry, whether it be ministry in the church or ministry in the home, is not the plan of God. God knows that isolation can lead to depression, disillusionment, and lost vision. A man or woman in ministry is on the front lines of battle, and if we become isolated, we are prime targets to be picked off by the enemy.

Amazing what we can learn from one little word, isn't it?

To sum it all up, the Levites focused on the religious ministry and life of the people. In return, they were honored and remunerated. Theirs was a high calling. And so is ours.

Somehow, in a society that is turned upside down, we have to figure out how to focus our hearts upon our homes once again.

Single mothers, even though your time at home is limited, *oikourous* may change the time you do have. It may mean that you and your children will turn off the TV or perhaps stop running about in such a flurry of endless ball games and lessons. Your children desperately need a home in which to learn how to love, how to stay committed, how to resolve conflict and forgive. And most of all, they need you.

Mothers who must work, *oikourous* may mean you will go to your boss for a more flexible schedule. Or it may mean you will ask God for a job that will give you the freedom to be there for your children and care for your home.

Mothers of young children, *oikourous* may mean that your personal career will have to take a back seat. Which brings us to the question of the day. *What about career?*

This question is answered in the second word used in Titus.

A CALL TO "WORK"

The second word, *oikourgous*, means "home-worker." The "work" part of this word implies very hard work, as a farmer or a vine dresser might do out in the fields. But this word is referring to hard work in the home. We know that in the days of Paul a woman labored at home. If a woman did not use her talents and skills well, then she was not only lazy, but her gifts were wasted and her family was left uncared for.

But what about the career women who worked outside the home? Such women did not exist. For the most part, work was tied to the home. We cannot forget this when we begin to interpret Paul's command. If a woman worked outside the home, she was probably a prostitute.

Look at Proverbs. There you see two women—the virtuous woman and the prostitute. One worked hard at home and brought honor to her husband and children. The other wandered the streets, ensnaring men and ruining their lives. Look at the book of Timothy. First Timothy 5 contrasts two women—the woman who fixes her hope on God (5:5) and cares for her home (5:14) and the woman who either gives herself to wanton pleasure (5:6) or becomes a busybody, preoccupied with sensuality and gossiping about ungodly things (5:11-13).

We simply don't find the "career woman" in Scripture. What we do find is that when godly women expressed their gifts, they did so through their work in the home. Today, since a large part of "work" has been moved outside of the home, the only way to express certain gifts and skills fully is through an outside career. How are we to resolve this problem?

First, we must examine what the Bible says about work and gifts. And, second, we must consider the thrust of Paul's words to these women in Titus.

WORK HEARTILY

The Bible tells us that work is to be done with a goal and an attitude: "Do your work heartily, as for the Lord" (Colossians 3:23). The goal of our work? To glorify and bring honor to God. The attitude? Joy and wholeheartedness.

No question about it. The Proverbs 31 woman worked hard. She rose early in the morning, hustled all day long, and burned the candle late at night. But she also worked heartily. This woman enjoyed her work: "She...works with her hands in delight" (31:13) and "She senses that her gain is good" (31:18).

You can almost see a smile on her face. I think one of the reasons she had so much fun was because she was operating in her area of strengths. She was skillful with her hands and good at turning a profit. And since she had found a way to put her skills to work on behalf of her home and family, she enjoyed it immensely. Her husband and children appreciated this. And the blessing of God was clearly upon her. This woman had learned the secret of doing her work "heartily, as unto the Lord."

What we see consistently in Scripture is that women of God worked hard on behalf of their families, using their talents and ingenuity to the maximum. But they also worked heartily, according to the circumstances they were in. Ruth, for example, became a worker in the fields. She did so as a widow and a daughter-in-law of a widow caught in a situation of need. Abigail was in an entirely different place. She was the manager of a huge estate, overseeing hosts of servants and handling the great wealth of her foolish husband, Nabal. Her situation was also a tough one, but this did not keep her from working heartily unto the Lord and using her talents to honor Him.

Joy in our work is not contingent on ideal circumstances. Joy comes from using our gifts to glorify God.

WORK UNSELFISHLY

Secondly, the beneficiary of our work is others, not ourselves: "As each one has received a special gift, employ it in serving one another, as good stewards of the manifold grace of God" (1 Peter 4:10).

What we see throughout Scripture is women taking initiative and creatively using their gifts on behalf of others.

Ruth worked because of her commitment to care for Naomi.

Abigail acted out of a commitment to Nabal—despite her husband's vulgar behavior—as well as to David, God's appointed leader of Israel.

Lydia, who appears to have been a widow, was a successful seller of purple who used her position of influence for the cause of Christ in her part of the world.

Priscilla, who apparently had no children, was a scholar and a teacher who studied the Scriptures fervently and used her gifts in equipping new believers in Christ.

Whatever the case, we know that God would not have so honored the work of these women had they been neglecting their families in the process.

According to the Bible our gifts are not given primarily for our own self-fulfillment. They are given to meet the needs of others. But our society has lost its impetus to serve. Service roles have become secondary. The roles that really count are the ones that carry power and status. Meanwhile, work has been turned into "career."

Career, as we know it today, is actually an invention of modern times. It is, in fact, the new religion of the baby boomer generation. While character was once the measure of a person's value, career has now become the measure. Career has been so elevated that it has become a god, reigning over our choices and establishing our priorities. Marriage, children, friendships, even morals, are expected to bow before its demands.

In their book *Your Work Matters to God*, Doug Sherman and William Hendricks peg this new religion of "Careerism." Baby boomers, they say, have thrown out the old rule of life, "Deny yourself," and have ushered in a new rule, "Fulfill yourself." They have exchanged the first and greatest commandment, "Love the Lord Thy God," for the commandment, "Love the lord thy self."[5]

Why does God enable men and women to work? The expression of gifts through work was given by God to provide for families and to serve others. Work is never an end in itself.

What happens when we pursue personal fulfillment? It eludes us. What happens when we serve others? We find fulfillment. Interestingly enough, work that seeks to honor God and serve others always ends up bringing the greatest long term fulfillment. But while self-fulfillment is certainly a by-product, it is never the focus. Work is a tool for meeting family needs. Therefore, when family needs clash with work, *family needs are the deciding factor*—not the other way around. This settles the issue of career versus home—clearly and simply.

WORK PATIENTLY

Finally, we are to use our gifts according to God's grace in our lives. "And since we have gifts that differ according to the grace given to us, let each exercise them accordingly" (Romans 12:6). What in the world does this mean?

First, it means to be happy with our gifts. God has gifted each one of us, and He has gifted us differently. With each gift comes a measure of God's grace to express that gift. We do what we do because *God has so enabled us*. Since every skill we possess is from God, it is foolish to hate our gifts or to wish we had the gifts He has given to someone else. We must embrace our gifts as given by God for a great purpose.

But I think there is another aspect of God's grace here. Just as we each have unique gifts, we also live in unique circumstances. Some of us live in circumstances which allow us to express our gifts fully and creatively. Some of us live in more limiting circumstances. This, too, comes from the gracious hand of God. And so we must adapt the expression of our gifts to the place and the seasons of life in which we find ourselves.

Put another way, God has a plan that weds our gifts with His priorities. Somehow in His great plan, He has provided a way to accomplish His will and still use our gifts. This is where we have to trust His timing and wisdom.

Perhaps you have a degree in law or business. Or perhaps you can sing or dance. Yet you find yourself at the moment caring for young children. Unless you can find a way to use your gifts without compromising the needs of your children, you must trust God to make a way for you eventually to use that skill and training, in *His* good time, according to *His* plan for your life. If some of your gifts and skills end up being put on the back burner, that's okay. You can still be you. God is not so concerned with your career as He is with doing a work in your life, and He is not finished with you yet.

In short, a person's gifts can never replace or override the commands of the Lord. Gifts have been given by God to *fulfill* His commands. If using our gifts requires us to compromise biblical motherhood, biblical unity in marriage, or our biblical calling to care for the home, we are violating the plan of God, and we cannot expect His blessing.

This brings us back to Titus. When Paul tells women to be "home workers," he is saying for women to work hard, with their focus towards the home. Try as we might, we cannot get around the apostle's clear implication without doing serious damage to the biblical text.

And herein is the big rub for modern Christian women.

Some women's gifts and bents lend themselves naturally to the care of the home. But other women have bents that create a great struggle in a postflood world. If you are one of these women, relax and understand that your struggle is normal and natural. The truth is that many of the women of Scripture would be struggling, too, if they lived in your shoes.

No doubt the Proverbs 31 woman would be faced with some tough choices if she lived in our time. But mark this—please. *She would never let her outside ministry and businesses get in the way of the care of her home.* My guess is she would get highly creative in operating those businesses or simply give them up altogether rather than compromise her family and home.

The godly women of Scripture were not gift-enamored. They were God-enamored.

They were not gift-bound. They were God-bound.

They were not gift-fulfilled. They were God-fulfilled.

Their primary concern was the well-being of their families and the furtherance of God's kingdom on earth.

This is tough for some of us to swallow. Yet if our homes are to survive the inferno raging about us, we cannot ignore these harder truths or lay them aside. Let's just face it. There are times when taking God's priorities as our own priorities will mean that we will lay aside the expression of some of our gifts and training for a season.

But consider this. While you and I are sacrificially meeting the needs of our children and families, God is preparing us, sharpening us, equipping us, deepening us, and re-directing us to use our gifts in ways we could never have foreseen.

There are other times, however, when accepting God's priorities as our own will mean becoming creative in using our gifts and training. As twenty-first century women, you and I are blessed to live in a time of unprecedented technology which has opened up a whole new world of possibilities our mothers never had. In fact, our entire last chapter is devoted to this idea.

The same may be true of your husband. Your husband may need to get creative or perhaps forgo a promotion that would bring prestige and a bigger salary—if he finds taking the promotion would prevent him from leading in his home or being available to his children.

These are tough, tough decisions. But they are absolutely critical.

Inevitably, the couples that make such agonizing choices testify to the incredible blessings of God. I am constantly running into couples with amazing stories of God's blessing on their lives—above and beyond their wildest expectations. And I have yet to meet a woman who has laid aside a career who has not been blessed in the end with a ministry or work that is even better than the work she left.

When you and I put God's priorities over our own personal fulfillment in this world, we will discover blessings we never knew could be possible in this life. We may not live high on the hog, or have huge homes, or be able to eat out every week. But the relationships of our lives will be so much richer and healthier that we would never want to go back and change a thing.

Count on it. God makes good on His promises. And couples who choose their children and homes over prestige in careers and wealth will find God's provision for them at every turn.

The equation is simple. You honor God by putting first things first. And He will honor you. "For those who honor Me I will honor" (1 Samuel 2:30).

A WARNING

Is it possible for a woman to get too focused on her home and children?

Yes, I believe it is. And therein lies a warning.

It is possible for a godly, committed mom to be so intensely focused on her home that she lives, eats, and breathes her children and her husband. Beside the fact that she will likely be overly protective and smother her family, she is also setting herself up for deep depression when the nest empties. An empty nest is hard enough for parents, but an empty nest for the unbalanced mother is death. Like the end of the world. The key to a healthy transition at this stage in life is to have lived a balanced life beforehand.

How does a woman find balance? She finds outlets. She continues to develop her mind and her skills. She looks beyond her home and models to her children a vision for the world. For the sake of her family, she sinks her heart into something *beyond* her family.

Children whose mother reaches outside of the home are doubly blessed children. They will value her, respect her, and rise up to catch her vision. And they will say, as did the husband and children of Proverbs 31, "Many daughters have done nobly, But you excel them all."

You can't do much better than that.

Chapter Seventeen

The New Pioneer

In a time of great change, we are most in need of creativity.

JOHN NAISBITT

In the beginning, God created....
And God said, "Let Us make man in Our image, according to Our likeness."

GENESIS 1

The summer of 1874 was a summer Kansas pioneers never forgot.

The crops were unusually plentiful and lush pastures promised a healthy herd of cattle.

And then came the grasshoppers.

Millions upon millions filled the sky. As their wings caught the sunshine, they appeared like a great, white, glistening cloud. One pioneer described it as looking like a midsummer snowstorm, in which the air seemed filled with enormous flakes. When the grasshoppers came down, they struck the ground so hard it sounded like hail. The sky soon became so thick with them that the sun could hardly be seen.

Mounding to a depth of four inches in some areas, to as much as a foot in other areas, these grasshoppers covered every inch of ground, every plant and shrub, every tree. Tree limbs snapped under their weight. Cornstalks bent to the ground. Potato vines were flattened. Quickly the grasshoppers devoured everything in their paths—whole fields of corn, wheat, and vegetables, trees, shrubs, turnips, tobacco, fruits, and even onions. They ate the onions from the inside, leaving the outer shell. The peaches they relished, leaving the pit hanging. The corn was consumed down to bare stalks.

In a desperate effort to save a portion of their crops, the pioneers grabbed whatever coverings they could find—sheets, blankets, quilts, shawls, winter coats, and burlap sacks. But the grasshoppers ate straight through them or wormed their way underneath.

When they had finished eating every edible plant in sight, they invaded the homes of the pioneers, and unless the food was enclosed by wood or metal, the grasshoppers consumed it all. One pioneer woman told how the grasshoppers settled on her green and white striped dress, eating every bit of green stripe before she had a chance to do anything. Besides devouring the food left in cupboards, barrels, and bins, they attacked anything made of wood, destroying kitchen utensils, furniture, fences, and even rough siding on cabins. Window curtains were left hanging in shreds, and families' clothing was heartily consumed. Craving anything sweaty, the insects took a special liking to the handles of pitchforks and harnesses of horses. They filled the bedding and climbed down children's shirts and through their hair. Men tied strings around their trouser cuffs to keep them from wriggling up their legs. Animals were helpless, as grasshoppers filled their ears, eyes, and noses.

Some of the pioneers tried building fires to ward off the grasshoppers, but within moments the fire was smothered by grasshoppers! In a matter of hours no part of the countryside was left unscathed. Even trains could not start or stop because the tracks were slick with crushed grasshoppers.

Once they had done their damage, they moved to the next valley, the next field, the next cabin. But to the dismay of the settlers, after they were gone, everything reeked with the taste and odor of the insects. The water in the ponds, streams, and open wells turned brown with their excrement and became totally unfit for drinking by either the pioneers or their livestock. Bloated from consuming the locusts, the barnyard chickens, turkeys, and hogs themselves tasted so strongly of grasshoppers that they were completely inedible.

Worst of all, the insects deposited their own eggs in the soil before departing. The following spring the whole earth began to crawl. Grasshoppers by the millions hatched into sickly white bugs, and once again they mowed down all of the farmers' work. Fortunately this time it was early enough in the summer that the farmers could plant more crops.

How did these people endure? How could they go on?

Some pioneers did give up and go back East. But most remained to face a life that was "wretchedly uncomfortable, poverty stricken without the means to sustain life through the coming winter." The secret of their endurance can be found in the words of one pioneer woman: "In those days there were no aristocrats on Spring Creek. We made the most of our circumstances and of one another. Life was yet before us, and it was the same danger that ever threatened us: hard times. Kind friends sent us 'aid' such as bedding and clothes, food and shoes. The men went back to work, with heavy hearts, putting in winter crops of cane and millet. And we lived on corn bread, cornmeal, coffee, gravy, sorghum for sweetening, while the men smoked grape leaves for tobacco. Yet, life was worthwhile, even then."

Those are the words of a true pioneer. What a spirit of endurance, of looking up and carrying on, of pulling together, encouraging, and helping one another through the tough times, of using sheer ingenuity to survive on almost nothing. Not a note of resentment towards God entered the writings of these Kansas pioneers regarding 1874, the Year of the Grasshopper.[1]

TWENTY-FIRST CENTURY PIONEERS

Christian women, we are the new pioneers, the pioneers of the twenty-first century—pulling together, encouraging one another in the tough times, using ingenuity to carry on with the tasks God has laid before us on the path of life.

And what a calling it is. What a challenge. There is not a better time to be alive, to make a difference in this world, to impact our families and our nation by the choices that we make.

Yes, we are in a flash flood. But God has provided higher ground. Yes, the home is in danger of being consumed in the inferno. But it will never be consumed as long as Christian men and women make a stand.

It is high time we said that our homes are too important, our children too valuable, our marriages too precious to be squandered in personal pursuits. It is high time we rose up and told the world that *it* will have to bend for a change, that *it* will have to accommodate the priorities of God. It is high time *we* were the ones defying convention, upsetting the rules, changing the game plans.

It is high time we started a new revolution. A revolution to return to womanhood. A revolution to renew the value of the home. A revolution to stand up for what is right when all around us are floating with the current.

How do we do this? We must become as tough as the Kansas pioneer women. We must become right-brained *creative* in our survival skills!

RELIGIOUS RIGHT-BRAINERS

I live in a household of right-brained people. Consequently, it's a miracle we get anything done. Right-brained people are artistic, creative, verbal, and unorganized. That's about as good a description of my family as you'll ever come up with. I asked God to give me a left-brained child, but He probably knew that such a child would die of exasperation just trying to function among the rest of us.

There is a time when right brains come in handy, however. In a bind or a tight spot, a right-brained person is handy to have around. Right-brained people can conceive of the inconceivable. They can take what is available to them and do amazing things. They are unafraid to break rules, smash categories, or color outside the lines. They enjoy the challenge of doing things a new way, putting a new twist on an old line. This is the kind of thinking we need out on the new frontier.

Johann Gutenberg was right-brained. He took two unconnected ideas—the wine press and the coin punch—and put them together to make the printing press. Nolan Bushnell was also right-brained. In 1971 he looked at his television and thought, "I'm not satisfied with just watching my TV set. I want to *play* with it and have it respond back." His creation of the interactive table tennis game "Pong" was the start of the video game revolution.[2]

In a nutshell Religious Right-Brainers (RRBs) are gifted, smart, ingenious Christian women with a great heart for God. They don't let a wall get in their way. They simply figure out how to get over it, around it, or through it. They have discovered how to take gifts from God and use them to their advantage: talent, education, resources, experience, and circumstances.

Perhaps you are left-brained. This need not stop you! The thing every woman must realize is that she has a creative side. You do not have to be right-brained to become an RRB. Some of the most ingenious people I have ever known have been extremely left-brained. The point is this. You are made in the image of God, and part of His image includes His creative bent. The great Creator has endowed mankind uniquely with the ability to conceive of new ideas and bring them into being. How else could Charles Goodyear come up with 32,000 uses for rubber?

We need only tap into this gift from God. And once He has given us a plan, we must be willing to step out and do it. As one person has said, "Don't be afraid to go out on a limb. That's where the fruit is." This is, in fact, what Christian women are starting to do all over the country.

Some RRBs have stepped into the home-business world, a world which has literally boomed in the last decade. Working together with other resourceful and gifted women, they are developing their own niche, expressing their gifts, and making a mark as entrepreneurs. Home-oriented businesses are popping up everywhere, providing services, using resources, tapping into talents, keying off of previous experience and education, or extending previous jobs from the corporate world creatively back to their homes. Other RRBs are working within the present system, paring down their hours outside the home, accommodating their workloads and schedules to their family's schedules and needs, or finding jobs that mesh well with family life.

My dentist is one such woman. She works one day a week (she calls it her "day off") on her husband's day off and has a thriving practice filling and straightening teeth. My doctor works one to two days a week, with a cooperative group of doctors who enjoy having her there on those days. My beautician set up her own shop so she could schedule appointments around her home and family. And several of my children's teachers and school employees have chosen their jobs so they can come home with their children from school.

There are hosts of women who have taken their original jobs in companies and created the means to continue those jobs in a limited fashion out of their homes. And there are hosts of other women who have come up with creative ideas for beginning businesses right out of their homes. Recently I have learned of a ghost writer, a publisher, a journalist, a learning specialist and tutor, a custom shopper for executives, a home headhunter, a stationery printer, an editor, a mural wall painter, a substitute Realtor, teachers of everything from music to Lamaze, a breast pump rental businesswoman, a volleyball referee, and a businesswoman who does advertising out of her home for Christian publishing. Some of these businesses have grown so big that these women have had to add other women to their team. One young friend of mine has a business of putting women into their own business. Now that's what I call creative!

But there is another thing this twenty-first century pioneer woman will need: the willingness to make extraordinary choices. Choices like Margaret has made. I first met Margaret, heavy with her first child, several years ago at a conference. Since then I have watched her grow from one tough choice to another, discovering with every step God's unusual blessing in her life.

But I would much prefer to let Margaret tell you her story herself.

MARGARET'S STORY

My career was a dream come true. My second summer of working for a large consumer products company, I was offered a position—if I would go back for a Master of Science degree. And so one year later I returned to take a job on the bottom rung of the professional ladder. In six months I was promoted, and a year later I was given my first management position. I was breaking new ground as the first female technical manager in the company.

My plan until now was not to marry—I was set totally on my career. That is until I fell in love with my best friend. This was the first major area in my life where God changed my plans and my heart for His. When we married, my husband became the biggest blessing in my life, next to Christ.

Before marriage, we had agreed that children would not be in our future. I felt that I had no maternal instincts, and I had no desire to be tied down by children or to sacrifice my career aspirations.

At work, I was promoted to upper management. My job required very long hours, usually 60 or more hours a week, but I did not mind. I loved the travel and benefits. My husband and I both worked and played very hard. I was on the fast track , with a plethora of management training experiences, and some of the best, most visible projects in the company. I even went back to get my MBA, better equipping myself for upper management. Soon, I was responsible for managing the entire New Products Group, tripling my initial salary. And from there I went on to become Marketing Product Manager. I honestly felt life could not be much better.

My husband and I were involved in a great church and a wonderful small group. Our friends in this group began praying that we would become open to having children. We just laughed them off, but after several years, our position weakened. Both of us began to independently wonder if we had made the right decision. Together we decided to allow God to make that decision for us.

My doctor assured us that our chances of becoming pregnant right away were slim. I was over 30, in a stressful job, and had been on the pill for seven years. In my heart, I was convinced that children were not part of God's plan for us. Having children would severely hamper our ministry in the church, not to mention our ability to financially give out of our lucrative salaries.

Then, one month after I went off the pill I got pregnant. And that is when the wrestling began. The only person I could go to was God. I did not know another woman who had faced the choices I was about to have to make. I knew some women who had quit work, but none with the positions and opportunities I had at the time, and certainly none with the same drive, desire, and love for their work.

In my heart I knew I couldn't care for a child and carry the job. It was hard enough fitting in my husband as it was. And so I wrestled. On the one hand in my mind were my wonderful memories of a childhood and teen years in which my mom was available to me. But on the other hand there were the finances. I was supplying over half our income. The thought of leaving my salary and more importantly my position of power, authority, and influence for diapers, spit up, and baby food was almost overwhelming. And what about fellow women with high aspirations at work? Would they see me as having let them down, as a traitor?

We happened to be in our third year of teaching a Sunday School class of four-year-olds. Roy and I had become amazed at how evident it was to us which kids had moms at home. Their behaviors and attitudes were, almost without fail, an outward sign of this. Then, as I studied the Scriptures it seemed that everywhere I turned God was speaking to me on this issue. I simply could not escape it. After months of wrestling with the decision, I finally came to grips with His inaudible voice speaking to my heart. My career would have to go.

Once the decision was made, my biggest battle began. I felt little support from within the company. But the real battle was inside myself. Many days after meetings in which I delivered an impressive presentation or sold an idea or strategy, I would flee to my office and close my door to hide the rush of oncoming tears. I had never been a crier, but giving up on almost ten years of success in a career I had always dreamed of was like losing part of ME.

Knowing my deep need, God planted a wonderful Christian woman in my group at work. She became my constant encourager and affirmer. At my toughest moments she seemed to be there with the words I needed. Then a second young woman also entered my life as an encourager. In one of my darkest moments when I was not sure I could really make the break, I closed my office door for another teary session. Then the phone rang. It was this woman with just the right words and a book to send.

The day the baby was born, something happened in me. I felt an instantaneous, overwhelming love for this little boy that I did not know I was capable of, and a nurturing spirit began to grow within me. I soon began to realize new depths of God's incredible love for me as His child.

Two weeks later I went to clean out my office. Stopping by to see my boss, he reminded me that I was slated to receive my next promotion in six months, a promotion in which I would receive an incredible pay increase, a company car, a home computer, and all sorts of benefits. This was the position I had worked so hard for so many years to achieve.

But as I sat in my boss's office it was abundantly clear. Our son was more valuable than all of that. Turning down the offer one last time, I said my good-byes. My boss turned to me and said, "Margaret, you are making the right decision." And he gave me his blessing.

In the years since, God has performed "heart surgery" on me. He really knows the deepest desires of our hearts far better than we do. I am busier today than ever, involved in more challenges than I could have dreamed of, and enjoying my children more than I ever imagined could be possible. My problem has not been boredom. Rather, it has been having *so many opportunities* that I have to constantly make sure I am not shortchanging my family.

It has not all been easy. I struggled with my "importance" for a while, feeling compelled to make sure that new acquaintances knew I had been "somebody" before I came home. It took time to deal with my lost identity, and find my new one. I have realized that God cares far more about what He does *in* me, rather than *through* me. That's a hard lesson for a Type A, driven, over-achiever.

At times people have commented that I have given up so much—finances, position, status, etc., and how hard that must be. It really is not that difficult to do, because when God calls you to do it, He enables you to do it. I believe in God's economy: loss equals gain. What a great God we have who can break through the most determined of human plans to give us the real desires of our heart.

Perhaps the most significant discovery about my children in the last few years has been how much they really do need me. Recently Roy and I accepted a call to full-time ministry. For several months we decided to trade responsibilities for the kids on a 50/50 basis. But not long into our plan, our six-year-old son began giving us discipline problems, and our three-year-old became exceedingly clingy and whiny. It began to sink in that even though our kids were getting more than the normal amount of parent time, they were getting far less of Mommy time. Even though my husband is the world's greatest Dad and is nurturing and affectionate with our boys, Daddy is just not Mommy. As soon as we went back to our primary roles, the boys quickly returned to their normal selves.

But perhaps the most significant discovery I have made about myself occurred only a few weeks ago, at the funeral of a good friend. This man had been a wonderful husband, father, and businessman. And he had lived an extraordinary life. Someone got up and referred to him as being "just an ordinary man." That bothered me a great deal.

I certainly would never want anyone to say that about me. I knew God used ordinary people, but this was not an ordinary person. I have striven all my life to be different, better than ordinary. As a child, I chose the most difficult projects, always feeling I needed to do more and better than everyone else. I even chose to play the oboe in our school band just because I was told it was the most difficult instrument to master.

But as the days have gone by, God has been speaking to my heart. I have begun to realize that He really does just want ordinary people. In fact, He will be able to use me in greater ways as I become more ordinary, allowing more of His power to flow through me to do extraordinary things.

And so that has become my highest goal: to become an ordinary woman through whom God can do His extraordinary work.

Though she may not realize it, Margaret is already that woman. Why? Because she has already made the extraordinary choices that God has asked of her. And extraordinary choices always lead to extraordinary living.

William Wilberforce was discouraged. After years of pushing in Britain's Parliament for the abolition of slavery, he felt he could not go on. And then a letter arrived. It was from an old, dear friend. The friend had written with trembling hands from his deathbed:

> "Unless God has raised you up for this very thing, you will be worn out by the opposition of men and devils. But if God be for you, who can be against you? Are all of them stronger than God? Oh, be not weary of well-doing! Go on, in the name of God and in the power of His might, till even American slavery shall vanish away before it."

Wilberforce felt his resolve return with the encouragement of these words. His friend died six days later, but Wilberforce fought for forty-five more years and in 1833, three days before his own death, saw slavery abolished in Britain.

It was no accident that the name of Wilberforce's friend was John Wesley. Wesley, the child saved from the towering inferno. Wesley, the man who went on to lead the Wesleyan Revival. Little did the two men who saved Wesley that night know that their choice would go on to impact their nation, much less an entire nation of slaves over a century later.

Do I hear a woman saying, "But what can one woman do?"

The answer is, *more than you will ever know.*

She can choose to follow Christ, she can choose to stand alone, she can choose to be accountable and hold others accountable, she can choose to love her children and her husband, she can choose to care for her home. And in so doing, she can taste of God's best in this life.

And in the end, one woman and the choices she makes can go on to impact this world for centuries to come.

N O T E S

CHAPTER ONE

1. Chuck Colson, as cited in *Focus on the Family Magazine*, (January 1994), 14.

2. William J. Bennett, *The Index of Leading Cultural Indicators 1* (March 1993), 1-4.

3. Barbara Dafoe Whitehead, "Dan Quayle Was Right," *Atlantic*, (April 1993), 4.

4. Joe Klein, "Whose Values?" *Newsweek*, (8 June 1992), 20.

5. Whitehead, "Dan Quayle Was Right," 1, 13.

6. Ibid., i-ii.

7. Maggie Gallagher, *Enemies of Eros* (Chicago: Bonus Books, Inc., 1989), 12-13.

8. William H. Chafe, *The Paradox of Change: American Women in the Twentieth Century* (New York: Oxford University Press, 1991), 224-25.

9. Gallagher, *Enemies of Eros*, 16.

10. Klein, "Whose Values?" 19.

11. Ibid., 20.

12. Ibid., 22.

13. "Sorokin: Prophet of Family Decay," *The Family in America* 8, no. 4 (April 1993), 3.

14. Carl Wilson, *Our Dance Has Turned to Death* , Worldwide Discipleship Association, (Fayetteville, Ga.: Renewal Publishing Co., 1979), 12.

CHAPTER TWO

1. William Manchester, "A World Lit Only by Change," *U. S. News and World Report*, (25 October 1993), 6.

2. "1933-1993, The Years that Remade the World and the Forces that Could Remake It Again," *U. S. News and World Report*, (25 October 1993), 2-3.

CHAPTER THREE

1. Carl Holliday, *Woman's Life in Colonial Days* (New York, N.Y.: Frederick Ungar Publishing Co., 1922), 95.

2. Francis B. Cogen, *All American Girl: The Ideal of Real Womanhood in Mid-Nineteenth-Century America* (Athens, Ga.: University of Georgia Press, 1989), 214.

3. Midge Yearly, *"Early American Women," The Atlanta Journal and Constitution"*, (17 October, 1976), as cited by Wilson, *Our Dance Is Turned to Death*, 57.

4. Cogen, *All American Girl*, 111.

5. Holliday, *Women's Life in Colonial Days*, 108.

6. Cogen, *All American Girl*, 250.

7. Linda Grant DePauw and Conover Hunt, *Remember the Ladies: Women in America, 1750-1815* (Plymouth, Mass.: The Pilgrim Society, 1976), 35.

8. Robert A. Caro, *The Years of Lyndon Johnson: The Path to Power* (New York, N.Y.: Alfred A. Knopf, 1982), 504-11.

9. DePauw and Hunt, *Remember the Ladies*, 48.

10. Holliday, *Women's Life in Colonial Days*, 111.

11. DePauw and Hunt, *Remember the Ladies*, 89-93.

12. Ibid., 134.

13. Ibid.

14. Ibid., 96.

15. Ibid.

16. Ibid., 99.

17. Ibid., 31.

18. Holliday, *Women's Life in Colonial Days*, 134.

19. Ibid.

20. Annegret S. Ogden, *The Great American Housewife: From Helpmeet to Wage Earner, 1776-1986* (Westport, Conn.: Greenwood Press, 1986), 11ff.

21. Ibid.

22. Ibid.

23. DePauw and Hunt, *Remember the Ladies*, 33, 97.

24. Arthur Calhoun, *The Social History of the American Family*, vol. 1, *Colonial Period* (New York, N.Y.: Barnes and Noble, 1960), 75-76.

25. DePauw and Hunt, *Remember the Ladies*, 33, 97.

26. Ogden, *The Great American Housewife*, 11.

27. Norman Cousins, *In God We Trust* (New York, N.Y.: Harper and Row, 1958), 48.

28. Edward M. Deems, *Holy Days and Holidays* (New York, N.Y.: Funk and Wagnalls, 1901), 340-344.

29. Wilson, *Our Dance Has Turned to Death*, 7.

30. Calhoun, *Social History of the American Family*, 72, 74.

31. DePauw and Hunt, *Remember the Ladies*, 11.

32. Carroll Smith-Rosenberg, *Disorderly Conduct: Visions of Gender in Victorian America* (New York, N.Y.: Oxford University Press, 1985), 17.

33. Cogen, *All American Girl*, 3, 10.

34. Holliday, *Women's Life in Colonial Days*, 139.

35. Cogen, *All American Girl*, 146.

CHAPTER FOUR

1. *World Book Encyclopedia* (Chicago, Ill.: World Book, Inc., 1949), 9:3752.

2. Ibid.

3. Leslie Parker Hume and Karen M. Offen, *Victorian Women: A Documentary Account of Women's Lives in Nineteenth-Century England, France, and the United States* (Stanford, Calif.: Stanford University Press, 1981), 2-4.

4. Glenna Matthews, *Just a Housewife: The Rise and Fall of Domesticity in America* (New York, N.Y.: Oxford University Press, 1987), 21-26.

5. Hume and Offen, *Victorian Women*, 274ff and Matthews, 31.

6. Matthews, *Just a Housewife*, 34-35.

7. Ibid., 6, 30.

8. Ibid., 19-34, 46.

9. Hume and Offen, *Victorian Women*, 250.

10. Dr. Frank Pittman, Ph.D., "Fathers and Sons: What It Takes to be a Man," *Psychology Today*, (September-October 1993), 52-54.

11. *World Book Encyclopedia*, 9:3752-62.

12. Pittman, "Fathers and Sons," 53.

13. Wilson, *Our Dance Has Turned to Death*, 54.

14. Pittman, "Fathers and Sons," 52-53.

CHAPTER FIVE

1. Hume and Offen, *Victorian Women* 274ff and Matthews, 31.

2. *World Book Encyclopedia*, 9:3752-62.

3. *World Book Encyclopedia*, 18:8921

4. Hume and Offen, *Victorian Women*, 4-5, 50ff.

5. *World Book Encyclopedia*, 9:3752-62.

6. Matthews, *Just a Housewife*, 92-93.

7. Hume and Offen, *Victorian Women*, 6-11.

8. Matthews, *Just a Housewife*, 92-93.

9. Ibid.

10. Ibid.

11. Hume and Offen, *Victorian Women*, 94ff.

12. Matthews, *Just a Housewife*, 32-33.

13. Ibid., 72ff.

14. Wilson, *Our Dance Has Turned to Death*, 7.

15. Matthews, *Just a Housewife*, 117ff.

16. Ibid.

17. Ibid., 127-29.

18. Ibid., 131ff.

19. Betty Friedan, *The Feminine Mystique*, twentieth anniversary ed. (New York, N.Y.: W. W. Norton and Co., Inc., 1963), 26.

CHAPTER SIX

1. Matthews, *Just a Housewife*, 216-17.

2. Lois W. Banner, *Women in Modern America: A Brief History* (New York, N.Y.: Harcourt Brace Jovanovich, Inc., 1974), 40.

3. Ibid., 214-16.

4. Ibid., 86-89.

5. Jane Gross, "Does She Speak for Today's Women?," *New York Times Magazine*, (1 March 1992), 38.

6. *Current Biography Yearbook, 1992* , 284.

7. Gross, "Does She Speak for Today's Women?," 54.

8. Mary A. Kassian, *The Feminist Gospel* (Wheaton, Ill.: Crossway Books, 1992), 59.

9. Ibid., 61-63.

10. Steven W. Mosher, *A Mother's Ordeal* (Fort Worth, Tex.: Harcourt Brace Jovanovich, Inc., 1993).

11. Kassian, *The Feminist Gospel*, 63.

12. Gallagher, *Enemies of Eros*, 8-9.

13. Alex Taylor, III and Barbara Hetzer, "Why Women Managers Are Bailing Out," *Fortune*, (18 August 1986).

14. Felice N. Schwartz, "Management Women and New Facts of Life," *Harvard Business Review*, no. 1 (January-February, 1989): 65-76.

15. Nan Stone, "Mother's Work," Harvard Business Review, no. 5 (September-October, 1989): 50-60.

16. G. Borger, "Behind the Wellesley Flap," *U. S. News and World Report*, (28 May 1990), 31-32.

C H A P T E R S E V E N S

1. Kassian, *The Feminist Gospel*, (Wheaton, Ill.: Crossway Books, 1992), 227.

2. Richard N. Ostling, "The Second Reformation," *Time*, (23 November 1992), 53-54.

3. "Christian Conference Takes Feminist Slant," *Dallas Morning News*, (13 November 1993).

4. "Goddess Groups Attract Female Faithful," *Dallas Morning News*, (15 January 1993).

5. William Hendriksen, *Exposition of the Gospel According to Matthew*, of *New Testament Commentary*, (Grand Rapids, Mich.: Baker Book House, 1973), 354.

C H A P T E R E I G H T

1. Bradford Angier, *How to Stay Alive in the Woods* (New York, N.Y.: Macmillan Publishing Co., 1956), 271.

2. Ibid., 273-285.

3. Ibid., 270.

4. Tom Brown, Jr. with Brandt Morgan, *Tom Brown's Field Guide to Wilderness Survival* (New York, N.Y.: Berkley Books, 1983), 11.

5. Jason Lehman, used by permission.

C H A P T E R N I N E

1. M. Scott Peck, *The Road Less Traveled* (New York, N.Y.: Simon and Schuster, 1978), 15.

2. John Haggai, *Be Careful What You Call Impossible* (Eugene, Ore.: Harvest House Publishers, 1979), 89.

3. James Dobson, *When God Doesn't Make Sense* (Wheaton, Ill.: Tyndale House Publishers, 1993).

4. Martin Lloyd Jones, *Spiritual Depression* (Grand Rapids, Mich.: Baker Book House, 1965).

5. *Leadership* (fall, 1991), 45.

CHAPTER TEN

1. Eugene H. Peterson, *Working the Angles*, (Grand Rapids, Mich.: William B. Eerdmans Publishing Co., 1987), 55.

2. Ibid., 52.

3. A. C. Hervey, *The Pulpit Commentary on Thessalonians, Timothy, Titus, Philemon* (London: Anson D. F. Randolph and Company, n.d.), 7.

CHAPTER ELEVEN

1. John Piper, *Desiring God* (Portland, Ore.: Multnomah Press, 1986), 19.

CHAPTER TWELVE

1. Linda Barry, "How Kids Grow," *Newsweek*, special edition, (summer 1991), 70.

CHAPTER THIRTEEN

1. Jill Bauer, *From "I Do" to "I'll Sue"* (New York, N.Y.: Plume Publishers, 1993), 57.

2. Steve Farrar, *Point Man* (Portland, Ore.: Multnomah Press, 1990), 58.

3. Ibid., 59-60.

4. Ibid., 62.

5. Stu Weber, *Tender Warrior* (Sisters, Ore.: Multnomah Books, 1993).

CHAPTER FOURTEEN

1. Nancy Gibbs and Jeanne McDowell, "How to Revive a Revolution," *Time*, (9 March 1992), 57.

2. Mary Renault, *The Bull from the Sea* (New York, N.Y.: Pantheon, 1962), 117.

3. Irene Claremont de Castillejo, *Knowing Woman* (New York, N.Y.: Harper & Row, 1973), 110.

4. Neil R. Lightfoot, "The Role of Women: New Testament Perspectives" (Memphis, Tenn., Student Association Press, Harding Graduate School of Religion), 11.

5. Ibid., 15.

CHAPTER FIFTEEN

1. Susan Feeney, "Women's Rights Advocates Temper Praise for Clinton," *Dallas Morning News*, (13 July 1993).

2. Loraine O'Connell, "Frankly Speaking: How Blunt Can You Be These Days,"*Dallas Morning News*, (18 August 1993).

3. Robert Knille, *As I Was Saying: A Chesterton Reader* (Grand Rapids, Mich.: Eerdmans, 1985), 120.

4. Chuck Colson, as cited by *Focus on the Family*, (January 1994), 13.

5. Levi Coffin, *Reminiscences of Levi Coffin* (New York, N.Y.: Ano Press and the *New York Times*, 1968).

6. Ibid., 13.

7. Ibid., 126-28.

8. Matthews, *Just a Housewife*, 50.

9. Ibid., 57.

C H A P T E R   S I X T E E N

1   Jeff Giles, "The Poet of Alienation," *Newsweek*, (18 April 1994), 47.

2. Steve Farrar, *If I'm Not Tarzan, and My Wife Isn't Jane, Then What Are We Doing In the Jungle?* (Sisters, Ore.: Multnomah Press, 1991), 103.

3. Leon Wood, *A Survey of Israel's History* (Grand Rapids, Mich.: Zondervan, 1970), 194-200.

4. Alfred Edersheim, *Old Testament Bible History*, (Grand Rapids, Mich.: William B. Eerdmans Publishing Co., 1975), 40.

5. Doug Sherman and William Hendricks, *Your Work Matters to God* (Colorado Springs, Co.: NavPress, 1987), 19.

C H A P T E R   S E V E N T E E N

1. Joanna L. Stratton, *Pioneer Women, Voices from the Kansas Frontier*, (New York, N.Y.: Simon and Schuster, 1981), 102-06.

2. Roger von Oech, *A Whack on the Side of the Head*, (New York, N.Y.: Warner Books, 1983), 6-7.

Study Guide

≈≈

Lesson One

Read: Towering Inferno (Chapter 1).

1. What is your definition of a *home*?

2. What *is* this inferno about which the author writes? What has caused it to burn out of control?

3. How has your life been touched by the "towering inferno"? Did your childhood home suffer from the inferno? Has the inferno reached your neighborhood? Your church? Your own home?

4. How is a family like an atom? Based on this picture, how would you define a *family*?

5. Do you agree with the author that our nation is in crisis? Do you feel the same sense of urgency? How do you tend to respond to crisis?

6. Why do you think our choices as women are so pivotal for the home? Have you already made some choices that have proven to be pivotal in the lives of your husband and children? Describe them.

7. Read Exodus 20:5-6. What effect did the choices of your grandmother and your mother have upon your own life? The lives of your children? How did their choices impact the lives of those around them?

8. According to Psalm 68:5-6, what kind of hope does God give to the husbandless and fatherless? To those who are lonely?

9. Read James 1:5-8. According to this passage, why is it so important for women to be anchored deep into God's wisdom? What does James say will happen to those who are not?

10. Read James 3:15-17. what are the two kinds of wisdom? Describe them.

11. Read 1 Corinthians 1:19-20, and 3:19-20. What does God say about the wise and clever of this world?

   How does God say that He will demonstrate His great wisdom (1 Corinthians 1:26-29, 1 Corinthians 2:4-5)?

   Perhaps you consider yourself to be ordinary—not particularly "mighty," "noble," or "wise according to the flesh." Why would God choose to work through ordinary people (1 Corinthians 1:29)?

12. What does Colossians 1:15-17 tell us about our Creator? Of whom is Paul speaking in this verse (look back at verse 13, or forward at verse 19)? What else does He do (verse 17)?

   What are the implications of these verses for our marriages and homes?

13. What does God promise us regarding the failures and mistakes of our past? Read Romans 8:28-29.

   According to this passage, what is God's ultimate goal for our lives? How can He use our failures to accomplish such a high goal?

Thought or Action Point for this lesson:

Lesson Two

Read: The Tide that Blinds (Chapter 2), and Hub in the Middle of the Wheel (Chapter 3).

---

1. Historically, as the home has gone, so has gone woman. Why do you think this is true?

2. Think back on a woman's world in pre-industrial times. Specifically:

   • How was she able to use her skills and abilities?

   • What kind of relationship did she have with her husband?

   • How did she influence her children? Society at large?

   • What would you say were her deepest struggles?

   • What gave her a sense of significance and worth?

3. What is the single biggest change for women since "pre-flood" days in your own estimation? Why do you think this is so?

   What has been the greatest change for men? For children?

4. What do you think is the difference between independence and *inter*dependence?

   How do you see these two ways of living in your own family?

   Does your family demonstrate more independence or interdependence?

   What forces in our culture fight against interdependence in families?

5. Were you surprised by what you read regarding life in "pre-flood" days? What surprised you most?

6. Contrast the role of Scripture in pre-flood times to the role of Scripture in culture today.

   What would you say is the plumb line (or basis) for governing society today?

7. What do you think of when you hear the word "feminist"? Is this a positive or negative term and why?

8. Can you recall a recent news report in which the mainstream media clearly slanted the public perspective?

Do you feel that the "political feminist" reporting of history has altered the true story of women? Why or why not?

9. Which time of history would you choose to live in—colonial days, or today? Why? What are some reasons that today can be an exciting time in which to live?

10. Read Isaiah 40:21-31 and 46:9-11. What do these verses tell you about God: His power? His moral character? His self-sufficiency? His infinite knowledge? His justice? His eternal nature? His mercy and goodness? His sovereignty?

Thought or Action Point for this lesson:

Lesson Three

Read: White Water Rapids (Chapter 4), and Niagara Falls (Chapter 5).

TIME LINE

FLASH FLOOD: FIRST WAVE		SECOND WAVE	THIRD WAVE
1700's	1815	1870's (WW's I &II, Depression)	1950's
Colonial Days			
	Industrial Revolution		
		Rise of Technology & Science	
			Rise of Modern Feminism

1. What most impressed you as you read about the flood of change?

2. Looking at the above time line, review how the home slipped from its central position.

   How would you say that the "quality of life" for women and children has improved during this time? How has it regressed?

3. How do you think the Industrial Revolution ultimately impacted the family you grew up in?

   Did you grow up in a father-absent or mother-absent household? If so, did such absence personally effect you as a child?

   Were your parents intimately involved in your development and training? Did they "know your heart"?

4. The devaluing of home in our society has influenced all of us, whether we are single career women, single mothers, or married women. How has the home's removal from the mainstream of society affected you personally?
   How has the understanding of recent history helped to explain your present struggles?

5. What impact has the Industrial Revolution had in your marriage and home today?

Would you describe your home now as father or mother absent?

Would you say that your family is more "fragmented" than it is "together"?

What are some creative ways that your family, or families you know, have overcome the fragmentation that results from work demands and activities?

6. What insights have these chapters given you regarding your father and the men of his generation?

   How have these chapters helped you understand your husband, or other men around you?

   How has it helped you understand the needs of our sons? Our daughters?

7. What has been the impact of the Industrial Revolution on the community around you? On the church you attend?

   How can the church become more involved with families in need? How can it help to restore the value of the home?

8. The author discusses five ways women in the mid-twentieth century began to suffer in their sense of influence, purpose and self-esteem:

   • The central roles of women in the home (except for child rearing) were *taken over by society*.

   • The high value of *serving roles lost out* to roles that drove a technological society.

   • *"Work"* in our language became synonymous with *"paid work."*

   • Women became *consumers* rather than *producers*.

   • The *de-skilling of work* in the home decreased the challenge of home work.

   Which of these factors are "hot buttons" for you. Why?

9. Was your life effected by the feminist revolution in your growing up years? Do you empathize with the midcentury feminist cry to be "liberated from the home"? Explain.

10. Did Darwin's influence upon modern day views of men and women surprise you?

    How has this view damaged the relationships of men and women and destroyed the "teamwork" mentality?

    Read Philippians 2:1-4. What attitudes does Paul urge us to have which directly oppose "selfish ambition and vain conceit" (vs. 3) and "looking out for number one" (vs. 4)?

11. Do you ever find yourself wanting to prove your worth? In what ways?

    Has the devaluation of the home colored the significance you feel in your role as wife and mother?

    What skills are you unable to express in your home today that you might have expressed in pre-flood times?

    What aspects of your womanhood are denied in your working world?

12. Do you tend to accept the propositions of science without question? Which would you say that you question more—the scientist or Scripture?

13. Read Matthew 7:24-27. In the midst of such bad news for the home, is there any hope for the future?

    According to this passage, what foundation can weather any revolution, storm, or sudden change?

    What (or who) is the rock—the higher ground?

    What must we do if we wish to build upon the rock?

Thought or Action Point for this lesson:

Lesson Four

Read: *Truth or Consequences (Chapter 6), and Roots (Chapter 7).*

1. Did you grow up with the message that "You can have it all"? What was (or is) the sentiment of your college, or university? Who gave you this message primarily? Did it motivate you? Overwhelm you? Explain.

   Is the idea that "You can have it all" appealing to you? If so, why?

   Have you seen the deception of this lie in your life? In the lives of others?

2. What truths has the modern feminist movement articulated well? What needs has feminism sought to address among modern women?

   Do you think the church has addressed these needs?

3. Feminism in its purest form means "advocate of women." In its effort to meet the need, how has modern feminism actually become a *destructive* force for women?

4. Of the influences listed below, which one(s) do you think touches your life— and the lives of your family—to the greatest degree?

   • The media

   • The academia

   • Friends, peers

   • Language, terminology

   Think of three ways—*without lecturing*—that we can teach our children to become discerning regarding influences in the media...In school...Among their peers. Be specific....

5. The evolving lie, "You can have *some* of it all," is much more subtle.

   What is *right* about the statement "I'm OK—my kids and husband are OK"? What is *wrong* with it?

   Read Matthew 6:33. What does this verse imply about true happiness and fulfillment?

6. The author outlines three tests for using Scripture to expose a lie. They are:

(1) Know the truth; (2) Observe the deeds of those who teach; (3) Look for the hook.

The first step is to "know the truth intimately." Read John 8:31-32. According to verse 31, *how* can we know the truth?

What do you think Christ meant when he told the disciples to *abide in His word*?

7. A second test is to "observe the deeds of those who teach a given philosophy." Their deeds will reveal whether they are from God. Read Matthew 7:15-23.

How does Jesus say that we can recognize a false prophet? Can a non-believer do good things? What is the difference between his good deeds and the good deeds of a believer?

8. Those who embrace God's word also embrace God. If God's primary attribute is holiness, what impact should that have upon those who claim to be His followers? (See Matthew 5:48, 1 Corinthians 3:16-17, and 1 Peter 1:15-16.)

What does it mean to be *holy*?

In light of God's holiness, how are we to respond to the modern cry for "tolerance" of immoral lifestyles and choices? What inevitably happens to a love that compromises holiness?

When we pursue truth, we become more holy; when we pursue deception, we are drawn down a path of ungodliness and sin. Were you surprised that feminist philosophy has led many of its well-meaning followers towards immorality and witchcraft?

9. According to the author, the "slippery slope" begins with *struggle* over biblical teaching, then moves to *questioning*, and then finally ends with the *rewriting* and eventual *abandonment* of Scripture.

Review the contrast between Scripture and feminist philosophy. Are there certain biblical teachings with which you have found yourself struggling?

Do you ever feel guilty when you struggle over a teaching of Scripture, or begin to question God? Why do you think it would be unhealthy never to struggle or question? What kind of struggle leads to deeper faith? Where can our struggle take a wrong turn?

What are some practical positive steps that you can take when you struggle and find yourself questioning God? (See Ephesians 4:17-23 for guidance.)

10. The final test of using Scripture to expose a lie is to "look for the hook." While feminism has spoken some truth, what has been the "hook" inside of the feminist philosophy?

11. Can you relate to the author's temptation to buy into the lie? Satan tempts modern women in the same way as he tempted Eve, using the following rational:

(1) You can have it all. Not only so, but you *deserve* to have it all.

(2) Look at all the fun and happiness that you are missing! (Is life hard? I'll show you the way out. Other women are much happier than you are. They have more money, an easier lifestyle, and greater fulfillment. If you aren't careful, life will just pass you by.)

(3) God cannot be trusted. He does not really love you or have your best interests in mind.

Have you experienced these enticements? How?

12. According to Matthew 6:33, how does God answer the lies, "You can have it all," and "You can have some of it all"?

What do you think it means to seek God first? What does it mean to seek His kingdom?

What do you think Jesus meant when He said, "...all these things will be added unto you."? (For help, look at the previous verse, Matthew 6:32.)

13. Do you agree that every choice exacts a price?

In Matthew 7:13-14, Jesus speaks of a narrow road and a broad road. What do you think is the narrow road today? The broad road? Have you ever felt that you are on a narrow road?

What good choices have you made that have carried a price? What blessings have you received from making these choices? What is the promised destination of the narrow road?

Thought or Action Point for this lesson:

Lesson Five

Read: Blazing a New Trail (Chapter 8), and ...But God (Chapter 9).

1. Do you agree with the author that modern Christian women must blaze a new trail? If so, does this perspective excite you, challenge you, or overwhelm you?

2. Read Psalm 46:1-3 and 10. The first verse can be literally translated, "God is our refuge and strength, abundantly available for help in tight spots." The author has suggested that modern women are in a tight spot. Would you agree?

   When you are in a tight spot, where do you typically first turn for help?

   The psalmist describes a catastrophic picture in verses 2 and 3. The events of our lives can seem just as catastrophic. What does the psalmist urge us to do in such times, according to verse 10?

3. Our world is full of noise. It is little wonder, then, that "God speaks loudest in the quiet places," as one person has put it. This is why we often refer to time alone with God and His word as a "quiet time." Do you find it difficult to find a quiet place or time in which to "be still and know God"?

   What roadblocks in your life are preventing you from time alone with Christ?

4. Would you like to become more consistent in this area of your life? If so, write down a *time* of day and a *place* in which you can begin to "abide" on a regular basis.

   What is a reasonable goal for you to have in terms of time alone with God? (Be realistic. If ten to fifteen minutes, three days a week is realistic for you, then begin there. The key is to set a goal and implement it for the next four weeks. Then you will be well on your way towards establishing a new lifestyle of abiding in God's word.)

   If you have young children, what are some creative ways that you can "abide" in the Word?

   Consider establishing accountability among yourselves throughout the duration of your small group. You may need to ask one another, "How did you do this week? What did you learn? What kept you from following through? How can you do better next week?"

5. Read Matthew 6:26-27, and verse 34. How do you think attitude can make a difference between conquering a challenge and becoming defeated by it?

   How can another person's positive or negative attitude affect your own attitude?

6. Are you a "one-day-at-a-time" type of woman?

   Why do you think it is so hard for the achiever, goal-oriented woman to have this attitude? What do you see as your greatest personal challenge in the road up ahead? How will attitude make or break you?

7. What are the attitudes that often tend to take over in the difficulty or panic of the moment?

   When things get tough, what is your natural tendency? (Do you tend to fear? To be anxious? To want to be "in control" of the present? To be discontented? Dissatisfied? Negative about the future? Do you need to be able to see what is around the bend?)

8. According to Philippians 4:11, Paul "learned" contentment. Is it possible for a person to change a natural *habit* of fear, anxiety, or discontentment to a *habit* of trust? How? (Look back at Paul's words in 4:6-8.)

9. Is there someone in your life who has modeled the principle of "living one day at a time"? How did it make you feel to be around such a person?

10. The author outlines four truths about life, and four "greater truths" about God:

    1. Life is hard...but God is good.
    2. Life is unpredictable...but God is sovereign.
    3. Life is unfair...but God is just.
    4. Life is short...but God is eternal.

    How has your own journey been a testimony to these four hard truths of life?

    Which one of these greater truths has meant the most to you? How have you seen this greater truth of God in the midst of your hardships? (Take as much time as you need on this question, for you will encourage one another by your life experiences.)

11. Is there a particular adversity in your life from which a "rose" has come? How long was it before you saw the blessing that came out of that hardship?

12. Do you find it difficult to let others, including your children, suffer?

    How has suffering built character in your life, or in the life of someone you know?

13. According to Romans 5:3-5, Paul gives us several blessings that eventually come into the believer's life through adversity. What are they?

    According to the author, hope is necessary for maintaining perspective in life. How do you think suffering can produce hope (see verses 4-5)?

Thought or Action Point of this lesson:

Lesson Six

Read: A Woman's VIPs (Chapter 10).

For this study, you will need a few sheets of paper and a pencil or pen.

1. Think through your life goals. Make a list of your five top goals (you can certainly list more). If you became a Christian as an adult, how has becoming a believer changed your life goals?

    Have you seen a dream or goal demolished through an unexpected circumstance in your life?

2. What perspective on priorities did you have going into this chapter (a ranking system, a stretching rubberband, other)? Did the author shed new light on the way you think about priorities?

3. Draw a circle, filling the open space inside with large letters: RELATIONSHIP TO GOD. Then, over these large letters, draw in and label the other priorities of your life, like pieces of a pie. Your life-pie will be different from everyone else's pie. Which priorities are pulling and stretching you most right now?

4. Have you, or someone close to you, experienced "burnout"? What brought it on? How can a clear sense of priorities prevent burnout?

    What could easily lead to *imbalance* in the lives of the following women: a career woman, a mother at home with young children, a mother of school-aged children, a widow or divorced mom, a gifted leader, a willing servant?

5. A woman can find herself on a particular path of life that she may have never anticipated. She may be single, when she expected to marry. She may be childless, when she expected to bear children. She may be divorced, when she expected to remain married for life. If you are on such an unexpected path, how has this changed or affected your priorities?

6. Every woman passes through various seasons of life. What would you say are the typical seasons in a woman's life? (The seasons will vary depending on her path in life.) In which season are you, and how does this tend to impact your priorities?

7. What do you think have been the most difficult choices you have faced in your life? What made them so difficult?

8. What happens when a woman is faced with choices in life without a clear sense of priorities? What difference do clear priorities make when we face the tough choices of life? Can you give an example?

9. Were you surprised by any of the top priorities of Titus 2:3-5? Which priority surprised you most?

10. Looking at your priority pie, do each of the priorities of Titus 2 touch your life in some way? How?

11. Look carefully at the original Greek meanings of the words in this Titus 2 passage. Do the original meanings lend new light or insight for you?

12. Which aspect from the background of this book of Titus was most helpful to you?

13. Read 2 Timothy 2:15. According to what you read in this chapter, what do you think it means to "handle accurately the word of truth"?

Has this chapter changed your own approach to interpreting the Bible? Explain.

Out of all of the principles of interpreting Scripture explained in this chapter (such as noting author, audience, and purpose for the book, original language, historical and cultural background, immediate context, context of all of Scripture), there is *one* principle every Christian can apply, using nothing but his Bible. *Every Christian can consider the immediate context.* Why do you think immediate context is so important in this particular passage?

Thought or Action Point of this lesson:

Lesson Seven

Read: VIP #1: Maturity (Chapter 11), and VIP #2: Mentoring (Chapter 12).

1. Read Matthew 18:35-40. This lawyer asked Jesus to tell him the single greatest commandment. But Jesus gave him *two*. What do you think Jesus meant when He said that the second commandment was "like unto the first"? Which of these commandments is most important (see verse 40)? Explain.

   Which key relationship does the first commandment involve? Which key relationship does the second involve?

   Which commandment most relates to the VIP of Maturity? Which most relates to the other four VIPs?

   Who is your "neighbor"? Which of your "neighbors" is found in Titus 2:3-5?

2. According to our passage in Titus, what are the marks of a mature woman? Make a list of these traits, and then list the contrasting traits of the popular woman of our world today.

3. A mature woman has learned that respect always outlives popularity. How have you seen this truth borne out in life?

4. If maturity is developed through a one-on-one relationship with Christ, can a non-Christian woman be a "mature" woman? Why or why not?

5. Are you presently "swimming upstream" as a result of choices you are making today? Do you find it hard to stand alone among your friends, your neighbors, your family? How do you feel when they do not understand your choices?

   How can you stand alone in the world, without "standing weird"?

6. Do you think there are times when God purposefully allows us to stand alone? How does standing alone strengthen our relationship to Christ?

7. While the first commandment of Jesus relates to our relationship to God, the second commandment relates to our relationship to one another. Does it seem contradictory to you that we must be willing to stand alone, yet, as believers, we still need one another?

266   M A R Y   F A R R A R

How does fellowship with other Christian women equip us to better stand alone? Explain.

8. Who have been your "mentors," or healthy role models, in life? How did they mentor you?

9. What kind of relationship did (and do) you have with your mother? Did she positively or negatively impact your life? In what ways?

   What are some ways that a woman can overcome negative mentoring relationships?

10. What do you think an "independent person" might need to overcome when it comes to mentoring? Is it possible to be skillful in life without help?

   What do you think a "people-person" might need to overcome? Is it possible to become too dependent on a mentor?

11. Do you feel a need for help and guidance from a mature woman in Christ?

   What are some mentoring alternatives if there are no mature Christian women available or willing to become involved in your life? Do you think you can be mentored by a book? Why or why not? What is the great advantage of "flying together," following the example of geese?

12. God commands us to mentor one another. If you are an "older" woman, have you ever considered yourself a mentor? Do you find it difficult to develop an ongoing relationship with the younger women around you? What are the obstacles? What are some creative ways to overcome these obstacles?

13. Do the women of your church teach other women from Scripture? How can a woman know if God is calling her to teach or disciple other women? What qualifications must she have, according to Titus?

14. The most powerful tool of mentoring is *life example*. Whose example has most powerfully touched and shaped your life?

   What kind of "life example" are you to the women around you?

Thought or Action Point for this lesson:

Lesson Eight

Read: VIP #3: Marriage, Part I (Chapter 13).

(As you answer the questions for chapters 13 and 14, if you are unmarried, think about your parents' marriage. If you are widowed or divorced, think back on your previous marriage and seek to glean from that experience.)

1. Why do you think it is so important to understand God's ideal for marriage? How do you respond to Jane Fonda's assertion that marriage for a lifetime is "unnatural"?

   What forces from the outside culture threaten to destroy oneness in your marriage?

   What do you see as the single greatest outside threat to your marriage right now? (What seems to cause struggle, or create the greatest sense of isolation?)

2. How do the differences between you and your husband threaten to destroy your marriage from within? (Different backgrounds, different personalities, different philosophies of parenting, different approaches to communication and problem solving.)

   What do you wish your husband could better understand about you?

   What does your husband wish you better understood about him? (You may need to ask!)

3. How did the author's discussion of male/female differences help you to better understand your husband?

   If you are unmarried, how have these male/female differences evidenced themselves in your relationships to the men in your life?

   Has your experience with the aggressive, conquering, protective side of men been primarily positive or negative? How have these experiences shaped your view of men in general?

4. Consider for a moment your husband's masculine traits. How do they complete you, complement you in your parenting, balance your family decisions, and so forth?

5. Why do these differences that strengthen a marriage tend to become a source of conflict?

Marriage is a two-way street. But one mate can still make a difference in a marriage by the choices he or she makes. What can *you* do to counteract conflict when differences seem to continually lead to disagreement?

How can the embracing of your differences help lead to greater oneness?

6. What would you say the ideal marriage should look like? (Use what you have learned in this chapter.)

Do you think that conflict should be part of the ideal marriage?

7. The truth is that conflict is inevitable in marriage. How can conflict lead to oneness in marriage? How can conflict lead to isolation?

How do conflicts between you and your husband usually end up? Do you resolve your conflicts and come to better understanding and communication, or do you usually end up without resolution and understanding? How do you usually feel when the conflict is over?

What can you do differently to help your conflicts move toward oneness?

8. Were you encouraged by the biblical concept of "help-mate"? Do you think this concept has been misunderstood by modern culture? Underrated?

Which particular words behind the concept of "help" were especially appealing to you?

Do you think that the image of Strong Relater is a good description of most women that you know? Do you consider yourself to be a Strong Relater? Do you think that a woman can be strong, without losing her femininity? How?

9. When is a woman most vulnerable to an affair?

What avenues can Satan use to hook the average woman into wrong thinking? Consider the books women read, the movies they see, the television programs they watch. How can the mere viewing of or reading about immorality hurt us?

How can a woman break the habit of reading unhealthy literature? What can you do when you are tempted to watch immoral programming?

10. Should a married woman spend time alone with another man, even if he is a friend? Under what conditions? How can she avoid an unhealthy emotional enticement ?

What are the trigger signs in a friendship/relationship that we should "flee"? When and how should we "flee"?

11. What are some ways that a woman can "pursue righteousness"?

It is supremely difficult to pursue righteousness when you are emotionally involved in a wrong relationship. What does God promise to those who do? (Look up 1 Samuel 2:30; 1 Peter 4:6-9, Psalm 34:15, 17-19; Psalm 37:3-5.)

If you have fled a wrong relationship and pursued righteousness, have you seen God's blessing on your life? In what way? Did your peers support you in this choice? (Share these things carefully, but nonetheless, share them. We need to be encouraged by one another when it comes to such difficult, life-saving choices.)

12. How important are *feelings* in your relationship to your husband? Would you agree that feelings ebb and flow in every marriage? Has this been your experience?

What do you think it means to be a "one-man-kind-of-woman"?

When your emotional needs are not being met by your husband, what are some positive ways that your emotional needs can be addressed?

What valid reasons do you think there may be for breaking a marriage commitment?

13. Read 1 Corinthians 13:4-7. Although this is a perfect, "ideal" love, God asks us to demonstrate this love to others! Jesus Christ even said that this kind of unselfish, unconditional love would distinguish us from the world (John 15:17 and 17:23, 26). The problem is that on our own, such love is humanly impossible. Let us consider then how we can have this kind of "uncommon" love.

According to Galatians 5:22, where does this love come from?

According to 1 John 4:19, and 5:1-3, what fuels and keeps this love nourished and alive?

What would you say is the difference between feelings and attitudes?

Is it possible for a woman to *act* in love towards her husband when the feelings are not there? What are some very practical actions that would demonstrate such unconditional love? (1 Corinthians 13:4-7.)

14. What are some areas in which you desire to see greater oneness in your marriage? The process of becoming one takes a lifetime. Do you find this to be an encouraging truth?

Thought or Action Point for this lesson:

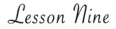

Lesson Nine

Read: VIP #3: Marriage, Part 2 (Chapter 14).

1. Describe healthy independence and self-assertion in a woman.

2. Do you see any unhealthy traces of the Amazon woman in your life? Explain.

   Where do you think these have come from?

   Do you agree that the Amazon woman of modern times cannot experience real love? Why or why not?

   Why do you think that strong, masculine men do not usually feel drawn to an Amazon woman?

3. Were you surprised at the image of "stepping into the ropes"? What is your natural tendency—to fight, or to run from the fight?

   How can the tendency to run have a negative impact on your marriage? On other close relationships in which you experience conflict?

   How can the tendency to fight have a negative impact on your marriage? On other close relationships in which you experience conflict?

4. What is our *offensive* piece of armor according to Ephesians 6:17?

5. In God's word, we are given an action plan in the battle for oneness.

   What two weapons has God given wives for the battle?

   What two weapons has God given to husbands?

6. Have you ever thought of love as a weapon? Why do you think love is such a powerful weapon?

7. Describe the "two vital sides" of love.

   How do biblical forgiveness and accountability reflect those two sides?

   What can happen when only one side of love is exercised?

   Which side do you feel you need to grow in?

8. What do you usually think of when you hear the word "submission"?

   Has the concept of submission in marriage been a "hot button" for you? Why?

Has this chapter changed your understanding of biblical submission? If so, how?

9. Take a few moments to read Ephesians 5:21-23. What do you think Paul meant when he instructed men and women alike to be subject to one another?

   What is the wife's responsibility in the marriage relationship (verses 22-24)? What is this compared to?

   What is the husband's responsibility in the marriage relationship (verses 25-31)? What is this compared to?

   Who do you think has the tougher responsibility and why?

10. How has inaccurate teaching on submission in the church damaged women? How has it helped to open Christian women up to feminist thought? Do you think it has also damaged men? Explain.

11. What did you learn about the attitudes of Christ and his followers toward women in the early church? How did this differ from your ideas going into this chapter? Did it help you to respond more positively to Paul's writings?

12. Based on what you have learned, how would you define biblical submission in your own words?

    Do you agree that submission is an act of strength?

13. Are you a volcano, or an underground cave? What do you need to learn most in developing biblical submission?

14. Of the three steps of submission, which is hardest for you: Looking, Loving, or Leaning?

15. How would you define biblical *leadership*? How does it differ from the "patri-archalism" from which feminists are so desperately seeking to free themselves?

    Describe Christ's sacrificial love for the church (John 10:11, 17-18).

16. Biblical submission teaches women to give the best of themselves for the purpose of encouraging their husbands to become the men and biblical leaders God has called them to be. It not only embraces tough and tender love, but it always seeks to do what is best for our husbands *and* families. In light of these things:

How can a woman who lives in an abusive relationship exercise biblical submission? Is separation a biblical option?

How can a woman who lives with a man who is far from God exercise biblical submission?

How can a woman who is a natural leader exercise biblical submission, and in so doing, encourage her husband to develop in *his* leadership?

When a woman disagrees with her husband, does biblical submission imply silence or rote compliance? If not, what does it require of her?

17. Christ is our greatest example of submission. To whom did He submit, first and foremost? Likewise, to whom must we submit first and foremost?

    Christ constantly communicated with the Father. Submission did not negate communication. When, however, do you think that communication stops and nagging begins?

    What does God ask us to do once we have communicated? (Proverbs 3:5-6) What role do you think prayer plays in biblical submission?

18. The biblical roles described in Ephesians 5:22-24 are specifically addressed to husbands and wives. This passage does not apply to employer-employee or brother-sister relationships in the body of Christ. But what about male leadership in the church? What can a woman do in the church? What can she not do?

    How is a man to lead in the church? (1 Peter 5:1-3.) How is this similar to a man's call to leadership at home? Do you think placing women in authority over men has hurt the modern church? If so, how?

    How can women become an asset to those who lead in the church?

19. What "unknown" would you like to trust to your "known" God as you finish this study on marriage?

Thought or Action Point for this lesson:

Lesson Ten

Read: VIP #4: Motherhood (Chapter 15).

1. What thoughts in this chapter touched you the most?

2. What does a woman without children have to gain from a discussion on motherhood?

   What aspects of the mothering instinct or nature do all women share?

   What kinds of experiences can cause women to squelch their natural mothering instinct?

   Did your experiences growing up encourage your desire to mother, or discourage it?

3. Describe "biblical motherhood" in your own words.

   From your own experience, do you think that the career world tends to encourage or discourage biblical motherhood? Biblical fatherhood?

   How is feminist philosophy at odds with biblical motherhood?

4. Did the question "When does motherhood begin?" give you any new insights into the abortion issue?

5. Were you surprised by the similarities between slavery advocates and the abortion advocates of today?

6. Why do you think a biblical view of adoption would be important today?

7. Were you surprised by Scripture's heavy emphasis on the father's role in parenting? Why do you think this is so foreign to us today?

8. How does the typical view of children's needs in our culture differ from the biblical view of parenting?

9. The author listed seven habits that God has commanded parents to practice in raising their children. What are those habits? Explain what each one means in your own words.

   Which of the seven habits do you feel you do best with each of your children?

   Make a list, considering each of your children. Which habit would you most like to improve upon with each child?

10. Read Deuteronomy 6:6-7. How would you describe this parent?

11. Summarize in your own words why the habit of availability, or "presence," is so fundamental to all of the other habits?

12. Some mothers have no choice but to be away from their children for long periods of time. What are some ways that these moms can implement maximum availability? (The final chapter of the book will expand on this idea.)

    How can a local church be vitally important for families recovering from divorce?

13. How have the changes in life brought on by the industrial revolution made it so tough to be a "Deuteronomy 6" kind of parent?

    Availability will require sacrifice of *every* post-flood parent. What can availability cost fathers? Mothers?

14. What our children want most from us is *us*. Looking back on your own childhood, what do you remember most? What would you wish to do differently in parenting your own children?

15. What tough choices have you made in order to meet the needs of your children? Have any blessings accrued into your life as a result? If so, please share them.

    What attitudes hinder God's blessing in our lives? What attitudes open the floodgates of His blessing?

    How does Romans 8:28-29 apply particularly to our failures with our children?

16. Is your mothering nerve more tender after reading this chapter? Is there one application from this study that you could begin to put into practice this week?

Thought or Action Point for this lesson:

Lesson Eleven

Read: VIP #5: Making a Home (Chapter 16).

1. Respond to this statement: A home is a *greenhouse* for human growth and development. How is a home like a greenhouse?

   Respond to this statement: A home is a *womb*. How is a home like a womb?

2. What kind of home did you grow up in? Were you emotionally nourished, protected? Did you feel safe?

3. In what ways is your present home a greenhouse? A womb?

4. Would you describe your childhood home as primarily *constructive* or *destructive*?

   Do you feel you were brought up in a well managed home that honored God? Why or why not?

5. How does a woman help to determine the constructive or destructive environment of her home?

   Do you need to become more constructive at home with your tongue?

6. How is a man best suited for the role of protector and provider of the home?

   How is woman best suited for the role of caregiver, nurturer, guardian?

   How have these roles become confused in our society?

7. Do you struggle with these responsibilities as God has laid them out?

   Who assumes the role of primary caregiver in your home? Who assumed them in your home growing up?

   Who assumes the role of primary provider? Who assumed them in your home growing up?

   If your present home is not in tune with biblical roles, do you see the value of returning to those roles? Why or why not?

8. What did you learn from the analogy between the Levitical priests and your own ministry in the home?

9. What does the concept of "double honor" mean to you?

10. Why do you think isolation is so devastating to mothers in our modern culture?

11. What insight did you gain regarding the biblical perspective of work and gifts?

    How is "work" different from "career"? What is the primary purpose of work? What has become the primary purpose of career?

    God has given us our talents and gifts for a purpose. What do you think that purpose is? What is God's greatest concern for us, beyond our present personal expression and fulfillment? (Ephesians 4:11-15.)

    How does God use the experience of motherhood and caring for a home to better equip us to use our gifts well?

12. Who or what, according to Titus 2, is to be the primary beneficiary of a woman's work?

13. Read Proverbs 31:10-31. What strikes you about the work of this woman? Who or what was the focus of her work? How was she able to use her talents and skills for the home? Where did she work? How was this woman's world different from our modern world? What struggles do you think she might have in our modern world?

14. What makes our choices regarding work so tough in these days? What are the major adjustments a woman will encounter if she leaves the work of a career to work at home?

15. Consider these three statements:

    •There are times when embracing the priority of the home will mean *laying aside* certain aspects of personal fulfillment, or perhaps the expression of certain gifts or training for a season.

    •There are other times when embracing the priority of the home will mean becoming *creative* in using our gifts and training.

    •There are times when the needs in our homes decrease, and God will open up opportunities for us to express our dormant gifts and training more fully.

    Which of these three statements most applies to where you are?

16. The choice of making the home top priority is one of the most pivotal choices you will ever make in your life. What insights have you gained from this chapter to help you and encourage you in this all-important choice?

Thought or Action Point for this lesson:

Lesson Twelve

Read: The New Pioneer (Chapter 17).

1. What idea affected you personally in this chapter?

2. Why would the author use the image of the new pioneer to describe modern Christian women?

3. Do you consider yourself to be creative? Resourceful? A risk taker?

4. Brainstorm in your group. What creative things have members of your group seen or done? You may wish to consider the following questions.

    What are some creative ways to work outside the home and still meet the needs of your home?

    What are some creative ways to work out of your home?

    What are some of the inherent negatives/positives if a woman chooses to work out of her home?

5. What special gifts and talents has God given to you? What training do you have? Are you presently able to use your gifts and training? Are you involved in service or ministry outside of your home?

6. What is the "wall" in your life keeping you from implementing Titus 2:3-5? Is there a way to go over it, around it, or through it?

7. Thinking back over what you have read in this book, what insights have given you new freedom?

    Which chapter touched you most in your place of need?

    Which chapter challenged you most?

    What aspect of recent history has given you new insight?

    How do you better understand God's calling in your life?

8. Can you relate to Margaret's story?

    What extraordinary choice have you decided to make as a result of reading this book?

9. Read Galations 6:9 and Ephesians 3:14-21.

How do these verses encourage you as you move forward on the path of life?

10. Spend some time in prayer. Pray that God will give you wisdom as you walk the path of life. Pray that He will honor your godly choices. Pray that He will bring blessing upon your children. And pray for your grandchildren.

Thought or Action Point for this lesson: